What Do You Do

with a

Chocolate Jesus?

An Irreverent History of Christianity

By Thomas Quinn

To Mom, Dad, Robin and David,
who are always there.

NOTE ABOUT TERMINOLOGY:

Scholars have recently taken to using B.C.E. (Before the Common Era) and C.E. (the Common Era) to reckon the years in order to avoid what some see as the Christian bias of using B.C. (Before Christ) and A.D. (Anno Domini, meaning "in the year of our Lord") when discussing historical events. Personally, I've never met anyone who lost sleep over this. Whenever I see "B.C.", I think of *The Flintstones.*

The newer terms are more awkward to read and to say. Further, they're not really a solution to the bias problem. The Common Era begins with the presumed birth year of Jesus Christ, so it's still a Christianity-based counting system. Hence, I'll go with the more familiar and readable "B.C." and "A.D." This will also help distinguish my book from scholarly works—as if there were any danger of confusion.

Table of Contents

Table of Contents

Fix reason firmly in her seat,
and call on her tribunal for every fact, every opinion.
Question with boldness even the existence of a God;
because, if there be one, he must more approve of the homage
of reason than that of blindfolded fear.

—Thomas Jefferson

Even the gods love jokes.

—Plato

What Do You Do with a Chocolate Jesus?

It was the last thing I expected from my high school party buddy. I was a sophomore at a Midwestern university and he called to invite me down to the art college he was attending in Florida, and to accompany him to a Christian revival fair. I thought he was kidding. He wasn't. Over the previous year, he had become a born-again Christian. "Jesus freaks" we called them. Hippies buzzed on Christ.

Clueless me had grown up in what I always figured was a Christian household. I said the Lord's Prayer every night. I cried when my Catholic mother told me the story of Jesus. Like most good Christians, we celebrated Christmas with evergreen trees and Easter with colored eggs. As for the Bible, I thought of it as kind of like *Aesop's Fables*—a collection of folktales that taught me to be nice to strangers and to not cheat on my math tests. (The results were mixed.) But the religion stuff pretty much ended there.

When it came to hardcore practices like faith healing or speaking in tongues, I thought that only happened on TV. The only seriously religious people I ever met were the unnaturally well-groomed folks who'd knock on our front door every Sunday afternoon wanting to talk about God. So it was a little shocking to me that a well-educated party animal like my friend had veered down this evangelical path.

Still, I was curious. Hell, I was in college. I was up for any new experience if it didn't cost too much. I thought of myself as a truth-seeker and had dabbled in stuff like Transcendental Meditation, New Age metaphysics, Buddhist chanting, and anything else I could fit between girlfriends and bong hits. (As a sophomore, it rarely occurred to me to find enlightenment at the campus bookstore.)

Now, here I was on a balmy Florida evening with my dear friend, driving to a big fundamentalist gathering that he promised would change my life. He was glassy-eyed with the spirit and certain that every green light we hit was a personal favor from heaven.

The revival event was huge. It was set in a city park with large white circus tents full of worshippers who took turns witnessing on how Jesus had healed their ills, saved their marriages, or warned them off liberal congressmen. It was a festive affair, like a traveling carnival, and, along with amusement rides and primitive Christian rock bands, there were kiosks with all kinds of churchy paraphernalia for sale, including a hand-sized portrait of Jesus made of chocolate.

Strange. I had never seen a marshmallow Mohammad or a Gummi Bear Buddha, so I wasn't sure what to make of it. But it did raise a question: What do you *do* with a chocolate Jesus? How do you eat something like that? Do you work your way up the legs or go right for the halo? Do you worship it? Share it with twelve friends as the Last Dessert? Was it like a communion wafer that became the flesh of Christ before it hit your lips? And if so, did that make it okay for a low-carb diet?

They were stupid questions, but they made me realize that there was a huge subculture in America that took these things very seriously. They talked about the Bible as if it were a history book. They believed in miracles. And they saw Jesus in everything. They claimed my values and my freedoms came from God—freedom being the last thing I ever associated with the stifling rituals of church. More disturbingly, they wanted to pass laws banning lots of things that, frankly, struck me as none of their business.

My first reaction to this was to think: Haven't these people heard of the twentieth century? But the experience launched me onto a personal journey to seriously explore this religion thing.

It was very unlike me. I was into science and skepticism, not to mention sleeping late, and most religions love to drag you up at the crack of dawn. But I made the effort. I attended services at different churches to find one that "spoke to me." I read the Bible every night, and read books about the Bible. I took religious history classes and joined a little Jesus group. I experienced the wave of love during services, saw the affection among worshippers, and came to realize how religion gave people hope in dark times and a sense of purpose in this life beyond leaving a carbon footprint. It was kind of nice.

As time went on, however, things got increasingly strange, and then a little scary. I mingled with folks who prayed to God when deciding how much to charge clients in their car upholstery repair business. I met a young woman who talked in hushed tones because she was "heavily into humility." (A lot of unreligious thoughts ran through my head.) Then there were the elders, who firmly believed that God supported tax cuts, semiautomatic weapons, the Alaska pipeline, and whatever war America had stumbled into at the time.

No issue in life was too grand or too trivial for them to consult Jesus about and, whatever he decided for them, it could not be questioned. Their personal agenda was now ordained by heaven.

I was expected to take stories about talking snakes and walking on water literally. I was supposed to put Jesus at the center of my life. I was instructed to rely upon God for everything. Plus I had to give up sex with my smokin' hot Jewish girlfriend. That one really hurt.

Then I saw a fascinating little Australian film called *The Devil's Playground*. Set in a 19th century boarding school, it featured a preacher lecturing to a roomful of horny pubescent boys about damnation and about how long their eternity in hell would feel if they sinned. He asked them to imagine a ball of steel the size of the sun and how, once every ten thousand years, a sparrow would fly by and graze a wing against it. By the time that ball had worn away to nothing, he said, only the tiniest fraction of their suffering would have elapsed. The guy could have given motivational training to Tony Robbins.

It eventually occurred to me that I wasn't exploring religion so much as I was buying it wholesale, and it seemed an ill fit. If I was going to dive into the deep end of this pool, I had to take a break from questioning my own sinful self and, instead, question the people who put all this together. Who were they? How did I know they were right? What made them any smarter than me?

I decided to submit all this religion stuff to the same harsh grilling my born-again friends applied to everyone else's beliefs. How well would it all stand up to...oh, let's call it an Inquisition?

My evangelical friends responded that I was a prisoner of the intellect. I needed to liberate myself from the "pride and arrogance" of reason and skepticism and, instead, become a dutiful servant of Christ, who specialized in goodness and niceness and alcohol-free beer.

The arrogance of *reason?* I thought about how science established its ideas. Someone observes nature for awhile and thinks he sees a pattern. He hypothesizes that a natural law might account for it. He then does experiments to test his idea. If it holds up, he publishes a paper and his colleagues get busy dissecting his work. Eventually, after more testing and debate, if the idea still works, it's accepted as a genuine discovery. That's a fairly humbling process. Nobody takes anyone's word for anything.

Contrast this with the way religion comes up with its own sacred truths. Historically, one guy has an emotional, subjective, shattering experience which *he* claims is personal contact with the Creator of the Universe. Then he stands up on a hill, or in a church, or outside a Michael Moore movie, and rails about it to anyone who will listen. If he's articulate, a crowd gathers around and someone says, "Hey, he sounds pretty good. Somebody write this down!" And suddenly we have sacred scripture and eternal truth.

Sure we do.

I finally came to see that religion was an invention, not a revelation. It was a choice, not a discovery. Yet, according to Reverend Ted Haggard (shortly before he was caught snorting methamphetamine with a male prostitute), a new megachurch goes up every couple of days in the United States and most of them are evangelical.

That statistic chilled me like the final scene of *Invasion of the Body Snatchers*. It meant that legions of voters were being lured into a mindset that said society should be organized in accordance with God's will. That always raised two key questions: a) who gets to define "God's will" and, b) why is it never me?

If war was too important to leave to the generals, religion was too important to leave to the preachers. Someone who hadn't drunk the Kool-Aid needed to weigh in. After all, you're not going to learn everything you should about communism if you only listen to avowed Marxists. I needed to explore and document the side of the religion story we didn't get in Sunday school.

Hence this book.

This is not a comprehensive history of Christianity. It's a look at the fantastic folktales, the scriptural inconsistencies, and the pious hypocrisies that have been sold to us as eternal truth over the past 2,000 years and how little of it is actually the foundation of our values today. It's religious history deep fat fried in irreverence for popular consumption, even if it risks a little indigestion.

Everyone has a right to their beliefs and, having been through the experience, I can appreciate why people sometimes believe incredible things. It's fine with me that Orthodox Jews think starting their car on Friday night might compromise their holiness, or that Mormons feel the need to wear sacred underwear, or that Pentecostal snake handlers drink strychnine to prove they're protected by the Almighty.

I also understand that not all Christians are conservatives, that not all conservative Christians are fundamentalists, and that not all fundamentalists see eye to eye. There's plenty of diversity and disagreement among the ranks—which is one reason why they keep building more churches. All this variety and imagination is a great thing.

The problems don't start when people have a deep faith in their beliefs. The problems start when they want *you* to have faith in their beliefs and, if you're not interested, they stop making good arguments and start passing bad laws. Next stop: the Dark Ages.

It's true that the motive for legislating faith is often an honest belief that, if God isn't happy with what's going on, he'll take it out on everyone. (He's been known to do that. Ask Noah.) But this is only a belief, and just because you believe in vampires doesn't mean you get to force everyone else to stock up on garlic.

Faith is personal opinion, which is why it's not called fact. It's what you ask of someone when you don't have the goods to prove your point. When we forget that it's always trouble. If someone is hawking a religious belief as Eternal Truth, it's fair to ask for some kind of proof. If the answer is, "have faith," well, anybody can say that no matter how sane or ditzy their claims—which is precisely why laws based on faith are a bad idea. *Whose* faith are we talking about and what if they're completely deluded? It's happened.

What's more, those in power who are certain they're doing God's work tend not to be shy about passing judgment on different views held by others (whom they identify as heretics, heathens, blasphemers, idolaters, atheists, backsliders, minions of the devil, sons of Satan, or the mainstream media). If you oppose these believers, you oppose God—and that means it's open season on you.

Nor is this just attitude on their part. The Bible itself is uncompromising about other modes of belief. Just what part of *"Thou shall hold no other gods before me"* don't you understand?

It's nice to have certainty, but we live in a democracy and democracy depends upon compromise because it assumes nobody has all the answers. When you introduce religious absolutes into a system that requires compromise to work, it breaks. We need to knock that off, and by showing the Bible as a work of human creativity, it helps us keep a little humility about our claims to knowledge of Eternal Truth.

Those claims begin with the Hebrew Bible, a.k.a. the Old Testament, which tells the story of God and his people. It begins at the dawn of time and meanders up through 3,000 years of history to the glory days of the Roman Republic. But the ending is more promise than fulfillment. Long after the last draft of it was completed, Jews were still under the rule of Rome, waiting for a messiah and wondering why it was taking so damned long.

Well, wait no longer. With the advent of Christianity, God makes his return engagement. From the Gospels of Jesus, to the rise of the Church, to the founding of America, we'll have a ringside seat to the Greatest Show on Earth. They'll be jaw-dropping magic, lots of animals, feats of derring-do, and plenty of clowns to scare the children. So step right up.

Jesus famously said, "You shall know the truth, and the truth shall make you free." He was talking about the freedom of the soul from sin, but I like the general sentiment. So, here's my little joust for freedom. Make of it what you will. And whatever you think of my yammerings, please remember—I can be forgiven.

Whew...

CHAPTER ONE

You Can't Keep a Good Man Down

*I've never understood how God could expect his creatures
to pick the one true religion by faith—it strikes me as
a sloppy way to run a universe.*

—Robert A. Heinlein

A Brief History of Creation

It all started with a god named Yahweh—the king of the cosmos, the master of existence, the Big Cheese of Cheeses. He was bored to death. As the all-knowing, all-powerful Lord of Creation, he could have pretty much anything he wanted. The problem was there wasn't anything to want because there was nothing *in* the universe. It was dark and without form and, apparently, hanging around all this nothingness being perfect wasn't fabulous enough. There had to be a way to liven things up.

So, Yahweh said, "Let there be light," and there was light. Not a bad start, but the novelty quickly wore off because there was nothing for the light to shine on. So he formed the sun, the moon, and the stars. All very lovely, but once they were up and running a big *"Now what?"* set in. The whole thing operated by the laws of nature, which Yahweh had also created, so he knew everything that was going to happen. Not much suspense there. Something was missing.

Life! He picked one of his favorite planets—earth—and he created living things that moved by themselves and multiplied and did lots of amusing stuff. But algae, dinosaurs, and alpacas got tiresome after a few millennia. No intellectual stimulation. What Yahweh needed was something interesting and unpredictable.

Thus he created man and woman. They were curious creatures that were smart enough to love and worship Yahweh, but not bright enough to realize they could pass the time having sex—something you'd think they'd figure out since they were naked all the time. Whatever. They seemed like a nice couple and everything appeared to run smoothly. Maybe a little too smoothly. They didn't *do* anything. Well, there was nothing for them to do except loiter around the Garden of Eden not having sex.

Then Yahweh created the Tree of Knowledge of Good and Evil, planted it in the middle of paradise, and told Adam and Eve to leave it alone. Which they did.

Well, Jesus, this was no fun. Something had to kick-start a little drama. So, Yahweh tossed a serpent into the garden. Not only could it talk, it also knew more about the local plant life than the two dimwit humans. The serpent lured the people into eating the tree's forbidden fruit and, suddenly, they realized they were naked. Not much of an insight when you think about it, but it was a start.

Adam and Eve thus disobeyed Yahweh, which meant he got to throw his first fit—as if he didn't know this was coming. The people were tossed out of paradise and they were no longer immortal. But at least they could have all that sex they were missing. The result, of course, was many children. Pretty soon one brother was slaying another, while the rest were fruitful and multiplied, until the whole world was filled with humans killing each other. Now *that's* entertainment!

Unfortunately, it was also an endless series of headaches. People acted very badly and, since swimming hadn't been invented yet, Yahweh flooded the entire world and started over. The next crop of humans tried to build a tower to heaven in Babel. So Yahweh, not a big fan of competition, broke up that little project. Then the residents of Sodom and Gomorrah started doing things a little *too* entertaining, even for Yahweh's boredom-killing agenda, and both cities got nuked.

As the centuries wore on, Yahweh became partial to the family of a Semitic tribesman named Abraham. He promised Abraham wagonloads of descendants to populate the land of Canaan. But Yahweh, never one to make things simple, didn't give him a son until after Abe knocked up his maid and then turned 100. Yahweh had a flare for soap opera.

The son was a nice boy named Isaac, Abraham's long-promised offspring. Naturally, Yahweh demanded that Abraham kill him. Abe was about to make a sacrifice out of him when—*psych!* That wacky Yahweh was just messing with Abraham's head. Abe didn't have to sacrifice his son; it was just a test. Instead, he was given an alternative: trim the end of his penis. Kind of bizarre, but it beat torching the kid, who probably slept with one eye open that night.

Thus began the begetting. Abraham had Isaac, Isaac had Jacob—who was renamed Israel—and Israel had twelve sons from two wives, who were sisters, and their two maids. Yahweh's scheme got ever more interesting, even if it wasn't exactly family entertainment.

A drought then drove the people of Abraham to Egypt, where they spent 400 years being slaves and leaving no evidence they were ever there. Eventually, Yahweh heard their cries and found a fixer: Moses. He was the son of Hebrew slaves, but he passed as a prince of Egypt. Well, he didn't *look* Jewish. *Ba-da-boom.*

One day, while Moses was herding sheep, Yahweh appeared as a burning bush and spoke to him. Who knew Moses talked to his plants? Or that the plants talked back? God then slammed the pharaoh with ten plagues and led the Israelites out of Egypt, across the Red Sea, and back toward Canaan. But first they had to endure forty years of desert campouts. Along the way, Yahweh issued the Ten Commandments and a few hundred other mitzvah to live by.

Once they reached Canaan, the Israelites found that it was full of Canaanites. Go figure. The Hebrews called it the Land of Abraham because Abe had lived there years before. (Gee, I used to live in New Jersey. Does that make the Garden State the Land of *Me?*) With God's help, they launched a war and conquered sixty-one cities—the commandments about not killing and not coveting apparently on hold for the moment.

Eventually, they settled in and organized themselves into two kingdoms—Israel in the north and Judah in the south. Each was dominated by a different version of the Hebrew faith. Around 1000 B.C., the valiant King David—of Goliath fame—came to power. He united the two kingdoms and reigned for forty years, followed by his son, Solomon, who built a great Temple in Jerusalem and ruled for forty years more. Along the way, Solomon collected 700 wives and 300 concubines. He was also very wise. Hey, any guy who could land *that* much action was no dummy. Plus he had to remember all those anniversaries.

Around 722 B.C., the huge empire of Assyria invaded Israel in the north. Then, in 586 B.C., the even bigger empire of Babylon conquered Judah in the south and kidnapped the leaders. Then, in 536 B.C., the even *bigger* empire of Persia overtook Babylon and everyone else in sight. With bigger fish to fry elsewhere, the Persians allowed Israelite leaders to return to Jerusalem and run their own affairs, sort of. The Persians remained in charge.

While it was nice that the Jews were back home and could rebuild their Temple, it wasn't like the good old days of David and Solomon. The Israelites wanted to rule themselves and Yahweh wasn't being as helpful as he used to be. No ten plagues or anything cool like that. So, the people waited and prayed for a bold new leader—some courageous warrior prince who would kick their conquerors out and set up an independent Jewish kingdom.

Unfortunately, around 332 B.C., a Greek commander named Alexander, who by all accounts was pretty great, stormed in and took over. He left behind a series of oppressive generals who tried to force modern culture down the throats of the locals. In the process, the generals abused their subjects and violated the Temple. This got everyone really cheesed off.

For a brief time, a Jewish clan called the Maccabees expelled these conquerors, and established a tiny independent state around Jerusalem. But in 63 B.C., the Romans expanded their growing republic into Judea and vicinity, and they were so well organized that it was going to take a miracle to get rid of them. More than ever, Yahweh's people wanted a divine deliverer. A heaven-sent redeemer. A messiah.

By the end of the first century B.C., half the families in Judea were hoping that one of their sons would grow up to become this messiah—a lofty goal even for Jewish mothers. A dentist with a nice practice wouldn't do. They needed something special. A game changer. And boy-howdy did they get one.

Resurrection Hall of Fame

This grand saga leads us, of course, to the subject at hand: the story of Jesus Christ as enshrined by the New Testament and the vast religion it spawned. It's shaped our history, reframed the way we think, and morphed our pop image of God from a sage old man in the sky to an invisible father whose son was a tall, fair-haired, white guy. I'm sure there were a lot of those knocking around first century Palestine.

But before we talk messiahs, we need to lay the groundwork for why any of this was necessary. Why all the pining for a savior? What was the appeal of this cosmic superstar approach to setting things straight?

It begins with a simple fact. Man is the only creature that knows he's going to die. Death is a spooky prospect given how much we know about it (that would be nothing) and what a raw deal it seems to be after enduring the demolition derby we call life. Humans want a better payoff.

Enter religion. Religion is based on what we want. It's about faith, belief, and hope. Its appeal is emotional, and if something has emotional appeal we'll buy it. This gives it a huge advantage over something like science. Science tells us we're pond scum that evolved an opposable thumb. Religion says we're God's top accomplishment. This may make him an underachiever, but it's reassuring to think the creator of the universe is personally interested in my health, my career, and my right to own guns.

What's more, Western religion traffics in the idea of God as a caring parent. Its popularity, I believe, is based on our wish to recapture the most perfect moment in life—you know, the one when you were about three years old and your mom held you snugly in her arms and said, "It's all right. It's going to be all right." It's the ultimate experience of love, security, comfort, and bliss. It's precisely what people seek from an anthropomorphic deity, and the reason is not complicated.

Humans depend upon their parents for longer than any other animal, and when you're a kid parents are very god-like. They're bigger than you, they're all-powerful, and they seem to know everything. You also have a covenant with them. If you obey their rules, they'll give you love and won't make you eat too many vegetables.

But right about the time you turn twelve, you start to realize that your parents don't know everything because...well, *you* do. They no longer provide the total security they once could. But you still long for it. So, you imagine an invisible super-parent who *can* deliver absolute security. Obey his rules and you won't catch hell. It's just like home.

Given this primal wish, it's not surprising that a successful religion would be based on the story of a fatherly God sending his son to console and protect the rest of his needy children. If we obey him, we get an eternity on a nice, comfy cloud. You might not be crazy about learning the harp, but it's a lot better than just dying and no longer existing, which would kind of suck. And so, the ambitious, innovative West came up with exactly what it wanted: a myth that told them how to attain eternal life.

6

Joseph Campbell famously listed the four functions of a myth: a mystical function (to explore the unknown), a cosmological function (to explain the universe), a sociological function (to establish values to live by), and a psychological function (the inner development or "hero's journey" of every literary figure from Gilgamesh to Bilbo Baggins). I think it's this last function that made Christianity such a hit.

The Greatest Story Ever Sold

A long time ago, in a land far away, a child was born. He was the son of a god and a mortal woman and he used his miraculous powers to do good and to serve others. Tragically, he was betrayed and was killed by his enemies. But ultimately he rose from death and rejoined his father in heaven. That child, of course, was Hercules.

Oh…wait a sec. That's probably not where you thought I was going. Sure, that was Herc's basic bio. But the person I'm talking about was born to a virgin, under a star, and stood for truth, peace, and brotherhood. He launched a following known as The Way, and his supporters called him the Good Shepherd. When he died, he was placed in a rock tomb. He ultimately ascended to heaven while, back on earth, his disciples waited for a day of judgment when those who believed in him would find paradise. People were baptized in his name and his birth was celebrated every December 25th. Clearly, the man in question was Mithras.

Wa…huh? Okay, what's going on?

The Messiah Motif

We've come face-to-face with something religious historians call the "Messiah Motif." It's a storyline most of us were told was unique to Christianity—the Gospel (meaning "good news") of Jesus Christ. As it turns out, his biography was a template that had been applied to dozens of ancient heroes, real and imagined, long before the Wise Men from the East started gift shopping.

Just as American politicians frequently use the rags-to-riches story to come off like deserving heroes, the tale of a heaven-sent liberator who conquered death and vowed to return with a big dose of divine justice was told about many great figures, historical and fictional. And they each had rabid followers who were determined to immortalize their guru.

I was taught that Jesus was the only one to pull this off. But a look at several pagan prequels makes it clear that the basic plot was routine. The similarities between these legends may be superficial or just coincidence. They don't necessarily mean pagan myths inspired the Jesus tale. But they do show that, what's usually sold as a one-of-a-kind drama was, in fact, a familiar story arc. To wit:

Osiris

In ancient Egypt, Osiris was the god of death, fertility, and resurrection. He was lord of the Underworld, where the souls of the dead were judged. Legend says he was chopped up into pieces by his sinister brother, Set, but that the good chunks were gathered and brought back to life by his wife, Isis—who was also his sister. Don't ask.

The Osiris story goes back to at least 2,500 B.C. Around 500 B.C. the Greek historian Herodotus witnessed a huge Egyptian festival wherein tens of thousands experienced a spiritual rebirth by reenacting Osiris' death-and-resurrection story. It was called "The Passion of Osiris." Here's a poem written about the day he was born:

> He is born! He is born! O come and adore him!
> Young like the moon in its shining and changing,
> Over the heavens his footsteps are ranging,
> Stars never–resting and stars never-setting,
> Worship the child of God's own begetting!
> Heaven and earth, O come and adore him!
> Bow down before him, kneel down before him!
> Worship, adore him, fall down before him!
> God who is born in the night.

I can hear Donny and Marie singing it on the Christmas album. Osiris was known as "He who giveth birth unto men and women a second time," and for centuries, January 6th (the twelfth day of Christmas) was called the "Day of Osiris."

Horus

Like father like son. Horus was the offspring of Osiris and Isis. He was Egypt's falcon-headed Sky God. Pharaohs, when they were feeling especially full of themselves, claimed to embody his spirit. Horus was called "the light of the world" and "the way, the truth and the life." Kinda catchy, huh? He was emblemized by a great eye—a symbol of salvation—and he claimed that "Eternity has been assigned to me without end."

He was the son of a virgin goddess and was the only begotten son of a god. He was born in a humble cave and his birth was heralded by a star. His nativity scene included shepherds and a visit by three solar gods.

Horus represented eternal life and was known as the Lamb, though he was also imagined as a Good Shepherd. He was identified with the Tat or cross. There's even a gap in his biography between his childhood and age 30. His deeds included walking on water, healing the sick, casting out demons, quieting the sea, and giving sight to the blind. His nicknames included "the fisher," "the bread of life," "the son of man," and "the Word."

Dionysus

Back in ancient Greece there was a whole category of cults called mystery religions—a generic term for rather shadowy groups that worshipped in secret and taught that godly myths were mere allegories created to reveal deeper truths.

One of the most popular mystery cults was built around Dionysus—the Greek god of grain, bread, and the vine. Belonging to most religions is no picnic, but this sure sounded like one. Small wonder his following lasted over a thousand years.

Being the god of wine, Dion's moods ranged from light and fruity to mildly tart with a smooth finish. But the lord of inebriants could also drive men out of their minds. He was the son of Zeus, king of the gods, and Semele, a mortal woman. Semele remained a virgin, however, because she was impregnated by a bolt of lightning. Must have been some honeymoon.

This *hieros gamos*—sacred marriage—produced a divine child. To honor him, ritual unions were staged in a stable in the Athenian marketplace. Not quite a manger, but we're in the same ballpark.

Euripides wrote that Dionysus shrouded his "Godhead in a mortal shape" in order to make it "manifest to mortal men." As an adult, Dion turned water to wine at his own wedding.

When Zeus's perpetually jealous wife, Hera, found out about Semele and her child, she made sure that Semele went up in flames and that—in a Greek version of the Osiris story—Dionysus was torn to pieces. He, too, was reassembled and brought back to life.

Long story short: Dionysus was a god-man who was persecuted, tormented, executed, and then reborn—like many deities celebrated in spring festivals. Once he was resurrected he was hidden for a time in the woods with the nymphs. Not a bad deal, especially with all that bread and wine.

Each autumn, some 30,000 Athenians made a barefoot pilgrimage to the shrine of Eleusis, where they acted out a divine drama called The Passions of Dionysus. Plutarch wrote that Dion's worshippers sought a "rebirth." Others called it a "voluntary death" from which one is "born again." Pretty awesome idea.

Attis

Born to yet another virgin (what *is* it with these gods and nookie?), Attis was a Greek god who was honored each spring with a three-day festival and a passion play. An effigy of Attis was tied to an evergreen, which was decorated with sacred flowers. His "body" was then placed in a sepulcher from which he was said to rise on the third day.

Under dark of night, new initiates were brought to the sepulcher and told, "To you likewise there shall come salvation from your trouble." These rites were celebrated around March 25th. Once upon a time, Christian tradition said Jesus was crucified on that date.

Mithras

Mithraism was a Roman religion that may have been an offshoot of Zoroastrianism, an ancient Persian faith. It's thought that sailors brought Mithraism to Rome around 70 B.C. and it later spread throughout the Empire. By the third century A.D. it was so popular, especially among soldiers, that it was the number one rival to Christianity. Top-flight orators like Cicero had this to say about the faith:

> "These mysteries have brought us from rustic savagery to the cultivated and refined civilization...We have gained the understanding not only to live happily, but also to die with better hope."

Nobody talks about him today, but Mithras was once a big deal. He was the god of goodness and light pitted against the evil Lord of Darkness, which makes him sound like Luke Skywalker. He had a thousand eyes so no one could hide their sins, which makes him sound like the C.I.A. He was also the god of Truth and the Lord of Heavenly Light, and was later adopted by the Romans as a sun god and a god of contracts—that is, he assured honest agreements among men. The handshake may have originated with this cult. Roman soldiers, his biggest fans, adopted it as a proof that they were unarmed and they spread the practice across the ancient world.

Now for the routine part: Mithras was born in a humble cave to a virgin called the "Mother of God." He was a messianic figure who stood for ethical brotherhood, self-control, and a rejection of worldly indulgences. He remained celibate throughout his life and fought for virtue and peace. He was worshipped on Sunday, his

11

purification rites included baptism, when he died he ascended to heaven and yadda-yadda-yadda...heard it.

His followers lived by his example to assure themselves of eternal life. In A.D. 274, Emperor Aurelian established the Feast of the Nativity which honored Mithras the sun god on his birthday—December 25th.

Mithras worshippers reenacted his death and resurrection, in which he was carried aloft in a sun-chariot. He was enthroned by the God of Light as ruler of the world. He was to remain in heaven until the day God destroyed the world, at which time he'd return to resurrect and judge the dead. After the Damned were plunged into the depths of the earth, the Spirit of Darkness would be vanquished and the universe could go on happily ever after.

Some claim that Christianity became the official religion of Rome because it borrowed from Mithraism. Others insist that Mithraism borrowed from Christianity. We can't be sure. But these two competitors told very similar stories. Tarsus, the home town of Saint Paul, was a center of Mithraism. Even Vatican Hill, where the pope lives, was once a sacred location for Mithraic ceremonies. You can still visit such places in and around Rome.

Apollonius of Tyana

Throughout Greece and Turkey 2,000 years ago, a penniless preacher named Apollonius became the central figure of a popular mystery religion. Some thought him the son of Zeus. He taught a philosophy of love and self-sacrifice. Stories have him healing the sick, casting out demons, absolving the wicked of sins, and raising the dead. People called him the Son of God, he was worshipped as a savior, and temples lasting centuries were built in his honor. He confronted the religious establishment of his day with wise comebacks, and he even wrote his philosophy down. He was later dubbed the "Pagan Christ," and we don't have to rehash the rest. Point made.

To this list of messianic biographies you can add similar life stories for Beddou (a Chinese god-man), Adonis (from Syria), Zoroaster (the Persian prophet), Bacchus (the Roman retread of Dionysus), Pythagoras (the real-life Greek mathematician), and even Socrates (the philosopher who taught Plato).

All of these are examples of the Messiah Motif; something Joseph Campbell called a *monomyth*—a heroic story template every bit as routine as those "triumph of the human spirit" profiles they make about Olympic athletes who overcome some unheard-of disease to strive forward and win the gold. It works.

And Now for Something Completely Familiar

All of this brings us back to the man of the millennium—Jesus of Nazareth—whose biography includes many of the same story points as these pagan god-men. It's clear that certain plot elements are common to many messianic tales, suggesting that the Gospels of Jesus are as much myth as history. As Campbell would put it, it's a story that's true on the inside even if it's not true on the outside. It's not based on fact. Of course, this isn't something you're supposed to say in polite company. But fundamentalists are rarely timid about asserting the absolute reality of it all, so I guess we're even.

The New Testament is a brilliant piece of work—inspiring, insightful, comforting, and educational. It has spurred millions to great acts of kindness and courage when everyone else was looking the other way. Many glean hopeful messages from its pages. And it's given loads of British actors a chance to play starring roles in Middle Eastern dramas.

But *wow*, let's keep some perspective kids! Fundamentalist firebrands insist every word of the book is *literally* true, as if they were eyewitnesses. They further argue that there is only one way to understand it, and they'll be glad to show you how. Oh, and if you don't believe them, you're a dupe of the devil. Just FYI.

Well, I won't consign anyone to hell. But I won't be shy about commenting on either the Bible's content or how badly that content is sometimes misrepresented. As we'll see, the Bible is a work of men, not of a god, and we know too much about it to pretend otherwise. If it were created by an all-knowing deity it wouldn't be chock full of historical errors, scientific impossibilities, or frequent disagreements with itself. Nor would there be such a lack of confirmation of its stories. Nor would it require decades of theological training to understand it. Nor would believers spend lifetimes imparting meaning to the text, when it's the text that's supposed to impart meaning to the believers. Nor would...well, you get the idea.

The New Testament is a fascinating weave of history, myth, philosophy, propaganda and, on occasion, off-the-charts lunacy. It's an adventure, and it can sometimes be hilarious. Since we live in a country with a lot of free speech lying around, why not use some of it to put the Good Book through the same wringer its defenders do with other religions and see how it holds up?

Jesus for Dummies

It all begins with the life of Jesus Christ. Most westerners know the story in their sleep, which is what a lot of us did in church. But just for the record, let's review the official account.

About 2,000 years ago, in the Galilean town of Nazareth, a Jewish virgin named Mary was told by an angel that she would miraculously give birth to The Messiah. Months later, the Romans decided to conduct a census for a new tax, and it required that everyone return to their city of birth to be counted. Bureaucrats. While on the road, a very pregnant Mary and her husband, Joseph, a carpenter, wanted to stop in Bethlehem that night, but found no room at the inn. They were forced to camp out in a stable, where the baby Jesus, the Son of God, was born. To mark the event, a new star appeared in the heavens and it guided "Wise Men from the East" to the site of the miraculous birth. Strangely, it didn't get much attention from anyone else in the neighborhood.

The regional king, Herod, caught news of this threatening new "King of the Jews," and he ordered the slaughter of all male children under two. But Joseph and Mary escaped to Egypt with the baby Jesus.

They eventually returned to Nazareth where Jesus grew up to become a simple carpenter. (I'm not sure how he could have lived in such obscurity. Apparently everyone had forgotten that whole miracle star episode.) At around age 30 he was baptized, aptly enough, by a guy named John the Baptist, and launched into a new career as a wandering preacher in the backwater of Galilee.

Jesus then recruited twelve disciples to follow him and to spread his philosophy of peace, love, forgiveness, and obedience to God. The disciples turned out to be slow learners but Jesus was patient with them. He claimed the Almighty was his father and that he had been sent to deliver a Gospel of hope about the coming Kingdom of Heaven. It might've been easier for God to just appear in the sky and say, "I'm here! Impressive, eh? Now straighten up!" But he didn't. Like I said, he often does things the hard way.

To prove he was the real deal, Jesus miraculously healed the sick, fed the hungry, and raised the dead. (Between him and all those other resurrected god-men, there must have been a lot of cadavers walking around in those days.) He then foretold of his own execution and declared that he had to die to take on the sins of the world so as to offer man redemption. But he would finally rise from death to rejoin his father in heaven and those who believed in him would do the same.

He took his message to Jerusalem, where his claim that he was The Messiah, along with his controversial spin on Jewish law, got him in trouble with the authorities. He was arrested on trumped-up charges of blasphemy and was crucified by the Romans.

Jesus died on the cross on Good Friday and was resurrected that Sunday, just in time for Easter. He spent the next forty days with his disciples before ascending to heaven, with the promise that God's justice was coming soon. Until then, his followers were encouraged to preach his message of love, hope, and salvation, and to not take money. Nobody pays much attention to that last part.

In the wake of all those earlier pagan myths, we can now see how many of the ideas we often think of as uniquely Christian had actually been kicking around for centuries. The stories may have arisen independently, but different mythmakers obviously fall back on the same tried-and-true storylines. Ask any movie executive.

Dummies for Jesus

The resurrected god-man myth was so familiar to the Greeks and the Romans that the early Christian Church was hard pressed to explain why their savior's story was so special. But they did come up with an explanation—and it's a hoot.

They claimed that once the devil knew the life story of Jesus, he went *back in time* to plant the same storyline amongst the pagans who lived before Jesus did. The Church claimed that Satan had practiced "plagiarism by anticipation," swiping episodes from Jesus' life and assigning them to earlier heroes. This way, once Jesus was born, his story would already seem familiar and everyone's reaction would be, "Been there, done that, got the toga." It was called Diabolical Mimicry and theologians argued this idea with a straight face. Amazingly, the Church came up with it about 1,900 years before Hollywood came up with *Back to the Future* movies, and it probably got just as many laughs.

The Old Testament

You can't have a New Testament without having an old one first. Since the Christian religion was an offshoot of Judaism, the Hebrew Bible (with all the stories of Eden, Noah, Abraham, and Moses) is part of that tradition. Because Jesus was supposed to be the fulfillment of Hebrew prophecy, and God's way of cutting a new deal (or new covenant) with humanity, the official stories about him came to be known as the New Testament. This meant that the Jewish prophecies he allegedly fulfilled, which were first compiled in a single book around 430 B.C., got stuck with being called the *Old* Testament.

At the core of the Old Testament/Hebrew Bible is The Law, which is found in the *Pentateuch*—the first five books. They were supposedly written before 1200 B.C. by Moses. The fact that they describe Moses' death is just one of the many reasons why most scholars don't buy this. Actually, they are collections of stories produced by two rival priesthoods from two rival Hebrew kingdoms—Israel and Judah—beginning around 900 B.C.

Those from the northern kingdom of Israel worshipped a more sophisticated deity, El, the high god of Canaan. He was a calm, aristocratic god who said blissful things like, "Let there be light."

By contrast, the southern Hebrew kingdom of Judah had a more rugged, desert culture. They worshipped Yahweh, a more primitive god of storms and fertility. He's the one that made man from a lump of clay, breathed up Adam's nose to give him life (yuck) and then cloned a woman from his rib. Yahweh worked with his hands, was big on vengeance, and had problems with anger management.

When the northern kingdom was invaded by Assyria in 722 B.C. the priests fled south to Judah. Now two competing priesthoods vied for supremacy in the one kingdom and both rewrote the old stories to justify their own authority. Around 430 B.C. these two sets of stories were sandwiched together into a single book, written in Hebrew. Later, more books about King David and Solomon and a dozen or so prophets were added to the mix.

Then, a landmark Greek translation of it all was produced by 70 scholars in Alexandria, Egypt around 250 B.C. It's called the *Septuagint*—the popular Greek edition of the Hebrew Bible. This was the version of the Old Testament used as a reference by the writers of the New Testament.

The New Improved Testament

The New Testament tells us all about Jesus, or at least about the first and last years of his life—not much in between. It's a collection of 27 books written between roughly A.D. 50 and A.D. 120. The Bible presents them in the order set by the Catholic Church, *not* in the order they were written. This was done to make it read like a chronological history of the religion. Many other writings about Jesus, some of them genuinely strange, never made it into the Scripture, though some churches include a few of them among their "apocryphal" books. It took about four centuries before the Church canonized the list of books we know today. Apparently there was no hurry.

The New Testament has two parts: the Gospels and the Epistles. The first part is comprised of the Fab Four of Faith—the Gospels of Matthew, Mark, Luke and John, plus *Acts of the Apostles*, by the writer of Luke. The Gospels are allegedly biographical accounts of Jesus' life, written at least two or three generations after his time.

The authors of these Gospels, however, were *not* guys named Matthew, Mark, Luke or John. They were written anonymously, in Greek, and it wasn't until the fourth century that the Church attributed them to four of Christ's followers. It was a nice gesture, but it gave people a really false impression. Nobody knows who actually wrote them or even where the authors lived. None of them are eyewitness reports. None of the authors ever claimed to have met Jesus. And the author of Luke specifically says he got his information second-hand. Tell me if any of this is reassuring.

The Gospel of Mark is the oldest of the four, written around the year A.D. 70. Matthew came along about a decade later, and Luke a few years after that—though some think it may have been as late as the early second century. John was likely written between A.D. 90 and 100. Interestingly, each Gospel is more fantastical than the last as Jesus gets kicked upstairs from Mark's gifted country healer to John's cosmic savior. You can choose your favorite Jesus.

Copyright laws were not in force in those days and it's a good thing, because a lot of the material in the Gospels is borrowed. Mark leans heavily on the Old Testament. Ideas like a voice crying in the wilderness, the raising of the dead, and details of the crucifixion scene—including Jesus' final words—are all taken from the Greek-language *Septuagint*.

The authors of Matthew and Luke then built their Gospels on Mark. They polished it up, slanted their rewrites toward their preferred audiences, and added material from something called the *Q document*—a theoretical collection of wise sayings that scholars think once existed. No *Q document* survives today, but it seems clear that Matthew and Luke took their cues from Mark and *Q*.

The Gospel of John appears to be written independent of the other Gospels, which is why its stories and timeline disagree most often with the first three. When someone proudly says they believe in "every word of the Bible," they are claiming the impossible. The Bible doesn't agree with itself. We'll get to all that.

Following the four Gospels is *The Acts of the Apostles*. Written by the author of Luke, it purports to document the post-resurrection work of Jesus and his apostles, as well as the history of the early Church. Scholars, however, rarely bet the farm on how credible this "history" actually is.

The second section of the New Testament is a series of letters—the Epistles—seven of them attributed to a restless evangelist named Paul. He produced them starting around A.D. 50, a generation *before* the Gospel of Mark was written. But they're presented in the Bible *after* the Gospels because they cover the two decades immediately following Jesus' life story, when Paul made a traveling nuisance of himself across half the Roman Empire.

While he trekked through Greece and Rome, Paul sent his epistles to the early churches back east in order to hash out various issues. In so doing he established the foundations of Christian theology, turning a faith aimed at local Jews into an international religion. He also managed to throw in a lot of puritanical ideas about sex, for which we are eternally grateful. Though he never claimed to have met the earthly Jesus, he wrote with great authority because he believed he was in communication with the resurrected Christ. Paul was a piece of work.

The Pauline epistles include *Romans, 1 & 2 Corinthians, Galatians, Philippians, 1 Thessalonians,* and *Philemon*. These are followed by more letters by other authors, though some of them are traditionally attributed to Paul.

The Bible's final book, *The Revelation to John*, almost didn't make it into the Scripture because it's so damned weird and depicts a more militant Jesus than the four Gospels do. It was written by a very angry man named John living on the Greek island of Patmos around A.D. 95. It's a cosmic drama of war between Jesus and the devil at the End of Time, concluding with the establishment of God's eternal kingdom on earth. This is summer blockbuster stuff and people still write reviews about it when they're not using pages from it to wallpaper their bomb shelters.

Scraps of Scripture

There is no definitive edition of the New Testament. Each church has its own preferred version and each is assembled from selected scraps of ancient manuscripts from many different places. And *all* of these scraps are copies of copies of copies of the originals. When editors decide to publish a new Bible edition, they rummage through these copies, cherry pick which manuscripts they like best, then translate them as they see fit. This is how the sacred, inerrant, eternal word of the Almighty ended up in your hotel nightstand. It makes you wonder—was this the *best* God could do to preserve his timeless wisdom? He couldn't have waited for video? Or at least the Xerox people?

The picture we get of Jesus today is based primarily on the four Gospels that gained the most popularity in the early years and which were used most frequently by "the Church"—by which I mean the early, centralized, mainstream sect of Christianity that claims it was founded by Peter, one of Jesus' own disciples. Today, we call it the Roman Catholic Church.

Eventually, as the Church won the contest of defining the faith (and you'll see it wasn't pretty), other Christian followings fizzled or were forced out of business. Their writings were lost or dispensed with. (Like I said, not pretty.) Only a few works by larger groups such as the Gnostic sect still survive. More on them later.

"They Ain't Makin' Jews like Jesus Anymore"

As the Kinky Freidman song suggests, Jesus was a different kind of Jewish holy man. He made waves by offering a new twist on traditional Jewish law. Judaism and Christianity have a co-dependent relationship. Without Jewish history and the messiah movement it produced, Christianity would never have existed. On the other hand, the only reason most of us know about Moses or the Ten Commandments or Charlton Heston is because all that material was carried forward by a more widespread religion—one that ultimately turned against its parent faith.

Well, what chip off the old block doesn't go through a period of rebellion? The problem stemmed from the fact that Jesus wasn't the kind of messiah the Hebrew Bible anticipated—a warrior prince who would overpower Israel's oppressors and rule the world. Instead, they got a charismatic hippie kid who wandered the countryside with no visible means of support performing faith healings and preaching love for everyone from your deadbeat brother-in-law to Roman tax collectors. You can understand why people were confused.

Even more baffling was what Jesus said about God. He recast the Almighty from the wrathful, moody, law-and-order cop of the Old Testament into the ethereal, forgiving spirit of the New Testament (except for the part about non-believers burning in hell). Hearing about this touchy-feely deity, Jewish priests must have reacted like a divorced woman listening to a description of her ex-husband by his new trophy wife. "You say he's what? *Sensitive and forgiving?* Are we talking about the same *guy?*" Then there was the part about God being Jesus' dad. That was even harder to swallow.

Jesus also surprised everyone with his uncompromising rejection of Mosaic Law—including the circumcision requirement, which was a big deal back then. Actually, it's no small potatoes today, especially if you're on the receiving end. It's probably why they do it before you're old enough to say, "You gotta be kidding me with this." Just a little off the top, please.

Finally, few expected their messiah to be executed. That's not what messiahs are for. The big disappointment, of course, was that Jesus left his followers before doing what everyone hoped their savior would do—save them. When he died, they were still stuck living under the Romans. Why bother having a messiah drop in if he's going to leave things pretty much the way he found them?

Well, there are a lot of complicated, migraine-inducing rationales for all this. Almost nothing in Christian theology is simple and a lot of it is just excuse-making. But let's give it try.

One explanation was that, before God judged humanity, he had to update the Jewish religion to give more people a chance to avoid damnation. Evidently, the Laws of Moses didn't do the job or were just a stop-gap. So, Jesus wiped the slate clean of all those odious rules and rituals and preached a basic philosophy of love, charity, and repentance. He focused on the heart of the law rather than the letter of the law. Judaism got a warm, fuzzy makeover.

As for why Jesus didn't vanquish the Romans and establish a Jewish world government based in Jerusalem as the Hebrew Bible foresees...well, some argue that it's already in the works. By leaving his message behind, he changed the course of history in his favor. After all, you don't see any Romans walking around these days, do you? (And no, your Italian grandmother doesn't count.)

Furthermore, when Jesus spoke of establishing a Kingdom of God, he wasn't necessarily talking about a castle surrounded by cow pastures. It was more a state of being. By dying, he'd be free to "prepare a place" for his followers to enter on Judgment Day, when "they will see the Son of man coming on the clouds of heaven with power and great glory." [Matt. 24:30] *Then* they would get their utopian kingdom. At least, that was his story. Frankly, to regard this mere promise as the fulfillment of that prophecy is setting the bar rather low.

It was all Greek to Them

The authors of the Old Testament came out of traditional Hebrew culture. But the New Testament writers were products of

Hellenism—Greek civilization and philosophy. As mentioned, they wrote in Greek and they used the Greek-language *Septuagint* as their Old Testament reference. Tradition says the author of Luke wasn't even Jewish. Rather, he may have been a *godfearer*—a Gentile who had converted to Judaism before he caught Jesus fever. There are some historians who even regard Christianity as more of a Greek religion than a Jewish one.

Christianity's biggest advantage over Judaism was the decision early on to not limit it to Jews. Anyone could sign on. It was kind of like Microsoft *Windows,* which runs on any personal computer, compared with *Mac* software, which only works on a kosher Apple processor. The results were similar: Christianity boomed while Judaism maintained a niche market.

In short order, Christian recruitment expanded to include non-Jews who knew nothing of Mosaic Law. So they dropped the circumcision requirement, which was a deal-breaker for many Gentiles, and other rules as well. Let's face it, if Old Testament rituals like burning goats and spattering bull's blood at the altar were still in force we'd be in constant trouble with public health officials, not to mention PETA. This had to stop.

Half of Everything You Know is Wrong

Before we explore what's in the New Testament, it might be useful to review what's *not* in there. Our culture is so saturated with stories, symbols, and sentiments of Christian tradition that even the non-religious among us credit the Bible with lots of stuff that isn't in there at all.

Words or ideas you *won't* find in the New Testament include:

Christmas
Easter
Original Sin
The Immaculate Conception
The Catholic Church
Popes, cardinals or nuns

Monasteries

Mortal Sin

Stations of the Cross

Protestants

Mormons

Jehovah, or his witnesses ("Jehovah" was a medieval
                                    mistranslation of "Yahweh")

Angels with halos, harps, or wings

Guardian Angels

A physical description of Jesus

Jesus condemning homosexuality

Jesus condemning abortion

Jesus condemning slavery

Jesus advocating marriage

Jesus advocating a steady job

Jesus advocating money-making

Jesus advocating a male priesthood

Jesus advocating war

Jesus advocating the death penalty

Jesus advocating Christian government

Christians being fed to lions

Christians folding their hands and kneeling in prayer

Saint Peter at the gate

Seventh Heaven

Stigmata

Democracy

Science

Human Rights

Freedom (as in the right to speak, vote or worship)

The Rapture

The Rule of Law

The Rights of Man

Family Values

Life begins at conception

Billy Graham

Tax-deductible Contributions

These are only some of the things people have shoehorned into the religion and then acted as if Jesus came up with them himself. It's part of a long, tired tradition of people deciding what they want to believe and then creating a vision of Jesus to fit it.

Example: In the Gospels, Jesus comes off as a homeless, socialist, pacifist Jew who never married, never mentioned abortion, and opposed killing for all reasons, even good ones. Yet, for many in the United States, he's a wholesome Gentile family man who puts banning abortion, the death penalty, and righteous warfare above assisting the poor. They've remade Jesus in their own image—the opposite of what they're supposed to do.

These folks earnestly feel they're conforming to the will of God. But their pastors, whom they rarely question, are sometimes crafty about which parts of Scripture they cite and which parts they ignore. What's more, all pastors don't agree, so there are endless variations on what it means to be a Christian. Then there's the fact that the faith has done a 180 on every values issue from slavery and women's equality to free speech and religious tolerance over just the past 500 years. This is somebody's idea of Moral Absolutes.

With all this in mind, let's begin our tour through the epic book in which almost everyone says they believe and which most of us have never read.

CHAPTER TWO

The Amazing Adventures of Joshua the Anointed

If Jesus died for my paltry sins, he overreacted.

—Matt Decatur

Marketing the Messiah

Thomas Jefferson once described the philosophy of Jesus as "the most sublime and benevolent" ever heard by man, and it's hard to argue with that. Even snarky skeptics have to admit Western civilization has benefited at times from Christian wisdom.

Where we get into trouble, of course, is when certain folks (and you know who you are) take perfectly good ideas and harden them into dogmas that treat legends as history and metaphors as fact. As kids, we can gain insight from *Aesop's Fables*. But as adults, do we really want to convince ourselves that a fox actually bitched about sour grapes? You don't eradicate smallpox or land on the moon with that mentality.

Even worse is when the same folks who swear by every word of the Scripture manage to ignore so much of it. Attitudes completely at odds with what Jesus talked about somehow get his imprimatur. It's false advertising and it has been going on for a couple thousand years now. That's not to say there isn't plenty to learn from Scripture. We don't want to throw the baby Jesus out with the holy bathwater. But when politically-active religion junkies use this stuff in an assault on history, science, freedom, and common sense, the rest of us need a little ammo to fire back. So, here goes.

What's in a Name?

As any Hollywood mogul knows, if you're in the business of getting attention, you need a marquee name. So, Curtis Jackson III becomes 50 Cent, and Paul Hewson becomes Bono. Even popes don't use their birth names. The late John Paul II was born Karol Józef Wojtyła, which was hard to spell and even harder to pronounce. From the earliest days, God's top pitchmen have known the importance of name recognition.

In the oldest manuscripts, the New Testament says Jesus of Nazareth was actually born *Yeshu*, which translates to "Joshua." This was a problem. For Jews, Joshua was already a household name. He fought the battle of Jericho under Moses. Well, just as the Screen Actors Guild won't allow two actors to join under the same name, Christian copyists wanted to distinguish the Hebrew Bible's Joshua from their new messiah. So, they translated the latter's name as Jesus. It's probably just as well. Mexico would lose some of its charm if it were full of guys named Josh.

As for Jesus' last name, it's not like his parents got mail addressed to Mr. and Mrs. Christ. Technically speaking, Jesus was *the* Christ—the English word for the Latin word for the Greek word for the Hebrew word for "messiah." It meant "the anointed one." Kings and holy men were anointed upon assuming office with oils poured onto their heads. As Israel's hoped-for warrior prince was re-imagined into a divine wonderworker, "the anointed one" became "The Anointed One." A messiah became *The Messiah*. You'd think the guy could walk on water.

Jesus and the Four Christs

The Gospels of Matthew, Mark, Luke and John are regarded as the official records of Jesus' life and each one presents a somewhat different view of him designed for a specific readership. Of the many Jesus stories written, these are the only four that made it through the 400-year sifting process of popular acceptance and Church approval. As I said, none of the writers ever met Jesus, and we have no independent accounts of the events of his life by non-Christians living at the time. These stories are essentially all we've got.

It also helps to remember that these writers were evangelists—religious door-to-door salesmen. They weren't writing newspaper reports of events they witnessed. They were scripting infomercials based on stories that originated through word-of-mouth... er, that is, Oral Tradition. (That sounds better than rumor.)

The Gospel of Mark—Jesus the Folk Healer

The most creative of the four Gospel writers was the man who produced his account first—the author of Mark. He wrote it around A.D. 70, but scholars don't know who he was or if he even lived in Palestine. Geographical errors in his stories suggest he didn't know the region all that well.

The year 70 was not a happy time in Jerusalem, to say the least. The Romans had ended a four-year Jewish rebellion by sacking the city and destroying the Temple, thus ending Jewish control. It was a historic disaster. The Gospel of Mark may be a product of that event; a bit of good news in a dark time.

The most remarkable thing about this book is how unremarkable Jesus is. It's the least fantastical of the Gospels.

There's no miraculous birth story. Jesus does perform miracles, but in Mark he's mostly a wandering sage and healer from Nazareth.

As mentioned, Mark depends a lot on the *Septuagint*— specifically, passages from the books of *Psalms, Isaiah* and *Wisdom*. Mark also borrows ideas from Old Testament tales about Elijah and Elisha, a mentor-student pair of prophets whose stories included oldies but goodies like faith healing and raising the dead.

The intended audience for Mark was country bumpkins—the poor and uneducated. The folks who could really use a savior. Mark's Jesus worked like a down-to-earth folk healer; a man with the common touch. The kind of guy you'd like to have a beer with, or at least a water-to-wine cooler.

The Gospel of Matthew—Jesus the King

If Mark pitched to the country cousins, Matthew went for the city slickers. This account was meant to impress sophisticated urban Jews and it wouldn't do to cast Jesus as an itinerant preacher with a bag of tricks. Matthew's readership cared about social rank, so Jesus had to be a king. To that end, Matt adds a preamble to Mark and opens by giving Jesus a royal bloodline stemming back to Abraham, David, and Solomon. Jesus is portrayed as the fulfillment of Old Testament prophecy—something educated Jews knew well. And Matthew doesn't shrink from taking verses out of context or bending their original meaning to make that point.

While this Gospel is the most Jewish because it so frequently cites the Hebrew Bible, it was also the favorite of the early Catholic Church. Mark's account starts with Jesus' baptism, but Matt does it one better by beginning with his birth. It's Matthew's Gospel that gives us the Star of Bethlehem story to establish Jesus as divine from the get-go.

The Gospel of Luke—Converting the Gentiles

If Matthew established that Jesus was special from day one, the author of Luke, writing years if not decades later and also basing his story on Mark, had to show that Jesus was special *before* day one. Matthew starts its genealogy with Abraham, so Luke begins with Adam. Luke also tells the story of angels announcing Jesus' birth and it even has the unborn John the Baptist leaping for joy in his mother's womb when she meets up with the pregnant Mary. Anti-choice advocates make a big to-do about this moment.

The author of Luke was a physician and probably a converted Gentile. He was interested in promoting Jesus to non-Jews. If Matthew's messiah was corned beef on rye, Luke's was ham on white with mayo. The author of Luke admits right up front that his entire story is second hand information and he doesn't cite Old Testament verses because Gentile audiences wouldn't know them.

Luke is also aimed at the pundits and opinion-makers of ancient Rome and it emphasizes Christ's relevance to current events, along with a concern for the poor, for women, and for everyone else. Luke was written sometime after A.D. 80, by which time Christians started concentrating on pagan recruits because most Jews seemed content with the religion they had.

The Gospel of John—Jesus the Cosmic Savior

Alright then. Mark begins with Jesus' baptism, Matthew with his birth, and Luke with a genealogy going back to Adam. The author of John tops this by making Jesus eternal, a cohort of God the Father, the "uncreated Creator." By John's time, around A.D. 100, the image of Jesus had evolved into ever more grand and mystical forms—from the roving healer of Galilee to God incarnate. Consequently, it was no longer his teachings you were supposed to obsess over—it was *him.* Jesus was now life's be-all and end-all, soup-to-nuts, everything but the kitchen sink, plus the kitchen sink, plus the bathtub, the YMCA swimming pool, and the Mediterranean Sea. You couldn't dwell on him enough.

The Gospel of John begins by referring to Jesus as the *logos*—a Greek word meaning "the word." This idea had many interpretations, both far out and far in. Some saw the *logos* as the great ordering principle of the universe. For John that meant Jesus because, for him, everything Jesus did had cosmic significance.

The Gospel of John is spiritual, abstract, and pretty woo-woo. You get the feeling the writer would've been comfortable sitting on the floor of a college dorm room around 3 a.m., twisting up a fatty and having one of those conversations about how the whole universe could be, like, a dust speck on the fingernail of some giant super-being. Or about how everything is kinda just vibrations in the fabric of ten-dimensional space-time. Or maybe we're all just like, uh…what are we talkin' about, man? Oh, yeah. The universe… That's kind of where John's head was at.

Among the Gospels, John is the odd man out. Because the first three Gospels are fairly similar, they're called the Synoptic Gospels (*optic* = look, *syn* = alike), and they clash with John time and again. Example: the Synoptic Gospels have Jesus on his mission for about a year before he's crucified while John's author puts him on the road for three. John's Jesus makes several trips to Jerusalem, not just one as in the others. His Jesus is always in control and never expresses any doubt about who he is or what he's doing, unlike the more human Jesus in Mark. You could call John's account revisionist history, if any of this was actual history.

To his credit, the author of John does come up with many poetic passages, some so compelling that even sign painters at NASCAR rallies advertise them. The favorite is *John 3:16—*

> For God so loved the world that he gave his only Son, that whoever believes in him shall not perish but have eternal life.

It's a beautiful verse, and you can understand its appeal. But there's a lot more than this to the story of God's comeback tour.

The New Testament

From the start, the Christian faith had to pull a neat trick. It was a very new take on some very old ideas. It sounds like every TV executive's dream—something fresh and new that's exactly like last year's hit. And, like a lot of what ends up in primetime, Christianity benefited from being a spin-off.

Jesus billed himself as the fulfillment of Jewish prophecy. He was, after all, Jewish. That was a good thing for him. Even the Romans, who opposed the political rebellions in Palestine, respected the depth and antiquity of Jewish philosophy. When they first took over Palestine in 63 B.C., they ended desecrations of the Jerusalem Temple and protected its worshippers. A century later, a great Jewish thinker named Philo of Alexandria even got himself an audience with the emperor. Okay, it was with Caligula, the imperial pervert. But still, that's something to write home about.

Anyway, let's begin at the beginning.

Virgin Birth

Every event in the life of Jesus was deemed so significant that it was given a formal title by the Church. The first such event is when the archangel Gabriel announces to the Virgin Mary that she's about to give birth to The Messiah. It's a moment aptly entitled *The Annunciation*.

> And behold, you will conceive in your womb and bear a son, and you shall call his name Jesus. He will be great, and will be called the Son of the Most High...and of his kingdom there will be no end." [Luke 1:31-33]

This is a high bar for any kid. But Mary isn't too thrilled with the news despite being spared the hassle of picking out a baby name. At this point she's still only engaged to Joseph, and she's a virgin. Yet here's Gabriel already talking babies. What will everyone think? What will *Joseph* think? If your fiancée got pregnant and told you it was a miracle, would you roll with that or would you go looking for this "Holy Spirit" guy with a shotgun?

Well, maybe there's more myth than fact to this virgin birth claim. It turns out the concept is borrowed, rather dubiously, from the Hebrew Bible. Matthew even points this out:

> All this took place to fulfill what the Lord had spoken by the prophet: "Behold, a virgin shall conceive and bear a son, and his name shall be called Emmanuel."
> [Matt 1:23]

This quote comes from *Isaiah 7:14* in a story set around 725 B.C., when the prophet Isaiah warns the king of Israel that, before this predicted child grows old enough to know good from evil, Israel will be wiped out by Assyria. It had nothing to do with predicting Jesus. The name Emmanuel is a good hint. What's more, the word translated from the Hebrew as "virgin" technically means "young woman." The specific word for a virgin isn't used here. No virgin is prophesized so no miracle is necessary.

If you're a Catholic, there's also the question of why there was no equally prominent "Annunciation" for when Mary was born. According to Church lore she was also the product of a virgin birth: The Immaculate Conception. (Contrary to popular belief, the term refers to the conception of Mary, not Jesus.) That event should have been a clue that something special was up with this family. But no big deal was made about it. Sounds more like myth than history, doesn't it?

There are several more problems with the virgin birth idea anyway. For one, it'll get you an "F" in biology. Second, it means that even abstinence is no guarantee against teenage pregnancy. Third, virgin birth is just a raw deal. The pain of childbirth without the joys of sex? Who thought this was a good idea?

What's more, Jewish tradition didn't require that The Messiah be born to a virgin at all. Impregnating mortal women was something Zeus did, not Yahweh. Jews expected a king to be sent *by* God. He wasn't supposed to *be* God. Again, we see the influence of Hellenism (Greek thought) on Christianity. This may be one reason why the new religion didn't sit as well with devout Jews as it did with Gentiles. Christianity is in many ways a Greek religion.

The Annunciation raises yet another question. Why should God go through the machinations of being born into this world at all when, in the Hebrew Bible, he appeared in human form *three times* with no special fuss? He walked in Eden, lunched with Abraham before Sodom and Gomorrah got snuffed, and wrestled with Jacob in a cave before Jacob was renamed "Israel." Now, suddenly, God needs virgin births and angels and whatnot to make a grand entrance. Did he have an entourage plucking the blue M&Ms from his stash, too?

The orthodox explanation is that these earlier appearances were just that—appearances. God didn't come as a flesh-and-blood man the way he did as Jesus. How they know this is a mystery. But if God was only an image, it didn't stop him from snacking on a meal of veal with Abraham. I'm not kidding. Check out *Genesis 18.*

God's Family Tree

To prove Jesus had a royal pedigree, both Matthew and Luke offer a genealogy of Christ's bloodline. But there are two problems here. First, the genealogies don't match—a major conflict. Second, they both end with Joseph, who wasn't the father of Jesus if you believe the virgin birth story. Jesus had none of Joseph's DNA, so the genealogies are basically moot.

To get around this problem, folklore claims that Mary was also descended from the same noble bloodline as Joseph. But this is an add-on. Nobody saw fit to include it in the Bible.

The Road to Bethlehem

> "But you Bethlehem of Judea shall be the birth place of the savior..." [Micah 5:2]

Jesus' biographers have another predicament. Mark establishes that Jesus is from Nazareth, a city in the province of Galilee. But the Hebrew Bible never mentions Nazareth and instead requires that The Messiah be born in Bethlehem—the city of David—some seventy miles away. What to do?

Luke comes up with a solution. The author claims Emperor Augustus decided to take a census of the Roman Empire for the purpose of a tax and this required that everyone return to their place of birth to be counted.

The idea is nuts. Yes, the Romans did take the occasional census, but not at the time of Jesus' birth and certainly not with the requirement that everyone drag their butts back to their home town. That would have glutted the roads and disrupted the entire economy. Nor are there any records of such a mass migration. But it's a whopper that gets Joseph and a very pregnant Mary on the road to Bethlehem, so stop looking for evidence or common sense.

Born in a Manger

> And the angel said to them, "Be not afraid; for behold, I bring you good news of a great joy which will come to all the people; for to you is born this day in the city of David a savior, which is Christ the Lord." [Luke 2:10]

As everyone knows, Mary and Joseph wander into Bethlehem one night and, when there are no rooms left at the inn, they settle for a stable. (You'd think the innkeeper would have accommodated an expectant mother and made someone else sleep with the animals.) There, Mary gives birth to Jesus, who is wrapped in swaddling clothes and laid in a manger (basically a food trough). It's an image with a nice populist touch, like Abe Lincoln's birthplace log cabin. It's a sweet scene of Jesus' humble origins, plus it looks good on a suburban lawn at Christmas.

Unfortunately, a lot of folks run off the end of the earth with the humble origins idea. They claim Jesus was born poor and homeless. Not so. Joseph had a job—he was a carpenter. They had a home back in Nazareth. They only wound up in a stable because the night they blew into Bethlehem all the hotels were booked. Jesus was born to a working-class family, not to poverty.

As for the Nativity scene we imagine today, it was actually the invention of Francis of Assisi, who came up with the classic tableau in 1223. In a town in central Italy, he assembled villagers and their animals to stage the scenario; a kind of medieval street theater. The idea caught on and it's been a staple of Christmastime ever since.

A Brief History of Christmas

Most of us love Christmas—the smells, the colors, the carols, the sentiments. And what else could move intelligent people to put a big, dead tree in the middle of their living room and create a fire hazard for several weeks? Good thing nobody came up with the Christmas buffalo.

Despite the recent habit of advertisers calling it "the holidays" (they gotta sell Hanukah gifts, too, ya know), and despite my home town of Los Angeles feeling about as Christmassy in December as a skateboard competition in May, Christmas *is* a magical time of year. The notion of everyone setting aside their differences and recognizing their mutual humanity has universal appeal—except for shoppers outside of Best Buy around 6:00 a.m. the day after Thanksgiving. In that case, all bets are off.

Even if you don't take the birth story of Jesus literally, Christmas is awash with sounds and emotions that resonate with the best days of childhood. You're even free to flaunt your bad taste in everything from schmaltzy music to garish broaches to hideous sweaters bearing giant snowflakes or reindeer. You have to wait for July 4th and American flag sweatshirts to witness as many fashion crimes. But whether Orthodox, Catholic, Protestant, Jewish, agnostic, atheist, or Wiccan, there's something about Christmas most of us can appreciate.

The explanation for Christmas we get as kids is pretty straightforward. Jesus was born on December 25, 0000 and we commemorate the holy event with gift-giving. This reenacts the Wise Men offering gifts to the Christ child, and it expresses Jesus' spirit of generosity and love. It also makes you wonder if he felt cheated celebrating his birthday on Christmas every year. Actually, the real story of Christmas is a lot more interesting, and more complicated.

If Jesus was a real historical figure, the day and year of his birth are unknown. This would be understandable if he was the usual great man of history. We don't know the birthday of many ancient heroes because nobody knew they were going to be great when they were born. But if you believe the believers, this wasn't the case with Jesus. The angels knew. The shepherds knew. His parents knew. The Wise Men knew. King Herod knew. Even the Little Drummer Boy had a clue. If anyone had doubts, the Star of Bethlehem should have tipped them off. Yet somehow, nobody made a note of it on their calendar.

Some folks can't resist trying to calculate Jesus' birth date using clues found in Scripture. Among the first was a sixth century Catholic monk named Dionysius Exiguus, who calculated Easter dates as well. He also came up with the idea of *Anno Domini* (in the Year of Our Lord) as a way to reckon the years.

Dionysius started with a passage from *Luke 3:23,* which says Jesus was "about thirty" when he began his ministry in the 15th year of the reign of Tiberius Caesar. This means A.D. 29, which puts Jesus' birth at 1 B.C. Other passages say he was born during the reign of Herod the Great, who died in 4 B.C. A lot of experts now think this was Jesus' birth year.

It's highly unlikely that Jesus was born at the end of the year and equally unlikely that he was born on December 25th. There's certainly no evidence of it. The story has shepherds tending flocks nearby—not something you normally do in the dead of winter. Dionysius decided he was born on March 25th. April 17th was another popular guess. Nobody knew for sure and changes in the calendar over the centuries made calculations even more iffy. But the early Christians didn't care. It was Jesus' death and resurrection that mattered most, not his birth, which is why Easter rather than Christmas is the most holy day of the Christian calendar. You can tell it's more holy because it's a lot less fun.

So why did we settle on December 25th? Well, almost every culture has a big blowout of some kind around December 21st during the Winter Solstice—the first day of winter and the shortest day of the year.

The Roman solstice festival was called Saturnalia—named for the god of agriculture who'd be back in business as the days got longer and spring approached. The week-long celebration was everything you'd expect from a civilization that wore sandals to work, rooted for gladiators, and held board meetings in public baths: parading mobs, raucous drinking, and lavish dining, along with gift exchanges and a Vegas-style sense of anything goes. The entire civilized world went on Spring Break. Gambling was legalized and courts were shut down. Even social roles were reversed—slaves dressed up like their masters and ordered them around. Try fielding this idea at your office holiday party.

Naturally, the straight-laced Christians were appalled by all this. There was nothing in the commandments about enjoying yourself, so for a long time they resisted the impulse to party on the solstice. But as the faith vied for more converts, the Church had to deal with it. So, instead of a festival they decided to observe the solstice in a Christian way, with a church service—Christ's mass. Christmas.

It was their way of turning all that debauchery, which was bad for you, into a spiritual message that was *good* for you. Rather like giving trick-or-treaters a box of wheat germ instead of Hershey bars. The Church also fudged a bit on the meaning of it all by replacing the popular worship of Mithras, the sun god, with worship of the "Son of God,"…another savvy marketing ploy.

From its earliest days, Christmas was a two-track event—a pagan rite of fertility and an observance of Jesus' birth. As all of Europe was Christianized during the Middle Ages, Christmas acquired a lot of local pagan trappings.

In Scandinavia, Norsemen called their Winter Solstice the Yule, and a huge log was burned to keep the house warm and free of dark spirits. An evergreen was brought inside as a symbol of survival through the cold months. Livestock were slaughtered and

38

the occasion was made a feast. In Germany, the god Odin was said to fly through the nights deciding who would have good luck in the coming year and who wouldn't.

In Christian homes, apples were hung from evergreens to recall Eve in the Garden of Eden and these evolved into tree ornaments. The holly shrub's prickly leaves and red berries represented Christ's blood-dappled crown of thorns.

In England there was a tradition of drunken revelry akin to Mardi Gras. Christmas became a kind of Halloween for grownups. The poor would knock on the doors of the rich and demand goodies. Today, of course, they'd only get a restraining order.

When Protestants broke from the Catholic Church about 500 years ago, many rejected Christmas as a papist holiday. In 1645, England's Puritan leader, Oliver Cromwell, overthrew the corrupt monarchy of Charles I and instigated a wave of religious reform that made almost everyone miserable. In 1652, he outlawed the observance of Christmas. Shops stayed open but the churches shut down.

Even so, people continued to celebrate in private. (After all, there was *drinking* involved and this was *England.*) Then, when Charles II restored the English throne in 1661, Christmas was revived by popular demand.

Meanwhile, in the Protestant-dominated American colonies, Christmas took a holiday. The ultra-orthodox Puritans launched the original "war on Christmas" and by 1659 Bostonians could be fined for observing it. Other towns outlawed it for decades. Down in Jamestown, Virginia, it was celebrated unofficially, and they managed to add eggnog to the tradition.

Right up through the American Revolution, however, Yankees largely ignored Christmas. This included the Founding Fathers, who generally didn't pay that much attention to the holiday. That famous painting of George Washington praying in the snow at Valley Forge on Christmas of 1777 depicts what is likely a fictional event.

By the early 1800s, Christmas was reworked into something more acceptable to Protestants. The Industrial Revolution created a growing gap between rich and poor, and nobody did much about it because poverty was seen as a character flaw or a deliberate choice. But now the urban poor were becoming violent in the streets. Reacting to this, social activists and writers made Christmas an occasion to help the needy.

In 1840, Queen Victoria married Prince Albert, who was German, and thus popularized the Tannenbaum—the Christmas tree. The first Christmas cards appeared in 1843 and were an immediate hit. And while the days of boozing it up in the streets were over, a touch of naughtiness was preserved through the Scandinavian practice of kissing under the mistletoe—probably the most action Victorian men got all year.

In England, Charles Dickens crowned the sentiment of helping the poor in 1843 with *A Christmas Carol*. He provided us with Tiny Tim, the first cutesy child star that everyone wanted to slap. Charity also became fashionable; it fit the Christian message of being your brother's keeper. Even so, Protestant churches only reluctantly held Christmas services, mostly to keep up attendance.

Americans didn't catch the Christmas spirit until well into the 19th century, but once they did they couldn't leave well enough alone. They made it more of a family event. This was the era when technology allowed mothers to leave the fields to become the domestic goddesses we idolize today. Up until then, childcare manuals were aimed at Dad and childrearing was more about fatherly discipline than motherly love. But with Mom now in charge, the modern nuclear family emerged. Children now deserved affection and Christmas was the time to indulge the little darlings. This meant making a bigger fuss about the holiday and spending more time at that great new innovation, the department store.

All of which brings us to the patron saint of the shopping mall, Santa Claus, or, as they call him in France and England, Father Christmas. The real Saint Nicholas was a 4th century bishop in the Greek Orthodox Church. His reputation as a traveling gift-giver made him popular throughout the Middle Ages. December 6th was deemed St. Nicholas Day, when the good children would be given presents while the naughty ones came up empty handed. Santa became training wheels for their relationship with God—an unseen supernatural dispenser of rewards for those who obeyed the rules.

The Dutch called the legendary saint "Sinter Klaus" and, once they brought him to America, the name morphed into "Santa Claus." In 1822, an Episcopal minister named Clement Clark Moore embellished the Santa legend with his classic, *A Visit from Saint Nicholas,* better known as *'Twas the Night Before Christmas.* Moore is the guy who named the eight reindeer and had Santa slipping into the house through the chimney. (You know, between Santa, the Easter Bunny, and visits from various angels, there's a lot of breaking-and-entering in Christian lore.)

There was no consensus on what Santa looked like, but Moore made him a jolly, jelly-bellied elf. Years later, political cartoonist Thomas Nast, who became famous for drawing caricatures of Boss Tweed and other New York robber barons, decided to draw the generous Santa Claus in the same tubby profile as the city fat-cats. The image stuck.

As a gift-giver beloved by children, it was only a matter of time before Saint Nick was co-opted by retailers, who enthroned him in their stores. By the time of the American Civil War the department store Santa was an institution.

The bearded, red-and-white clad Santa image gradually emerged in the early 20th century and was later popularized in the 1930s by famous Coca-Cola ads in which he wore the company colors. His emergency reindeer, Rudolph, was created in 1939 in a jingle written by an advertising copywriter at Montgomery Ward. The song was recorded by Gene Autry and it became a hit.

Since then, every generation has carped about the increasing commercialization of Christmas. Yet, in America, more people attend church on Christmas now than ever before. Personally, I miss the drunks in the streets.

Wise Men from the East

Okay, a couple things about the Wise Men from the East who came to visit the Christ child. First, the Book of Matthew is the only one they appear in. Second, the Bible doesn't say how many there were. Some traditions said two. St. Augustine thought there were twelve. It was a 2nd century pope who started the tradition of *three* Wise Men, apparently because they brought three gifts: gold, frankincense and myrrh—the last two items being forms of dried tree sap used in perfumes and incense. What every newborn needs.

The Wise Men are called the Magi—a Persian word for a priest or astrologer from the Zoroastrian religion (the one that likely produced Mithraism). As astrologers, they paid attention to the stars, which Jewish priests didn't do. This is why three rabbis didn't show up with a jug of Manischewitz and a mutual funds starter kit. But notice something here:

> ...wise men from the East came to Jerusalem, saying, "Where is he who has been born king of the Jews? For we have seen his star in the East, and have come to worship him." [Matt. 2:1-2]

Now, if the Wise Men were *from* the east and they saw a star *in* the east, they would have journeyed *toward* the east, which would have put them in Afghanistan and not Judea. (Unless, of course, they meant they were in the east when they saw the star.) More importantly, who told them the star signified the King of the Jews? The Jews didn't; they didn't practice astrology. And why would Persian astrologers want to worship a Jewish king anyway?

As for them being three *kings* from the Orient, that idea was dreamed up by Tertullian, an early Church father who wanted to tie Jesus to an Old Testament prophecy about "kings bearing gifts." It was meant to symbolize the submission of the highest earthly authorities to Christ. But Tertullian made it up.

By the 8th century, the Wise Men had become individual characters: Melchior (an old man), Casper (middle-aged), and Balthazar (a youth, probably from Ethiopia, and therefore black).

The Magi followed the star to Jerusalem, and there they met up with Judea's King Herod, who felt threatened by the birth of this so-called "king." He asked the Wise Men to find Jesus and report back so that *he* could worship the child as well. (Yeah, sure.) The Magi smelled a rat, so after they swung by Bethlehem to drop off their gifts they hightailed it back to the East.

While Matthew depicts Herod as quite the monster, he wasn't all that bad. He was a competent Jewish king with the thankless role of reigning over Judea under the watchful eye of the Romans. It was a difficult balancing act and he generally pulled it off. He tried to win the respect of his subjects, but with a kingdom full of zealous priests dreaming of a messiah to replace him, he wasn't going to win any popularity contests.

The story's claim that Herod worried about a would-be Jewish king isn't quite credible because he was old by this time; he'd be unlikely to sweat the prospect of a rival who wouldn't come of age until he was dead. Furthermore, if he was intent on locating Jesus, he didn't need the Magi to tell him the infant's location. His troops could have followed the Wise Men to Bethlehem. Or they might have followed that giant star pointing right at the manger! You know...the one the Magi used? The one they saw from another *country?*

The Star of Bethlehem

Just what was the Star of Bethlehem? A miracle? A myth? A natural phenomenon? A lot of science-can-explain-the-Bible types have agonized over the Christmas Star, attempting to explain it as a real astronomical event. They calculate the orbits of comets and search the past for supernovas that might have coincided with Jesus' birth. They speculate that it wasn't a "star in the East" but rather a "*sign* in the East" that might have been the conjunction of Jupiter and Saturn in the constellation of Pisces—the constellation of the Jews. Something like this may even have inspired the story. A lot of Discovery Channel airtime has been consumed with these attempts to reconcile science with folktale. Unfortunately, they all fail, and for a couple of simple reasons.

First, there's no astronomical phenomenon of any kind that could guide Wise Men for hundreds of miles to a pinpoint location on earth. Except for a meteor, which would have put a crimp in the whole evening, what happens in space stays in space. You can gallop towards a star all you want. It will never lead you to a particular city, much less a specific Motel VI in Bethlehem.

The only kind of "star" that could do this would be the thingy you typically see on a Christmas card: a glowing orb hovering a few hundred yards above the sleepy suburbs of Bethlehem, beaming a spotlight down to where Jesus lay asleep in the hay.

Okay, fine then. It was a miracle star. Well, why not? It was a night when virgins were giving birth. Ah, but there's another problem. If Wise Men could see it from another country, anyone living closer to Bethlehem would have seen it, too. By the time the three wise guys showed up there'd be standing room only at the inn. Everyone would have flocked to the manger, including the Romans.

The Gospels, however, have nobody but the Magi seeing the star. Even shepherds tending their flocks nearby were told by an angel about the baby Jesus. Fact is, there's no real object that would be visible to astrologers hundreds of miles away but not to shepherds down the street. Nor would so many people ignore something like that. It doesn't add up. The Star of Bethlehem is a myth, just like the stars reported over the delivery rooms of other virgin born god-men.

Oh, and here's a bit of trivia you can share over your next cup of eggnog. According to Matthew, by the time the Magi found Jesus, he was living in a house:

> When they saw the star, they rejoiced exceedingly with great joy; and going into the house they saw the child with Mary his mother... [Matt. 2:10-11]

Maybe the innkeeper came through after all.

The Slaughter of the Innocents

> Then Herod...killed all the male children in Bethlehem and in all that region who were two years old or under, according to the time which he had ascertained from the wise men. [Matt. 2:16]

It would have been awfully sloppy of Herod to order the death of all males under two if the baby he was after was a newborn. Some think the passage suggests Jesus was two years old by the time the Wise Men found him. Whatever the case, this "slaughter of the innocents," a phrase Matthew borrows from the prophet Jeremiah, had to be fictional. As a puppet king of Rome, Herod didn't have the authority to order mass executions. While the Romans could be brutal in warfare, they did follow the rule of law. Given the manpower such a massacre would require, they'd need a really good reason to do this, and Jewish prophecies about a messiah wouldn't cut it. Besides, if such an event had actually occurred, there would've been an insurrection. Judean Jews had rioted over far less egregious offenses than this, yet there's no record outside the Bible of a mass infanticide or of any reaction to it. Surely somebody would have written this down long before the author of Matthew did eighty years later.

To skeptics, the story is an echo of the Moses legend, wherein the pharaoh ordered Egyptian midwives to kill Hebrew babies at birth to control the growing population. It's why the baby Moses ended up floating down the Nile. As it is, Jesus was saved when his parents retreated to another country—Egypt—until Herod died. Matthew is the only Gospel that mentions this major side trip. Because the writer is so set on linking Jesus to the Old Testament, it's no surprise that he got the baby Jesus into the birth country of Moses.

Furthermore, the two Gospels that tell this birth story disagree with each other. Matthew never mentions the census, the manger, or the shepherds tending their flocks. Luke never mentions the Star of Bethlehem, the Magi, or Herod's slaughter of the innocents. Instead, Luke simply has Jesus circumcised eight days after his birth. (The early Church claimed at one point that they possessed his foreskin; apparently they didn't throw anything away.) After this, Luke says Jesus is taken to Jerusalem for ritual purification and then back home to Nazareth. No slaughter, no flight to Egypt, none of Matthew's horror story. If it were true, how could Mark, Luke and John miss all that? It's a mystery.

The Year of Living Dangerously

We know almost nothing about the first thirty years of Jesus' life beyond an eerie little episode when he's about twelve and is found praying to his "Father" in a synagogue. He must have had an unremarkable childhood because, when he begins his missionary work at age thirty, everyone is surprised by the miracles he performs. You'd think being born to a virgin under a star would have prepared them for this.

By the reckonings in Mark, Matthew, and Luke, everything we know of Christ's adulthood comes from the final year of his life. Jesus became a carpenter like his father. That is, his *other* father. The human one. (I suppose he had to buy two neckties for Father's Day.) There is no indication he ever married or even had a girlfriend—and no, I'm not suggesting *that*. Not being married, however, would have made him the exception in first century Palestine. Young men, especially a teacher or rabbi, would normally have been set up with a wife. Even today, unmarried men of a certain age (like mine) are considered a bit suspect. And no, I'm not suggesting *that*. (Not that there's anything *wrong* with it, of course.)

Some scholars looking at heretical accounts of Jesus speculate that he had an intimate relationship with Mary Magdalene, who was one of his most prominent disciples and a financial supporter. Many get hot and bothered about this point. But even some clergy admit that being married with children would not have undermined Jesus' message or authority. It might even have helped the so-called Family Values argument.

Also, just for the record, Mary Magdalene was not a prostitute. That was the idea of a sixth century pope who figured that, if she *had* been a prostitute and could still be forgiven, anyone could attain God's grace. It was a nice idea, but Mary's rep paid a price for a long time. Eventually, however, they did make her a saint.

Many religions, biblical and otherwise, equate celibacy and virginity with purity, and people like their religious leaders pure. But in the early centuries A.D., Catholic priests had the option of getting married and having families. Even medieval popes had children, sometimes with wives and sometimes with concubines. The celibate, unmarried, hands-off priesthood we think of today evolved over centuries and didn't become official until 1139. At that point, Pope Gregory VII made existing marriages among priests null and void. Their wives were demoted to concubines, which basically meant live-in whores—except there was no sex allowed. I'm sure everyone was thrilled.

There are disagreements over why this was done. One claim is that celibacy represents a body-and-soul commitment to God. Another says it was instituted to ensure that a deceased priest's property ended up with the Church instead of with his descendents. Thomas Aquinas argued that celibacy was a Church idea, not God's. Nowadays there are calls by some Catholics to allow priests to marry again. Don't expect any quick action on this, however. Popes aren't generally worried about the issue and it's not as if women are lining up to land a man who wears a flowing frock on holidays and has no experience in bed.

Another controversy rages over whether or not Jesus had siblings. If he did, they must've spent years in therapy dealing with their overachieving brother. Clues in Scripture about this issue are inconclusive. References to James as "the brother of the Lord" or to Jesus as Mary's "firstborn son" are hotly debated. For traditional Catholics, the idea of Mary having additional children is blasphemous. As the Holy Virgin, she had to be a virgin for life, virginity again being equated with purity. Some even claim that, after she gave birth, her virginity was restored. There's a doctor in Beverly Hills who does this, too.

> "Behold, I send my messenger before thy face, who shall
> prepare thy way;
> the voice of one crying in the wilderness:
> Prepare the way of the Lord, make his paths straight—"
> [Mark 1:2-3]

Before rolling out a feature event, it helps to generate some advance buzz with previews of coming attractions. For Jesus, this meant John the Baptist. Essentially the warm-up act for God's headliner, John was the quintessential ranting holy man and one of the few biblical personalities mentioned by writers outside of the Bible. His job was to "prepare the way" for Jesus, and Matthew describes him as "the voice of one crying in the wilderness." That he was. He wore camel skins and ate locusts. He was barking mad. Not the advance man most of us would prefer. But Mark, which first gives us this story, borrows from Old Testament prophecy:

> "Behold, I send my messenger to prepare the way before
> me, and the Lord whom you seek will suddenly come
> into his temple;" [Malachi 3:1]

> A voice cries:
> "In the wilderness prepare the way of the Lord, make
> straight in the desert a highway for our God."
> [Isaiah 40:3]

If prophecy says The Messiah needs a voice crying in the wilderness, he gets one. Except it doesn't say this. It says "a voice cries." And what does it cry? "In the wilderness prepare the way of the Lord." It's *the way of the Lord* that's in the wilderness, not the crying voice. Crying in the wilderness is stupid because nobody lives in the wilderness. John would be preaching to mountain gazelles. Much better for the voice to cry in the center of town where there'd be crowds to hear it. Unfortunately, "A voice crying in a bus station" lacks a certain zing. So, the wilderness it is.

This is a nice example, by the way, of how the New Testament writers disingenuously employ the Hebrew Bible. They unapologetically lift phrases from it to reinforce their stories and, if they have to change the meaning of the line or plug it into a new context...well, God will understand.

The story paints the character of John the Baptist with Old Testament material. John is described with the same language the *Septuagint* uses to describe the prophet Elijah. They even wear the same leather belt (*zonen dematinen*) around the waist (*peri ten osphyn autou*).

John preaches a Gospel of repentance, baptism, and the coming of The Messiah:

> "After me comes he who is mightier than I, the thong of whose sandals I am not worthy to stoop down and untie. I have baptized you with water; but he will baptize you with the Holy Spirit."
> [Mark 1:7-8]

He claims a mighty one is coming who will separate the wheat from the chaff, and that "the chaff he will burn with unquenchable fire." [Matt. 3:12] This is the New Testament's first reference to hell, which isn't yet an actual place run by Satan. It's just a vague notion of a dire fate. But stay tuned.

Today, we react to a sidewalk doomsayer like J-the-B by handing him a dollar or prescribing lithium. But in days of yore a pious wild man screaming the apocalypse pulled in the crowds. John was a master at this.

John pleaded for everyone to confess their sins and come to the Jordan River to be baptized—a purification rite to wash away sin without the need for pricey oils. Christianity was more affordable than Judaism. But baptism didn't start with John. Sumerians, Greeks, and Persians had been doing it for millennia.

When Jesus shows up to be baptized, John recognizes him, which is quite a feat because they last met while both were in their mothers' wombs. Since John was born six months before Jesus, he also survived the slaughter of the innocents, though we never learn how. But when he baptizes Jesus, it's a special moment:

And when he came up out of the water, immediately he saw the heavens opened and the Spirit descending upon him like a dove; and a voice came from heaven, "Thou art my beloved Son; with thee I am well pleased." [Mark 1:10-11]

Mark says the Spirit, or Holy Spirit, descended like a dove, while Luke says it descended "*in bodily form* like a dove upon him." Whether it was a metaphor or an actual bird, both the vision and the voice were only experienced by Jesus.

My question is: Who was this voice from heaven? God? I thought he and Jesus were one and the same. Is Jesus talking to himself? Like a ventriloquist act? No, that wouldn't work because only Jesus hears the voice. So, I guess, he was listening to a voice in his head which was actually himself talking as if he were his own father. You wonder why people didn't get him at first.

The Holy Spirit

So, what exactly is this Holy Spirit that descends like a dove? It's mentioned many times in both the Old and New Testaments and there have been big fights over what it's supposed to be. It's never clearly defined, but it seems to work as a kind of otherworldly tutor:

> ...do not be anxious how or what you are...to say; for the Holy Spirit will teach you in that very hour what you ought to say. [Luke 12:11-12]

It sounds like a state of mind, mysterious and awesome—a feeling of God's presence. Jesus, the king of forgiveness, takes it very seriously:

> "...all sins will be forgiven the sons of men, and whatever blasphemies they utter; but whoever blasphemes against the Holy Spirit never has forgiveness, but is guilty of an eternal sin..." [Mark 3:28]

Yeow! That's heavy duty. For centuries after, Christians would stay up late at night arguing over what exactly Jesus is referring to when he says "Holy Spirit."

These are the popular choices:

1. The presence of God
2. Something that emanates from God
3. The same thing as God
4. One third of God
5. A separate entity that sort of works for God

Since you can't see it, touch it, or stuff it in a box, it's hard to define. But whatever you do, don't blaspheme against it because it's the only sin that even Jesus won't forgive. This Christianity business is starting to look like a bit of a minefield.

John's baptism of Jesus raises an embarrassing theological question for the early Christians. Baptism is a ritual of purification, the washing away of sin. If Jesus was born without sin, why did he need to be baptized? Even J-the-B says that it's *he* who should be baptized by Jesus. Perhaps as an acknowledgement of this dilemma, Matthew has Jesus being a good sport and saying they should just roll with it for the moment. But this still doesn't solve the problem.

The easiest way to solve this conundrum is to write it out of the story. In Mark's baptism scene, Jesus seems like a normal person who is suddenly possessed by the Holy Spirit. This is called the Adoptionist Theory—the notion that he was baptized into perfection at this moment. The idea later became a heresy when it was decided that Jesus had always been divine.

By the time the author of John writes his Gospel, about thirty years after Mark, John the Baptist sees the Spirit descending as a dove while *talking* to Jesus about baptism, but he never actually performs one. Theological problem solved. See how easy it is?

Jesus vs. Satan: Round 1

The Holy Spirit leads Jesus to the desert where he fasts for forty days and nights. This being the Middle East, the desert was the usual testing ground for holy men-in-training—Moses, Elijah the prophet, John the Baptist, and others. You may recall that, after they crossed the Red Sea, the Israelites spent forty years being tested in the Sinai, living such tidy lives that they left no evidence of their stay.

While out there, Jesus meets the devil himself, who is given a much bigger role in the New Testament than he played in the Hebrew Bible. You'd think a meeting like this would be a kind of "King Kong vs. Godzilla" clash of titans. But no, that will come at some unspecified future time—the Second Coming. This first confrontation isn't very thrilling. Mark keeps the story simple: it says Satan tempted Jesus. That's it. Matthew expands the scene with some invented dialogue, but still keeps it brief. There's no Old Testament prophecy for this event, you see. So, the author of Matt, writing for Jews, isn't going to dwell on it.

Luke, however, further embellishes the story. Satan tempts Jesus by turning a stone into bread, and Jesus responds, "Man shall not live by bread alone, but by every word of God." Frankly, this isn't much of a temptation. After weeks in a parched desert, the last thing you'd want is a French roll. Now, if Satan had turned up with a keg of cold beer, history might have been very different.

The devil then offers Jesus all the kingdoms of the world in exchange for worship. If you buy the traditional theology, this makes no sense. The Gospel of John says Jesus was "the Word of God" who existed from the beginning of time. This means Jesus and Satan have known each other for ages, which means Satan knew that Jesus was God. How could he tempt God with a piece of the Lord's own creation? Did God give the devil the pink slip to earth? And if he did, why would he want it back? He could just whip up another planet.

The scene doesn't work unless neither of them knew Jesus was God. That's not something you forget. God knows everything, so

Jesus had to know who he was, right? Or was Jesus' lack of knowledge about himself part of his human condition? If so, how did he know he was The Messiah? You getting a headache yet?

Jesus makes it clear that The Messiah will be a spiritual king, not a political one. He essentially tells the devil to go to hell and Satan departs "until an opportune time." In other words...he'll be back. Why Jesus allowed this, I don't know. He could have saved us a lot of trouble if he had just extinguished the bastard then and there.

A Fish Story

You know what they call a leader with no followers? A guy taking a walk. If Jesus was going to spread his message in an age before junk mail, viral videos, or Twitter, he had to put together a P.R. team. Otherwise, how would the Gospel writers have learned about his life story three generations later? In fact, we're not really sure how they knew it. They never cite their sources, which would have helped their credibility. We can only assume they heard it through the grapevine, which makes them about as reliable as your average blogger.

Since twelve was the number of Israelite tribes in the Old Testament, that's how many disciples Jesus decides to enlist. The four Gospels greatly disagree on the order of events surrounding his recruitment drive, but he doesn't sugarcoat the job of becoming a disciple:

> "Beware of men; for they will deliver you up to councils,
> and flog you in their synagogues..."
> [Matt. 10:17]

> "Then they will deliver you up to tribulation, and put
> you to death; and you will be hated by all nations for my
> name's sake."
> [Matt. 24:9]

Gee...hold me back. This doesn't sound like a cruise gig. But if the work was hazardous and the pay was lousy, the fringe benefits were awesome. A front row seat to eternal life. With this promise,

Jesus turns out to be a master recruiter. His first two conscripts are brothers: Simon Peter and Andrew. Both are fishermen.

> And Jesus said to them, "Follow me and I will make you become fishers of men." And immediately they left their nets and followed him.
> [Mark 1:17-18]

What's striking is how easily Jesus convinces these rough-hewn fishermen to drop their nets and become wandering peaceniks. How many working stiffs could you convert into homeless philosophers with that "fishers of men" pun? In Luke, Jesus fills their net with fish before they sign on. It's odd that such an impressive miracle isn't mentioned in the two earlier Gospels. But as with any fish story, maybe it gets bigger with each retelling.

Among the twelve disciples are:

1) Simon Peter: A fisherman, also nicknamed "the rock," which makes him sound like a wrestling star. He'll become the foundation stone of the Catholic Church. ("Peter" comes from "petros," the Greek word for rock.) Technically, he was the first pope, and he's allegedly buried under St. Peter's Basilica in the Vatican, where you can see his alleged tomb. Allegedly. I'm not sure why he isn't called Simon.

2) Andrew: He's Simon Peter's brother, also a fisherman, and a manly man because that's what "Andrew" means.

3) James the son of Zebedee: Yet another fisherman.

4) John, brother of James: Still *another* fisherman. Jesus must have had a thing for seafood. After all, he was symbolized by the fish long before the cross became the official Christian logo. It's a peculiar trademark, but I suppose he could have done worse. Nobody's going to stick a Jesus chicken on their bumper.

The remaining eight disciples, whom we know little about, were Philip, Bartholomew, Thomas (the doubting one), Matthew (a tax collector; *not* the guy who wrote the Gospel), Thaddaeus, then another Simon, Judas the son of James, and last and most certainly least, Judas Iscariot (the bad guy). More on him later.

It's generally assumed by Church historians that "the Twelve" were real people, though it's not as if there's any independent evidence of a dozen spiritually-imbued evangelists spreading the Jesus story around the Middle East at the time. If Jesus really existed, somebody had to pass on his story and may even have added the supernatural flourishes. What happened to these guys? Where is the verifiable chain-of-evidence that links Jesus' own disciples to the people who wrote the Gospels a half-century later? Answer: There isn't any.

Anyway, Jesus initially instructs the Twelve to preach only to Jews. This policy would change. He also tells them not to accept any money. This policy would change, too. And how.

Jesus then tells his men what to take along on their evangelical journeys:

> He charged them to take nothing for their journey except a staff; no bread, no bag, no money in their belts; but to wear sandals and not put on two tunics.
> [Mark 6:8-9]

It's a minor point, but while Mark has Jesus suggesting they take a staff and wear sandals, Matthew and Luke have him saying they should take no staff, and Matthew says no sandals either. [Matt. 10:9-10, Luke 9:3] Would the perfect author of the Gospel truth make a boo-boo even this tiny?

A bigger question is over how Mark can have Jesus send out his disciples in chapter six when they don't learn that he's The Messiah until chapter eight? *Mark 8:29* is when Peter figures out that Jesus is the Christ. How can they preach the Word before they know it themselves? *Mark 6:13* also says they cast out many demons, yet they don't learn until *Mark 9:25* that they need to say a prayer first for it to work. They become teachers before they've learned their subject.

Can't Get No Respect

Mark's Gospel has two sections—Jesus preaching in Galilee and Jesus preaching in Jerusalem. In the early going, Jesus and his troops don't have much luck winning converts in Galilee. One of his first moves is to sermonize in his home town of Nazareth. We don't get the details of what he said, but the folks he grew up with are a little worried and they seem ready to fit him for a straightjacket:

> And when his friends heard it, they went out to seize him, for they said, "He is beside himself." And the scribes who came down from Jerusalem said, "He is possessed by Beelzebub, and by the prince of demons he casts out the demons…" [Mark 3:21-22]

They think he's losing it. Well, let's face it, the folks back home are going to be a tough audience if you come off like, uh, God's gift to the world. They'll cut you down to size.

> "Is not his mother called Mary? And his brethren, James, and Joseph and Simon, and Judas? And his sisters, are they not all with us? Where then did this man get all this?" And they took offense at him. But Jesus said to them, "A prophet is not without honor except in his own country and in his own house." [Matt. 13:55-57]

Religious leadership requires a certain mystique and it's hard to engender this in the people who knew you as a snot-nosed kid (not that Jesus ever had a cold, of course). Apparently irked by their reaction, Matthew says Jesus doesn't even bother to prove himself with a miracle. He claims they aren't worthy. This gets the crowd so angry they almost throw him off a cliff! Jesus gets the hint and leaves.

What doesn't make sense about this episode is that the folks from his hometown don't seem to remember anything about his celebrated birth thirty years before. You don't forget stuff like the miracle star or the Wise Men. How did Joseph and Mary explain all that frankincense and myrrh? John's Gospel says Jesus' disciples knew immediately that he was The Messiah. So why didn't the folks who knew him since childhood? Did everyone forget all those innocents who were slaughtered?

This strongly indicates that Matthew's Nativity story, which Mark never mentions, is entirely invented. The author gives the pagan myth of the virgin born god-man a kosher makeover. But it never really happened.

Also notice that *Matt. 13:55* makes reference to Jesus' "brothers and sisters." This line, and others like it, keeps some people up late at night arguing about who these folks were. Catholics suggest they were Jesus' cousins, or perhaps his "spiritual" brothers and sisters. Anything but his actual siblings. The Church doesn't want to think of Mary as anything but a perpetual virgin. Yet another explanation says they were Joseph's children from a previous marriage. If that's true, where were they the night Jesus was born? And why didn't anybody write this down?

In any case, as the whole mob scene with Jesus takes place, a couple of spies for the religious leaders in Jerusalem look on. And they don't see a messiah; they see a troublemaker. Storm clouds are gathering on the horizon.

But what exactly is Jesus saying that gets these guys so upset?

CHAPTER THREE

Stumping for God

What reasons do the Christians give for
the distinctiveness of their beliefs?
In truth, there is nothing at all unusual
about what the Christians believe...

—Celsus, ca. A.D. 178

The Sermon on the Mount

As Jesus made his healing tour throughout Galilee, his fame spread far and wide. He was bigger than John Lennon. Matthew says Jesus healed "every disease and every infirmity." Galilee must have been the healthiest place on earth. Nothing like single provider, non-profit healthcare, huh?

His following grew, and Jesus sensed it was time to deliver his major stump speech. He made it from a hilltop, unless you believe Luke, which says he stood on a plain. (Was the author blind?) The speech is known as the Sermon on the Mount—a clear set of moral prescriptions to which countless believers would spend the next 2,000 years giving lip service.

For many, these lines are the core of Christian philosophy, which makes it strange that Mark doesn't even mention them. Isn't this like telling the story of Moses and leaving out the Ten Commandments?

The Beatitudes

The opening verses of the sermon are called *The Beatitudes*—a list of qualities that would get you into the Kingdom of Heaven. What strikes you about these bits of wisdom is how little they resemble the attitudes of so many politically-active evangelicals today. Of course, we can't be certain of exactly what Jesus said anyway because Matthew and Luke disagree on what he said. Some lines sound similar, but do they really mean the same thing?

> "Blessed are you poor, for yours is the kingdom of God."
> [Luke 6:20]
>
> "Blessed are the poor in spirit, for theirs is the Kingdom of Heaven." [Matt. 5:3]

These statements suggest two different criteria for who is blessed. Blessing "you poor" sounds like being penniless gets you in the door. Being "poor in spirit" could include billionaires suffering from low self-esteem. *The Catholic Encyclopedia* says this is pretty much the case. They regard "poor" not to mean economic poverty but rather a meek or wretched state of mind. Sure, poverty and wretchedness often overlap. But a homeless man with a bad attitude might not make the cut while an A-list celebrity could sail right in if he's wretched enough to be projectile-vomiting at the Betty Ford Clinic.

Others believe Luke's line about "the poor" *does* in fact refer to a lack of material wealth because that writer was reaching out to the masses, most of whom didn't have two shekels. The author of Matthew, on the other hand, writing for a prosperous, educated readership, might have wanted to bless the "poor in spirit" in order to keep his more affluent audience on board. Matthew continues:

> Blessed are those who mourn, for they shall be comforted.
> Blessed are the meek, for they shall inherit the earth.
> Blessed are those who hunger for righteousness, for they shall be satisfied. [Matt. 5:3-6]

And now here's Luke:

> Blessed are you that hunger now, for you shall be satisfied. [Luke 6:21]

Okay...Matthew's upper class audience wants justice while Luke's readers, the working class, have the munchies. One promises spiritual nourishment, the other a decent meal. Religious uplift vs. meat and potatoes. It's your choice.

> Blessed are the merciful, for they shall obtain mercy.
> Blessed are the pure in heart, for they shall see God.
> Blessed are the peacemakers, for they shall be called sons of God.
> Blessed are those who are persecuted for righteousness' sake, for theirs is the Kingdom of Heaven.
> [Matt. 5:7-10]

There's a certain karmic flavor to these ideas. Send out good vibes and the good vibes will come back to you. It's the Golden Rule, which was taught by everyone from Confucius to Socrates, though I do think Jesus put it most eloquently.

Next, Jesus introduces an idea that raises a lot of questions.

The Kingdom of Heaven

The Gospels have Jesus spending a lot of time in his early sermons telling people to prepare for the Kingdom of Heaven or the Kingdom of God. But nobody seems entirely sure what he's talking about. As usual, there are plenty of theories. In the Old

Testament, there's no heaven to look forward to. But there is the promise of a messiah who will establish an idyllic kingdom based in Jerusalem. That's a clear vision.

The Gospel of Mark, however, has Jesus tampering with these traditional expectations and putting a new spin on what everybody thought they understood:

> "The kingdom of God is as if a man should scatter seed upon the ground, and should sleep and rise night and day, and the seed should sprout and grow, he knows not how." [Mark 4:26-27]

This doesn't really clear it up for me, nor do the other metaphors Jesus uses to define the Kingdom of God. It sounds like something good, but I was hoping for a bit less ambiguity than lines that liken it to a mustard seed, buried treasure, a pearl hunter, or a fish net:

> "...the Kingdom of Heaven is like a net which was thrown into the sea and gathered fish of every kind; when it was full, men drew it ashore and sat down and sorted the good into vessels and threw away the bad. So it will be at the close of the age. The angels will come out and separate the evil from the righteous, and throw them into the furnace of fire; there men will weep and gnash their teeth." [Matt. 13:47-50]

Whoa! Wait a second! When did *hellfire* come into this!? You're telling me there's a "sorting out" at the End of Time? I'm supposed to live my life wondering if I'll avoid eternal teeth-gnashing? And if I'm good, my reward will be spending forever with poor, meek, hungry, persecuted peacemakers? This is the *good* news? What's the bad news?

> ...the kingdom of God is at hand... [Mark 1:15]

Yikes! Looks like I'm not getting any sleep tonight. So, how do I know exactly when this kingdom is coming?

The Kingdom of God is not coming with signs to be
observed...for behold, the Kingdom of God is in the
midst of you." [Luke 17:20-21]

Huh...Now he makes it sound like a state of mind again. Or
perhaps this refers to Jesus being in their midst. I think so...but I'm
not sure. Fortunately, the only thing at stake is my immortal soul.

Jesus on Economics

The Sermon on the Mount continues, and it has Jesus weighing
in on a range of practical issues. Among them is money. One of the
more twisted developments of modern Christianity, at least in the
U.S., is that Jesus has become a hero of free market conservatives.
Somehow, this penniless preacher has been morphed into a profit-
seeking, laissez faire investment banker.

Personally, I have no problem with the free market so long as
it's understood to be a human contrivance and not holy writ. But
capitalism is about material gain—how to make stuff, how to
acquire stuff, how to get people to produce more stuff using less
stuff so they end up with more stuff. No wonder economists are
stuffy. But not Jesus; he didn't care much about stuff:

"No one can serve two masters...You cannot serve God
and mammon." [Matt. 6:24, Luke 16:13]

Trinity Broadcasting and a lot of free market fundamentalists
seem to have forgotten this. They raise oodles of mammon pitching
God's 800-number for contributions. Archangels are standing by.

"...it is easier for a camel to pass through the eye of a
needle than for a rich man to enter the kingdom of
God." [Matt. 19:24, Mark 10:25, Luke 18:25]

Not really Rupert Murdoch's motto, is it? The Gospels make a
clear point—the same one Plato made centuries earlier: "It is
impossible for an exceptionally good man to be exceptionally rich."

Of course, lots of for-profit pastors and evangelical entrepreneurs are willing to give it a try.

> "...woe to you who are rich, for you have already received your comfort." [Luke 6:24]

I wonder if this makes the pope nervous? Here's a guy who can fly to some destitute country, preach the virtue of renouncing worldly wealth, then rise up from his throne, gather his satin robes, ride off in his popemobile, and wing his way home on a personal jet to a palatial estate whose interior decorators included Bernini and Michelangelo.

When Pope John Paul II passed away in 2005, his funeral was attended by the world media, half the U.N., and enough cardinals in flowing robes to make Vatican City look like a gay wedding cake. But when they laid the pontiff to rest, he was placed in a simple pine box because he was a "humble man," and we wouldn't want the event to look *ostentatious* now, would we? It seems clear that, if popes lived a little less like Caesar and a little more like Christ, they'd be easier to take seriously about the virtues of salvation over material greed.

Of course, a lot of people who vote traditional values don't pay much attention to what Jesus says about money, and for good reason. It's kind of depressing:

> "Sell all that you own and distribute the money to the poor, and you will have treasure in heaven."
> [Matt. 19:21, Mark 10:21, Luke 18:22]

Hmm... Sounds like socialism. Think you'll see this in the Republican Party platform any time soon?

> "...if any one should sue you and take your coat, let him have your cloak as well..." [Matt. 5:40]

It sounds like Jesus is giving legal advice. Bad legal advice. Give the guy who's suing you *more* than what he's asking for? Actually, the word "sue" in this case is taken to mean "beg" or "ask." So, if someone asks for a buck, give him two. It's a generous attitude, but hardly that of the economic do-it-yourselfer. You start to see why it's hard to be a genuine Christian in the modern world. It's not just because you can't curse or go bed-hopping. It's because you have to live by rules like this:

> "...lend, expecting nothing in return; and your reward will be great..." [Luke 6:35]

That would put an end to the banking industry.

> "Give to him who begs from you, and do not refuse him who would borrow from you." [Matt. 5:42]

When it comes to money, Jesus is more Dalai Lama than Adam Smith. Nowhere does he extol hard work, private property, personal ambition, wealth creation, efficiency, investment, or saving for the future. Quite the contrary:

> "...do not be anxious about your life, what you shall eat or what you shall drink, nor about your body, what you shall put on...Look at the birds of the air; they neither sow nor reap...and yet your heavenly Father feeds them...Consider the lilies of the field, how they grow; they neither toil nor spin..." [Matt. 6:25-29]

I had a roommate like this. He neither toiled nor spun. He never did anything—though the father that fed him wasn't in heaven. He was in St. Louis paying the credit card bills. Jesus' model citizen doesn't sound like a visionary planner with the industrious drive of the capitalist. He sounds like a ne'er-do-well. And as for the birds—of course they neither sow nor reap. They eat worms and sleep in trees. Naked. Is this part of your retirement plan?

Jesus continues, sounding vaguely like Scarlet O'Hara:

> "Therefore do not be anxious about tomorrow, for tomorrow will be anxious for itself." [Matt. 6:34]

He comes off as totally unconcerned with wealth, work, or even planning ahead, because ultimately none of it counts. He promises the *meek* shall inherit the earth, not the hucksters, the inside traders, or the born-again P.T. Barnums running tax-free theme parks. Money isn't important. In fact, it's kind of bad.

There are few, however, who take this advice seriously. Most people give themselves a lot of interpretive leeway when it comes to Jesus and money. Those who take him literally don't end up on Wall Street or praying with the power elite in "The Family" on C Street. Monks live in communes, not penthouses. Nuns take a vow of poverty, they don't pledge a monthly sales quota. When the salvation-happy Pilgrims landed in the New World, they didn't even acknowledge private property at first. Everyone worked for the collective and the church leaders decided who got what—from each according to his abilities and to each according to his needs. Does that sound like capitalism to you?

Of course, these groups were the exception. Historically, most churches had no objection to accumulating art, gold, jewels, or land, even as they venerated a man who rebuked the cult of money. Kind of a bait-and-switch. Or just hypocrisy.

Even industry-worshipping philosophers like Ayn Rand, whose birth certificate probably paid dividends, have pointed out how absurd it is to try and reconcile Christianity with capitalism. Here's just a sliver of what the godmother of supply side economics wrote about altruism and the spirit of giving vs. the profit motive:

> "Capitalism and altruism are incompatible; they are philosophical opposites; they cannot exist in the same man or in the same society."

Jesus seemed to agree.

> "Do not lay up for yourself treasures on Earth...but lay up for yourself treasures in heaven." [Matt. 6:19-20]

In other words, don't sweat about money. There's no toll for getting through the gates of heaven. At least, they don't want cash.

Another area where Jesus seems at odds with today's conservative Christians is law and order. They're both supposed to be tough on crime, right? Well, here's the way Matthew has Jesus handling bad guys:

> "You have heard that it was said, 'An eye for an eye and a tooth for a tooth.' But I say to you, do not resist one who is evil. But if anyone strikes you on the right cheek, turn to him the other also..." [Matt. 5:38-39]

Scholars point out that this isn't just about letting somebody slug you. When a person slaps your face they usually do it forehand. By turning your cheek you force the offender to backhand you—a despicably weak act. It's how a brute strikes a woman or a cruel master his slave. It turns the offender from a person of power into a slime bag. Unfortunately, it still means you get smacked in the kisser, twice, while the other guy keeps all his teeth. That's a problem because some people don't realize that they're slime bags.

But Jesus knows that violence begets violence. Retaliation has been the standard response to injury since we started clobbering each other around black monoliths. *Not* responding to an attack and letting God handle the punishment is what frees you from this vicious circle, even if it doesn't free you from a broken jaw.

According to *Matthew 5:38*, Christians are not supposed to fight evil. They're not even supposed to *resist* one who is evil. By rejecting "eye for an eye," Jesus rejects vengeance-based justice, and that includes capital punishment. Your job is to be good; it's not to punish evil. Punishment requires passing *judgment* and you're supposed to leave that up to God:

> "Judge not, that you shall not be judged." [Matt 7:1]

Following this rule is tougher than you think. Never judge *anyone?* How would you decide who to hire, or convict, or marry, or vote for? What would Simon Cowell do for a living?

There's another interesting rule that Jesus tells a crowd in Jerusalem when they grab a prostitute and want to stone her as the law prescribes:

> "Let him who is without sin among you cast the first stone." [John 8:7]

By this standard only Jesus or Mary could execute anyone, which means there really can't be any executions—which seems to be the point. Jesus appears to want a world *without* executions. Judgment is coming *soon* and God can dish out the punishment without human assistance, thank you very much.

To execute someone, even if they deserve it, isn't taking Jesus' advice, which is to walk the straight and narrow and never you mind making judgments about life and death. That's God's job. Even a skeptic can understand this.

Ironically, many of the folks who purport to take the New Testament literally have a hard time sticking by this revolutionary rule. They *love* to judge, despite the clear example in Scripture of how dangerous this can be. Jesus himself was wrongly judged and executed, and he didn't lift a finger to save himself. Instead, he stuck to his principles and took it like a savior. Aren't his followers supposed to emulate him?

We sometimes hear that Christians can avoid judging if they "love the sinner and hate only the sin." But the folks who say this don't often distinguish between the two. Case in point: Bill Clinton and Monica Lewinsky. You're telling me evangelicals actually loved President Bubba and only hated the blowjob?

Jesus wasn't the first to come up with the idea of avoiding judgment, by the way. Four centuries earlier Socrates said, "So, we should never take revenge and never hurt anyone, even if we have been hurt." He went on to say, "It is never right to do wrong and never right to take revenge..." Sadly, neither Jesus nor Socrates is on the Texas State Supreme Court.

Avoiding evil is Christian. Fighting evil is not. Even as Jesus is arrested, one of his followers pulls out a sword to defend him and Jesus says:

> "Put your sword in its place, for all who take up the
> sword will perish by the sword."
> [Matt. 26:52]

Not exactly *"Bring it on!"* is it? Jesus' attitude toward war has been tremendously unpopular over the centuries because it doesn't satisfy our bloodlust, nor does it get rid of the bastards who keep bothering us. So, we ignore it. Countries buy weapons and make war in the name of Christian values all the time.

And please don't justify that with passages like *Matthew 10:34:*

> "Do not suppose that I have come to bring peace to the
> earth. I did not come to bring peace, but a sword."

Here, it's *Jesus* wielding the sword, not you. He's the Son of God; it's his job to pass judgment. The Lord never said, "Vengeance is *ours.*" The sword is an instrument of divine justice, not human law enforcement.

In one other passage, *Luke 22:36,* Jesus recommends that his disciples buy a sword before he sends them out to evangelize. Apparently he anticipated how people might react to strangers at their door wanting to talk about religion. Maybe a little insurance was in order. But it's not as if he sent them out on a military campaign. He doesn't say, "Blessed are the sharpshooters," despite what the NRA might think. Jesus was not about killing, even the bad guys, and that drives us absolutely crazy. How do you deal with a guy who says stuff like this:

> "You have heard that it was said, 'You shall love your
> neighbor and hate your enemy.' But I say to you, Love
> your enemies and pray for those who persecute you..."
> [Matt. 5:43-44]

> "Love your enemies, do good to those who hate you, bless those who curse you, pray for those who abuse you." [Luke 6:27-28]

Can you imagine running for office on this platform? "Love the terrorists and forgive those who attacked us." Not a winning campaign slogan—especially in the churchy parts of the country. Ironic, huh? We're such a Christian nation that anyone who bases his candidacy on the Sermon on the Mount can't get elected.

Spin the Gospels all you want, there is absolutely nothing Jesus said or did that justifies war for any reason. Not even to defend your country. The whole idea of the Christian Soldier is an oxymoron. Sure, you want to fight evil. The problem is *everyone* thinks they're fighting evil, even the evil guys. The result: everyone fights. Yet evil never seems to go away—especially when we try to eliminate it by killing people.

I admit this pacifist philosophy isn't a formula for a country's longevity. But Jesus kept insisting, "The Kingdom of God is at hand." Longevity wasn't the priority. Holiness was.

Jesus on Family Values

Despite today's pious bellowing about so-called Family Values, Jesus was not much of a family man. He never married, never had kids, never officiated a wedding, never paid much attention to his mother, and never promoted family life. When asked how one could serve him, he didn't say, "Find a nice Jewish girl, settle down, get a job, make babies..." He told people to drop everything and follow him. That's the response of a cult leader, not a family man.

> "If anyone comes to me and does not hate his own father and mother and wife and children and brothers and sisters, yes, and even his own life, he cannot be my disciple." [Luke 14:26]

He's really serving up the Kool-Aid here; this is very cultish talk. It hardly squares with "Honor your father and your mother." Nor does it jibe with *Matthew 15:4*, where Jesus quotes God (a.k.a. himself) saying, "'He who speaks evil of his father or mother, let him surely die.'" Kind of a mixed message we're getting here.

Generally speaking, family wasn't much on his mind. The day he preached in his home town, his mother and brothers wanted to talk to him. But they couldn't reach him for the crowd. When Jesus was informed of this, instead of having the mob step aside to make room for his mom, he said, "My mother and my brothers are those who hear the word of God and do it." [Luke 8:21] His very own mother couldn't get a word with him and she was the Holy Virgin!

In another instance a new recruit tells Jesus, "I will follow you, Lord; but let me first say farewell to those at my home." Jesus responds, "No one who puts a hand to the plow and looks back is fit for the Kingdom of God." [Luke 9:61-62] Yet another initiate asks for time to bury his just-deceased father before joining the disciples. Jesus replies, "Follow me, and let the dead bury their own dead." [Matt. 8:21-22] Whoa...pretty cold. Also pretty weird given that it usually requires the living to bury the dead.

There are even parts of Scripture that seem ardently *anti*-family. Check out this quote from the Prince of Peace:

> "I come to cast fire upon the earth; and would that it were already kindled...Do you think I have come to give peace on earth? No, I tell you, but rather division; for henceforth in one house there will be five divided...father against son and son against father, mother against daughter and daughter against her mother, mother-in-law against her daughter-in-law..." [Luke 12:49-53]

Wanna bet James Dobson doesn't have this etched on a plaque in his office over at Focus on the Family? Admittedly, it doesn't take a commandment to get people sniping at their in-laws, but wow! This sounds worse than my family on a cross-country trip.

Given that early Christians expected Jesus' imminent return, there was no need to worry about family. The end was near. Three Gospels quote him as saying the Kingdom of God will come before "this generation" is passed. He was wrong. But wrong or not, family relationships didn't appear to be his primary concern.

Traditional Marriage

While we're on the subject of Family Values, it's worth mentioning a point about so-called "traditional marriage." Through most of Western history, marriage was not the sacred union of hearts we idealize today. It was a property arrangement. The bride was barter handed over from one clan to another in exchange for land, or a peace treaty, or a whole lot of fresh melons. Yet three millennia of marriage as an economic swap or a political deal didn't undermine the West. It was part of it.

Another traditional form of marriage was polygamy. It was practiced by most of the heroes of the Old Testament. It seemed perfectly acceptable to God and was evidently part of the plan. In fact, the Twelve Tribes of Israel are descended from twelve men who came from one father—Jacob—and *four* different mothers—two wives, who were sisters, and their maids. God didn't condemn this and it went on for centuries. Somewhere along the way, however, he changed his mind, because now it's forbidden. Yet historically, polygamy is one of the most traditional forms of marriage.

Jesus did cherish loving couples and caring parents, but they were less important to him than loyal followers and ardent missionaries. It didn't matter that the family was the cornerstone of civilization—civilization was about to become yesterday's news. If you were really on board, your job was to forget about family, money, work, pleasure, punishment, and your waistline, and prepare instead for the Kingdom of God.

While marriage wasn't a top priority, Jesus did condemn divorce for any reason other than a cheating spouse. To get around this inconvenient rule, the Catholic Church came up with the concept of annulment—that is, pretending your marriage didn't happen in the first place. I'm not sure why this loophole doesn't apply to any other contract. Can't I annul my two-year cell phone plan?

Jesus was also tough on adultery, or naughtiness of any kind:

> "And if your right hand causes you to sin, cut it off and throw it away; it is better that you lose one of your members than that your whole body go into hell."
> [Matt. 5:30]

If pubescent boys followed this rule, most of them would be left-handed by the sixth grade. This zero-tolerance for error leads to unreasonable ideas like, "...everyone who gazes at a woman to lust after her has committed adultery..." [Matt. 5:28] or, "Everyone who hates his brother is a murderer." [1 John 3:15] Wow. If you glance at a nice tush, you're a rapist? If you fight with your bossy sister, you're a killer? If you let loose a fart, you're guilty of chemical warfare and should be tried at The Hague? Aren't we losing perspective here?

Unfortunately, evangelical leaders often do. Reverend John Hagee (the guy who said Hurricane Katrina was God's way of bitch-slapping New Orleans for planning a gay parade) uses this technique in his church. He guilts people who've committed the slightest offense into thinking they're criminals in need of industrial-strength salvation. But he does it out of love.

Pro-Life?

Of course, no discussion of Family Values is complete without touching on the touchiest of touchy issues, the abortion debate. It's not surprising that the issue evokes emotion and controversy, but what does Jesus say about it? Answer: Not a word.

This is pretty astonishing given that virtually everyone who opposes legal abortion cites religion as the chief reason. Yet, claiming the Bible to be anti-abortion is legislating from the bench. It's reading stuff into Scripture that isn't there. The fact is the Bible doesn't ban abortion. It's another one of those policies invented by churches and then treated as if it were holy writ. It ain't.

Anti-choice activists are quick to haul up verses wherein God or Jesus asks us to "choose life." But choosing life isn't the issue. *Everyone* is pro-life. The question is: Does the word "life" include the unborn? Some assume it does, some assume it doesn't. The Bible never takes sides.

Most of the time, the word "life" in the New Testament refers to *eternal* life rather than biological life; the life of the soul. Nor does it specify at what point a fetus acquires a soul. There are a lot of theories about all this, but nothing in the Scripture. The Bible never teaches that "life begins at conception."

The only verse in the entire Bible that comes close to commenting on how we should view the unborn is from the Old Testament, *Exodus 21:22*, which says that, if men fight and cause a pregnant woman to miscarry, a fine shall be paid. But if the woman herself is killed, it's eye for an eye—a death sentence. There's a huge difference in the penalty for killing a mother versus killing her fetus. One is treated like murder, the other like a parking ticket. Clearly, Scripture regards the born and the unborn as different—which is the pro-choice view. An acorn is not an oak tree. So, if anything, the Bible is pro-choice. Point this out at your next Bible class and watch everyone's expression. Bring a camera.

Jesus on Homosexuality

Nothing. Sorry. Apparently he didn't sweat the issue.

Prayer

Before Jesus winds up the Sermon on the Mount, he delivers what we all know as the Lord's Prayer. When it comes to how one should pray, he offers this wise instruction:

> "And when you pray, you must not be like the hypocrites; for they love to stand and pray in the synagogues and at the street corners, that they may be

seen by men...when you pray, go into your room and shut the door and pray to your Father who is in secret...and in prayer do not heap up empty phrases as the Gentiles do; for they think that they will be heard for their many words." [Matt. 6:5-7]

This pretty much wraps it up for your local megachurch, along with every sidewalk prophet with a sandwich board reading, "Honk if you love Jesus." Jesus doesn't want you to honk. He doesn't need mass prayers staged in a titanium tabernacle big enough to be seen from orbit. He says go to your room, be humble, and pray with the sincerity of someone who isn't doing it for an audience. The Mormons can send their choir on tour, but that's it.

The Purpose Driven Cult

What's most remarkable about the Sermon on the Mount is that Jesus comes off as a forgiving, anti-materialistic, socialist pacifist—light years from the Christian warriors of the Middle Ages or the judgment-crazy, gun-loving, free market firebrands who routinely invoke his name today. Here is the role model for quiet monks, pious Pilgrims, Amish communes, the Salvation Army, and cozy little prayer groups. He's the Jesus of humility, kindness, and tolerance—the one who asks us to be our brother's keeper. So where did all those other guys come from?

Well, it turns out there's Jesus and then there's *Jesus.* That is, there's the benevolent Jesus of the Sermon, whom we just met, and then there's the Jesus yet to come—the Jesus of the Cross. The icon of righteousness, authority, power and, inevitably, conquest. Under the banner of the Cross, it's not about communing with your brothers and sisters. It's about Yahweh or the highway. Follow the leaders, don't ask too many questions, and march lockstep into glory. Not much live-and-let-live *Kum Ba Yah* there.

While the Sermon lays out a creed of peace, love and forgiveness, the Cross will become the battle standard of martial religion. The Jesus of the Sermon may charm the humble crowds with an affectionate, charismatic persona, but the Christ of the

Cross is the favorite of authoritarians—the people who are certain that God wants them in charge. For these guys, it's less about emulating Jesus and more about obeying him. If you're not sure what that means, they'll be glad to explain it to you. And they'll do so with the zeal of a holy cause, because that's exactly what it is. Medieval monarchs, crusading knights, and autocratic popes fell into this camp. It was an imperial power trip.

With the emergence of the Protestant Reformation some 500 years ago, however, one branch of the faith broke from the regal trappings of the Church hierarchy. You no longer needed a priest as the go-between for you and Jesus; you had direct access. This idea went over well with the pious utopians who washed up on America's shores in the early going. They now had a Jesus suited to people fleeing the church-state combo of European regimes. One that spoke to the *"Don't Tread on Me"* individualism of the American Revolution and the Western frontier.

Unfortunately, this also produced a culture of homegrown demagogues who ruled their local parishes in the name of Jesus, exalting their authority from their own churches. They defined God's will, gave marching orders to the faithful, and any authority that might thwart their agenda—even a democratic government— would be vilified as un-Christian and be labeled "oppressive." The Jesus of *"Get the hell off my lawn!"* was now on tap to oppose any kind of government "intrusion" a preacher didn't particularly like—such as the abolition of slavery, the New Deal, the Civil Rights Act, teaching evolution, abortion rights, or Medicare.

Ironically, this faith-based subculture found an ally in the ultimate materialist cause—capitalism. While it sounds strange today, big business has traditionally been a friend of big government as far back as the Dutch East India Company. Uncle Sam has always been corporate America's biggest customer—ask any canal builder, investment banker, railroad baron, or military contractor. But as 20th century government turned its concern to workers and consumers with laws governing monopolies, fair wages, safe products, and clean air, big business became annoyed with Washington as well. Industrial aristocrats and conservative country pastors found common ground.

Of course, the damned communists only made things worse. Disdainful of both private property and faith (except in their own cult), the Reds helped move evangelicals and multinationals onto the same political platform. By the end of the Cold War, these two minorities had merged into a movement bent on characterizing any activist government as a harbinger of totalitarian rule. Big business got religion and religion became big business. Economic elites teamed up with right-wing preachers to rev up the flocks with cries of "Freedom from big government!", as if regulating Exxon-Mobil were the same thing as telling Joe Six-pack which brand of beer he had to drink.

The result of this corporate con job is an update of the feudal system that kept starving peasants loyal while the papacy filled its coffers. Working stiffs now side with zillionaires, over whom they have no control, against their own democracy, over which they do. Instead of a healthy skepticism of government, they buy into conspiracy theories concocted to turn them anti-regulation, anti-union, anti-social welfare, anti-*anything* that crimps the corporate bottom line, their own economic interests be damned. And if guns offer compensation for this with a bogus sense of empowerment, then stock up. The people have to defend the Constitution against, uh…all the guys we keep voting for.

Anyway, this development of both a humble Jesus and a crusading Christ is a major reason for Christianity's long success. It's not because the faith represents a clear set of edicts, like the Sermon on the Mount. Quite the contrary. It's become the Swiss Army knife of religions, with something useful for almost everyone: imperial churches, utopian cults, industrial empire-builders, and gun-slinging holy rollers.

All this started on a hilltop with a clear, peaceful message. Sadly, this would be the last time following Jesus would be so simple—as he and his disciples were about to find out.

CHAPTER FOUR

Road Show

God loves you, and I'm really trying.

—Bumper Sticker

Tricks of the Trade

Offering crowds sound advice in the Sermon on the Mount is one thing, but it was going to take more than wise words from a hilltop to build up a real following for the new faith. Jesus had to dazzle 'em. One way to stoke the masses, especially in the rural outback of Galilee, was to offer free food, or free medicine, or free entertainment. Being both generous and resourceful (not to mention omnipotent), Jesus managed to provide all three.

The First Miracle

The Gospel of John skips over the Sermon on the Mount and goes directly to Jesus performing his first miracle at a wedding in the town of Cana. Here, he turns twenty or thirty gallons of water into wine, which makes him the go-to dude for the beer run. But certain fundamentalist teetotalers claim that Jesus would never sanction alcohol use and insist that the word usually translated as "wine" actually means "grape juice." This is what linguists refer to as bullshit. In the story, when the miracle drink is tasted (a nice '29 Chardonnay, perhaps?), the steward remarks:

> "Every man serves the good wine first; and when men have drunk freely, then the poor wine; but you have kept the good wine until now." [John 2:10]

It's the old trick of serving the vintage stuff while everyone is sober and then breaking out the cut-rate swill once they're all hammered. Nobody does this with grape juice.

My Son, the Doctor

According to the three Synoptic Gospels, Jesus never changes water to wine at all. Instead, after the Sermon on the Mount, he goes immediately into the doctor business. His healings go far beyond what physicians could offer then or now. He instantly cures Simon's mother of a fever, causes a paralytic man to walk, heals a leper, restores a man's withered hand, and purges demons from the possessed. In the Gospel of Luke, the demons he casts out exclaim, "You are the Son of God!" As if he didn't know.

Born Again

A story found only in the Gospel of John [John 3:3] is a conversation Jesus has with Nicodemus, a Pharisee—one of the mainstream Jewish leaders. One night, he tells the wise old man that the faithful must be "born again." For Nick, this brings up a bizarre picture: reentering his mother's womb. Ew. Jesus explains that people must be first born of the flesh and then born *again* of the spirit.

It's a powerful idea. In fact, it's so powerful that a good portion of today's evangelicals make it the central experience of their faith and sometimes they can be really obnoxious about it. For them it's the spiritual dividing line between the saved and the damned.

Catholics generally take a more sober approach to this "born again" line. For them it's a gradual process of growing in one's faith. But for others it's like a bong hit of Acapulco God. A transcendent buzz. A holy high. A shattering Bogart of bliss that has them writhing in the aisles or keeling over backwards with a slap to the forehead at the altar, and they emerge from it with the glassy-eyed look of *The Stepford Wives*.

In a way, this is a Christian version of the quick-fix therapies of Dr. Phil and his ilk. Who needs years of self-reflection when Jesus is your life coach? Born again, rebirthing, nirvana, transcendence, cosmic consciousness, getting it, becoming "clear." It all hovers around the same hope: *fix me now!* I want a microwaved mental breakthrough that'll rearrange me before lunch. Instant salvation; Cup-o-Soup for the soul.

Sometimes the Gospels have Jesus sounding like he buys into the claptrap of *The Secret*—that best-selling book which claimed that, by putting out the right vibrations and asking the universe for anything in a positive, heartfelt way, it will come true:

> Ask, and it will be given you; seek and you will find;
> knock and it will be opened to you.
> [Matt. 7:7, Luke 11:9]

Note: This seems to apply only to requests for salvation. It doesn't usually work if what you seek is to get laid by the Homecoming Queen before you get your driver's license.

Exorcisms to Go

Jesus continues his healing tour through towns and villages, and his twelve disciples are now called his apostles—a shift from students to ambassadors. He sends them out as "sheep in the midst of wolves." [Matt. 10:16] He instructs them to be "wise as serpents and innocent as doves." He also empowers them to perform the same miraculous healings and exorcisms he does, which is kind of cool. One wonders why we never hear about most of them again. You'd think guys like that would've made headlines across the ancient world.

Jesus and company then cross the Sea of Galilee, where they confront a man possessed by demons. [Mark 5] He's so frothing-at-the-mouth insane that he can't even be chained up. Jesus calls to the demons and they respond, "My name is Legion; for we are many." (A legion was roughly 5,000 Roman soldiers.) Jesus casts them out, yet he's rather accommodating about it. When they ask to be sent into a herd of 2,000 swine nearby, he complies. The pigs then stampede into the sea and drown. That's a lot of lost breakfast sausage. Oddly, the reaction of the locals is to ask Jesus to leave town. Maybe the whole episode was just too creepy. Or maybe they were friends of the rancher who just lost all his pigs.

One thing this story does suggest—the author of Mark doesn't seem to know the geography of Judea. He states that the pigs were feeding on a mountainside near a town that most historians believe was miles from the sea. The pigs would have died of exhaustion before reaching the water. This is only one of several places where the writer of Mark shows he's unfamiliar with the lay of the Holy Land and why some credible researchers think he didn't live there at all.

Peculiar as this story is, a suspiciously similar tale is told about a pagan religious rite in Eleusis, Greece. There, 2,000 new initiates to a mystery religion were purified by bathing in the sea with pigs— which absorbed their evils and were then driven over a cliff.

Exorcisms like these are practiced in many religions, and they always feel half creepy and half stupid. But they do pull in the faithful. I once produced a TV documentary about evangelist Bob Larson, who performs mass exorcisms in convention halls. After several hundred paying customers listened to a brief sermon, he asked if there were any demons in the audience. In short order, people groaned and growled and did everything but throw up pea soup. I thought it was considerate of the demons to wait until Larsen's sermon was over before making pests of themselves.

Bob would lay a Bible on a victim's forehead and call on the authority of Jesus to cast out the evil spirits. If he focused on one victim and another started making too much noise, the second subject would be gently escorted from the room. I later found several of them behind the convention hall, on their knees, clawing at the shrubbery and roaring like kids playing dinosaur. Back inside, all the victims were cured of their horror movie syndrome just in time for the hall to close. Demons are not only considerate, they're punctual. Afterwards, Bob told me there was a "demon gene" which made some people more susceptible to possession than others. Harvard Medical is on the case.

The Plot Thickens

Still making the rounds in Galilee, Jesus pulls out the heavy artillery and raises the daughter of a local leader from the dead. [Luke 8:49] He then asks her parents not to tell anyone about it. I'm not sure what the strategy is here because his other miracles have been public spectacles and his traveling medicine show has already popped up on the radar of the authorities.

His miracles, parables, and twists on traditional law annoy the Pharisees, who come off as sticklers for the rules. He forgives sins, which tradition says only God can do. He says it's okay to pick grain or to save your sheep on the Sabbath, all of which are scandalous to some. Plus there are the exorcisms, which educated people found hard to swallow even back then.

Meanwhile, his front man, John the Baptist, is arrested by King Herod (a different Herod than the one in the Christmas story). John's been railing against the king for marrying his brother's wife. This irks the new queen, so, at a birthday party for her daughter, she has the girl ask the king for a birthday present—John's head on a platter. Literally. Apparently she had enough Barbies.

Trouble is now brewing in official circles over this upstart preacher and his radical friends.

Feeding the 5000

If there's anything more popular than free first aid, it's free food. Small wonder, then, that Jesus feeding a crowd of 5,000 with only five loaves and two fishes is the only miracle that's mentioned in all four Gospels. Mark and Matthew then report an almost identical story a few pages later. This time, Jesus feeds a crowd of 4,000 with seven loaves and "a few fish." Strangely, his followers are every bit as surprised by *this* food miracle as they were by the first one. It's as if they'd never seen the stunt before. Isn't fish supposed to be good for short-term memory?

This problem, by the way, pops up throughout the New Testament—the denseness of the Twelve Apostles. Despite the miracles they routinely witness, they're kind of slow on the uptake when it comes to figuring out who Jesus is and they often forget events that would never slip anyone else's mind.

Walking on Water

Water plays a big part in Christian lore. Jesus is baptized with it. His followers are fishermen. His first miracle is to change water to wine. In *Matthew 8:23*, he and his disciples get caught on turbulent waters in a small boat and Jesus calms the seas. It's all very impressive. But none of these tricks compare with his signature feat: walking on water.

Jesus prays alone on a mountain while Peter and the other disciples sail across the Sea of Galilee in their boat. When high swells prevent them from nearing the shore, Jesus just strolls out across the water to meet them. He even has Peter step out of the boat and stand next to him. But when the wind kicks up, Peter freaks out and—rather like Wile E. Coyote, who only starts to fall once he realizes he's standing in mid-air—Peter begins to sink. "Oh man of little faith, why did you doubt?" Jesus asks. Evidently he never saw a Roadrunner cartoon.

Walking on water is actually part of an age-old motif in which water represents absolute chaos, or evil, and the control of it represents order, which is good. It's found in many creation myths, including the Bible's, wherein the universe begins as a turbulent sea or primordial sludge (chaos) from which either gods or dry land (order) emerge. Good wins over evil.

The walking-on-water event is so iconic that, in Central America, there's an animal called the Jesus Christ Lizard because it dashes across streams on its webbed hind feet. It does not, however, perform exorcisms.

The Rock

With events picking up speed, Jesus does a little polling and asks his disciples who the people think he is. The people, as it turns out, aren't too sharp. They figure he's a reincarnation of the executed John the Baptist, or an Old Testament prophet like Elijah or Jeremiah. But Peter (originally Simon Bar-Jona) declares that Jesus is "the Son of the living God." Fair enough. But Jesus offers a peculiar response to Peter's confession:

> "Blessed are you, Simon Bar-Jona! For flesh and blood has not revealed this to you, but my Father who is in heaven." [Matt. 16:17]

Oh, really? *God* tipped Peter off? I thought maybe he got a clue from Jesus walking on water, or calming a storm, or curing lepers, or raising the dead, or exorcizing those demons who shouted, "You are the Son of God!" Or how about the fact that the Gospel of John has the newly-recruited disciples declaring he's The Messiah the moment they meet? Peter didn't need a Ouija board to figure this out.

Still, Jesus is impressed by Peter's insight and he assigns him a special role. Jesus has begun to forecast his own imminent demise at the hands of his enemies. He says that, just as Jonah was in the belly of a whale for three days, he too will spend three days and nights in the heart of the earth and then rise again.

Technically, the whale story couldn't happen. First of all, according to the *Septuagint* (that Greek translation of the Old

Testament), Jonah was swallowed by a great fish, not a whale. There aren't any whales in the Mediterranean (or great fish for that matter) that could swallow a man. Furthermore, Jesus died late on a Friday and rose on Sunday morning. That's one day and two nights, not three days and nights. This may be hair-splitting, but if you booked a hotel for one day and two nights and were billed for three days, you'd bitch.

Anyway, if Jesus is not long for this earth, it means someone will have to carry on the good work. So, according to the Catholic Church, he establishes...well, the Catholic Church:

> "And I tell you, you are Peter, and on this rock I will build my church, and the gates of hell shall not prevail against it. I will give you the keys of the Kingdom of Heaven..."
> [Matt. 16:18-19, Mark 8:27, Luke 9:18, John 6:67]

According to the Church, the "rock" in question is Peter himself, who will become the first Bishop of Rome—eventually known as the pope. The Church will own the keys to the kingdom; they'll man the velvet rope. And the Church will be built upon Peter, both figuratively and literally. The Vatican is located on Peter's alleged burial spot.

Protestants claim that Catholics misinterpret this line about "the rock" and insist it refers to Jesus, not Peter. After all, there's nothing in the Bible that says Peter ever went to Rome or that he became a bishop. Those are Catholic folktales. They also note that Paul calls Jesus "the chief cornerstone." [Ephesians 2:20] Hence, Protestant churches are built upon the rock of *Jesus*, which is why they don't provide a priestly go-between for talking to God. It also makes it easier for some of them to call the pope the antichrist.

The Transfiguration

With all the questions about his real nature starting to bubble up, Jesus figures it's time to let his closest followers know the full story. Peter declared that Jesus is The Messiah. To confirm this,

Jesus takes him, along with James and John, up to a high mountain. There, his face and clothing begin to glow the way Moses did when he came down from Mount Sinai. Then, wouldn't you know it, Moses himself appears, along with the prophet Elijah. And *then...*

> ...a bright cloud overshadowed them, and a voice from the cloud said, "This is my beloved Son, with whom I am well pleased; listen to him."
> [Mark 17:5, Matthew 9:7, Luke 9:34-35]

It's nice that we've gotten away from the water-to-wine parlor magic and are back to some old-fashioned, Yahweh-class special effects: glowing clouds, booming voices, and resurrected prophets. But if Jesus is God himself, then who's the booming voice from the sky? Debates have raged for centuries over this point. The Catholic answer says that God is a Trinity—Father, Son, Holy Spirit. Three "persons" in one deity. Therefore he can be both in heaven and on earth at the same time. And you thought there was no logical explanation.

Son of Man or Son of God?

So who exactly is Jesus? Eighty-eight times he calls himself the "Son of Man," which technically means any normal human being. The term shows up in a half-dozen Old Testament books, and it always refers to mere humans. But then listen to the prophet Daniel:

> "...there came with the clouds of the sky one like a son of man, and he came to the Ancient of Days and was presented before him. And to him was given dominion and glory and kingdom..." [Daniel 7:13]

It's a messianic vision of a human-looking figure that appears before God (the Ancient of Days) after an evil beast is defeated. But some folks have a problem with similes. For them, the Son of Man and "one *like* a son of man" are the same thing, and both are messianic. After all, it *sounds* a little like "Son of God." So, when the Gospels have Jesus calling himself the Son of Man, it has a messianic flavor but it isn't actually blasphemy.

In the Gospels of Mark, Matthew and Luke, Jesus is rather coy about his messianic nature. But the author of John, ever the ardent mystic, writes about a Jesus who is a tad full of himself:

> "I am the bread of life which came down from heaven; if
> any one eats of this bread, he will live for ever..."
> [John 6:51]

> "I am the light of the world; he who follows me will not
> walk in darkness, but will have the light of life."
> [John 8:12]

> "I am the way, the truth and the life; no one comes to the
> Father, but by me." [John 14:6]

Jesus occasionally calls himself the Son of God, not so much in the messianic sense as in the loving-relationship-with-the-Lord sense. He's beloved of God, but he never says he's God's *only* begotten son. The writer of John came up with that one.

Will it play in Jerusalem?

After a few more healings, parables, exorcisms, raisings of the dead, and prophecies of resurrection, the story finally heads for the big town—Jerusalem. The Gospels have Jesus arriving one week before the Passover, and he enters the city exactly the way a Hebrew messianic prophecy predicts:

> Lo, your king comes to you;
> triumphant and victorious is he,
> humble and riding on an ass,
> on a colt, the foal of an ass.   [Zechariah 9:9]

This is supposedly a prophecy of the entry of Jesus into Jerusalem on the back of an ass or a colt...or maybe both. (His disciples actually buy both, suggesting he entered like a stunt rider.) But let's get real. Matthew says Jesus claimed to be The Messiah. Naturally, then, the story would have him entering Jerusalem the way the messianic prophecy predicts. It was self-fulfilling. He even had a choice of two messianic entrance scenes because, as we just saw in *Daniel 7:13,* The Messiah also comes "with the clouds of heaven." Of course, that would have been pretty tough to pull off. It was easier for Jesus to rent a nag.

Moneychangers

No sooner does Jesus enter the city than he heads for Jewish HQ—the Jerusalem Temple. By this time the thousand year-old shrine is a combination church, shopping mall, and campus quad where everyone meets to pray, trade, and chew the fat. When people come to worship, the rites involve sacrificing doves or donating other trinkets and doodads, which visiting pilgrims would purchase. Hence, the place is surrounded by merchants and moneychangers. But the commercial aspect of things had apparently gotten out of hand. There was plenty of activity but not much God worship. This rankles Jesus, so he upsets the tables of the moneychangers, then rails against them for turning a house of prayer into a "den of thieves." It's a scene.

Actually, the infamous moneychangers at the Temple were not out to debase the faith. They aided pilgrims who came from afar to worship. Jews considered the use of Roman coins an act of idolatry because they featured the graven image of the emperor. The moneychangers would swap Roman coins for non-offending currency. They were actually preserving the sacredness of the Temple, not defiling it. Jesus, being new in town, may have gotten the wrong impression. Oops.

Jesus Junk

Of course, religious purists throughout history have always been quick to condemn the commercialization of their faith, whether it was Martin Luther arguing against the selling of indulgences or present-day objections to Christmas becoming an Olympic event for your credit card. But gods have long been invoked to generate booty. Back in the Sinai, all the gold and fresh meat the Israelites could produce was kept nice and safe by the priests in the Tabernacle. Medieval popes drained the lifeblood of the peasantry to build churches, bribe kings, and finance armies. I once saw Pat Robertson brag that a poor, blind woman sent his ministry a check for her last $25, and the sonofabitch cashed it.

These days, Christianity seems especially prone to turning belief into ready cash. A quick Google search reveals so much Christian paraphernalia online it makes the marketing of Starbucks look like your niece's lemonade stand. The amount of royalty-free Jesus junk available would put the moneychangers to shame.

There are books, CDs, nightlights, lunch boxes (to keep your Eucharist fresh, I suppose), coloring books, graphic novels, clever T-shirts ("BODY PIERCING SAVED MY LIFE" heh-heh), dishware, bumper stickers, hood ornaments, puzzles, video games, and dust collectors of every sort, not to mention lots of Christian jewelry—some of which only God himself could afford.

Most of this stuff is aggressively tacky—good taste evidently not being among the blessings of the Holy Spirit. Examples:

✟ A windup Jesus action figure that reaches up to heaven.
✟ Jesus bubble bath. (Makes baptisms friskier!)
✟ Christian candies. (One brand is called Testa-Mints)
✟ *Last Supper* neckties. (Definitely a Father's Day gift)
✟ A bobble-headed dashboard Jesus.
✟ Jesus Beer. ("The King of Kings of Beers")
✟ Jesus Sneakers. (For walking on water?)
✟ Jesus throw rugs. (Nothing says devotion like stepping on Christ's face...)
✟ Jesus ashtrays. (...or snuffing a cigarette out on his nose)
✟ Jesus air freshener. (Now *your* home can smell like a first-century carpenter)

There are crucifixes made of everything from taffy to kryptonite. (And yes, there are even ones molded out of chocolate. One brand comes on a stick.) For Old Testament fans there's a Plague of Locusts snow globe and Apocalypse Hot Sauce. You can even buy a 47-foot high inflatable church for when you're on the road. And speaking of the road, in Los Angeles there's a car dealership called "Jesus is Lord Motors." I guess if their cars run, it's a miracle.

As a kid, I thought the idea of a Christian theme park was a joke, until Jim and Tammy Faye Bakker came up with Heritage U.S.A. in 1978 (well before Jim was indicted). In 2001, something called The Holy Land Experience was built in Orlando, Florida, where visitors can walk through a faux ancient Jerusalem and see replicas of the Ark of the Covenant and Christ's tomb. Some claim it was designed to convert Jews to Christianity. It doesn't seem to have worked. Maybe if they added a Mary Magdalene kissing booth.

Me = God

Since Jesus has been hinting that he is God incarnate, maybe his tirade against the moneychangers was just some of Yahweh's trademark moodiness; a little Old Testament ire coming through. The next morning, when he wakes up hungry, Jesus spots a fig tree. But there's nothing on it except leaves. So, this is what the Gospels claim Jesus says...to the tree:

> "May no fruit ever come from you again!" And the fig tree withered at once. [Mark 11:13, Matt 21:18]

I always felt sorry for that fig tree, though I suppose the scene would've been uglier if Jesus had been thirsty and came across a cow that didn't give milk. We're told this episode demonstrates the power of faith. I think it also shows that Jesus wasn't a morning person. Actually, there's debate about what this episode really means since a fig tree wouldn't be producing fruit at that time of year anyway.

By now, a lot of folks are talking about Jesus, and public opinion is split. The crowds are astonished by his wisdom, while some of the Pharisees think he's possessed. What really riles the authorities, though, is his promise of eternal life and the suggestion that he is something more than a man.

"...before Abraham was, I am." [John 8:58]

"I and the Father are one." [John 10:30]

These are touchy words to say in a synagogue, especially since nothing in Hebrew scripture says The Messiah has to be God incarnate. Jesus is coming up with new stuff, and the religious honchos are ready to stone him. Before they can, however, he goes into hiding. Good thing. If they had killed him right there, the emblem of Christianity would have been Jesus under a pile of rocks. Not very inspiring.

Jesus on Church and State

The Pharisees meet to decide what to do about this man. Since the Romans have the legal authority, and since they don't care much about Jewish religious arguments, the only way for the Pharisees to get Jesus out of the way is to goad him into violating Roman law. They try to snag him with a trick question: Is it lawful to pay taxes to the pagan government of Rome? Since it's blasphemous to use Roman coins, they figure he'll say "no" and thus land himself in hot water with the Empire. Instead, he famously answers:

"Render therefore unto Caesar that which is Caesar's, and unto God that which is God's." [Matt. 22:21]

In other words: Yes, pay up! This not only gets him off the hook with both the Romans and the Jews; it tells us that Jesus Christ favored Church-State separation. He saw both government and religion as legitimate institutions, each deserving of their due. Pay your taxes to the government and dedicate your soul to God. Keep those priorities straight and you'll be fine. He never said to convert the Empire to Christianity and *then* pay your taxes. He never advocated passing laws based on his teachings. If a good Christian lives a moral life, he does so freely out of a love of God—not out of fear of the feds. A believer doesn't need the government to save his soul.

The only ones who get ticked off by this clever answer are the Zealots, who *do* want to overthrow the government and make theocracy the law of the land. For them, it's not enough to freely worship God. They want *everyone* to freely worship God and, if everyone won't, they'll make sure everyone has to. You know the type.

Heavy Weather Ahead

With the cat now out of the bag on his messianic claims, Jesus continues working the nerves of the religious leaders, who keep trying to trip him up. They send a lawyer to ask him what the greatest commandment is, and he responds:

> "You shall love the Lord your God with all your heart, and with all your soul, and with all your mind...And a second [commandment] is like it, You shall love your neighbor as yourself." [Matt. 22:37-39]

Hard to argue with that. So, for the moment, the Pharisees back off. Then Jesus turns around and rails against them as elitist and ritual-obsessed.

> "...for they preach, but do not practice...they love the place of honor at feasts and the best seats in the synagogues...Woe to you scribes and Pharisees, hypocrites! For you...have neglected the weightier matters of the law: justice and mercy and faith...You serpents, you brood of vipers, how are you to escape being sentenced to hell?" [Matt. 23:3-33]

91

Well, if you're going to burn a bridge, might as well make it a spectacular fire. To be fair, he's being a little hard on the Pharisees, who are actually middle-of-the-road Jews, not purists. He's condemning mainstream Judaism—one reason why he's often seen as a revolutionary and why so many Jewish leaders had a hard time with him.

No matter. Jesus is on a tear and, as he marches out of the Temple, he tells his disciples that:

> "...there will not be left here one stone upon another, that will not be thrown down." [Matt. 24:2]

The man who deftly avoided trouble with elusive answers to loaded questions finally gives up the soft sell. Some of the religious authorities regard this statement as a threat. But the destruction of the Temple isn't the end of what Jesus claims the corrupt priesthood has wrought.

> "For nation will rise against nation, and kingdom against kingdom; there will be earthquakes in various places, there will be famines; this is but the beginning of the sufferings." [Mark 13:8]

> "For in those days there will be such tribulation as has not been from the beginning of the creation of which God created until now, and never will be." [Mark 13:19]

Yow!! He's talking about tribulations *worse* than the wars and mass slaughters of Moses and Joshua? Worse than Sodom and Gomorrah? Worse than the Great Flood!?

Welcome to Doomsday—a belief inherited from the Old Testament prophets and which we'll see again in the book of *Revelation*. These verses are called "the Little Apocalypse" and they are part of what will turn out to be one of Christianity's most potent recruiting tools: scaring the hell out of everyone.

But now comes a challenge. The whole expectation of The Messiah had been of someone who would vanquish Israel's enemies and create a holy realm of the chosen. Great. With a living messiah now on tap, it's time to start remaking the world into God's kingdom. Isn't it?

The Second Coming

Well, not so fast. You see, according to the plan, Jesus must first die and then come back from the dead on some future day and *then* he'll fix everybody's little red wagon. Frankly, this sounds like a carpenter talking—he keeps promising he'll come back to finish the job, but he never tells you when. The Hebrews have waited a millennium for a messiah to free them, and now here's another delay. Instead of eliminating their oppressors, this savior will allow their oppressors to eliminate *him.* Who came up with this plan? If George Washington had this defeatist attitude, we'd all still be speaking English.

Jesus assures his followers that his *second* appearance will be much more impressive than his first:

> "At that time men will see the Son of Man coming in clouds with great power and glory. And he will send his angels and gather his elect from…the ends of the earth to the ends of the heavens."
> [Mark 13:26-30, Matt. 24:30-34, Luke 21:27-32]

Wow. Most Jews just want him to send the Romans packing. Now he's promising to return as king of the cosmos. That's great, except, why must he go through the trouble of dying and coming back? Do it now and be done with it! He can't save himself from the executioner today…oh, but *next* time he'll conquer the universe and make it all better? Miss America wants to bring about world peace, too, but until she does she's just a babe in an evening gown. Bold promises are great, but I'm not seeing much follow-through, especially after Jesus proclaims:

> "Truly, I say to you, this generation will not pass away before all these things take place." [Mark 13:30]

"This generation?" Here we are 2,000 years later, the generation of Jesus is long gone, and none of these events have taken place. What happened to "The Kingdom of Heaven is at hand"? Jesus is doing the same thing the Old Testament prophets did—declaring the Day of the Lord is coming soon to a planet near you but never delivering on the promise. Somebody needs to explain the word "soon." And please don't give me the old, "To God, a thousand years is like a day" routine. He's not talking to God; he's talking to us. The Lord keeps pledging he'll settle accounts any day now, but whenever he shows up it's always, "I'll catch you next time." He acts like a guy who owes us money.

Apocalypse When?

None of the harrowing prophecies he spells out in these verses have come true, or, if they have, nobody's seemed to notice. So, to rescue Jesus' reputation as a prophet, his supporters sift through history to find events that might match his Doomsday prediction.

A favorite nominee is the Roman sacking of Jerusalem and the defeat of the Jewish rebellion in A.D. 70. Couldn't this count as the end of their world? Well, time out. The destruction of the Temple and the scattering of Judean Jews into the Diaspora was a historic catastrophe, but it was hardly the worst tribulation since Creation. The earth didn't quake and stars didn't fall from the heavens. If this was the Apocalypse, Jesus really oversold it.

Actually, these visions are borrowed from the Old Testament. Back in 167 B.C., after the Jerusalem Temple had been desecrated by the Greek general Antiochus, the prophet Daniel wrote of an imminent apocalypse. But it never happened. So, Mark reinterprets Daniel's doomsday predictions and reapplies them to A.D. 70.

Problem was, The End didn't happen in Mark's time either. No apocalypse took place before "this generation" had passed. So Luke, written many years after Mark, had to account for this delay. The solution: Luke changes Jesus' words from "the end is still to come" (Mark 13:7) to "but the end does not follow at once." (Luke 21:9) Luke gives the prophecy more shelf life.

Matthew also adds weasel words to Jesus' unfulfilled prophecy:

> "...of that day and hour no one knows, not even the angels of heaven, nor the Son, but the Father only." [Matt. 24:36]

It's a classic rule of prophecy: No timetables. This is a copout that, at least for some, gets Jesus off the hook for a bad call. But it doesn't negate his prediction that Judgment Day would come within the lifetime of his audience. So, Christians are stuck with two choices: a) they backed the wrong horse and the real messiah is yet to come, in which case they're all suddenly Jews, or b) Jesus didn't mean what he said. Some claim words like "this generation" really mean "this era of history" or some such double-talk. Apologists do this all the time. They'll insist the story of Noah's flood be taken literally, but when Jesus plainly forecasts the end of the world within a generation, it's just poetic license. This is the biblical literalist's stock-in-trade—spinning the meaning of verses that don't agree with their beliefs into ones that do.

Between evasive answers, blasphemous claims of raising the dead, the moneychangers outburst, and the diatribe he levels at the Pharisees, Jesus has dished out as much as the priests can take. They're worried that the controversy he's creating will have the Romans on their case. They want him arrested.

So, they recruit a mole—Judas Iscariot. Regarded as the most craven skunk in history, his name is synonymous with betrayal. He accepts 30 pieces of silver (a sum Matthew borrows from the Hebrew Bible) in exchange for revealing where Jesus is camped out for the night. It's then that the Pharisees make their move.

Passion Play

While the label given to the final episodes of the story sounds like a romance, "The Passion" actually comes from the Latin word for suffering. These are the most critical events of the whole saga and much of it is lifted directly from the Old Testament books of *Isaiah, Psalms* and *Wisdom*. For believers, the similarities between the Passion and the Old Testament verses are proof that Jesus was the fulfillment of Jewish prophecy. For skeptics, it suggests the story is a legend assembled from hand-picked lines of the Hebrew scripture.

The Last Supper

On the eve of Passover, in a room within Jerusalem's city walls, Jesus has his final meal with his disciples and a few others. During the supper, Judas slips out and makes his arrangement with the plotters. But when he returns, the boss is on to him:

> And as they were at the table eating, Jesus said, "Truly, I say to you, one of you will betray me, one who is eating with me." [Mark 14:18]

It's a prediction apparently borrowed from *Psalms*:

> Even my bosom friend in whom I trusted, who ate of my bread, has lifted his heel against me, [Psalms 41:9-10]

He then passes around bread and wine, and says something truly strange:

> "... unless you eat the flesh of the Son of Man and drink his blood, you have no life in you; he who eats my flesh and drinks my blood has eternal life..." [John 6:53-54]

Most of his followers hear this and back away, probably creeped-out by the statement's cannibalistic flavor, so to speak. Only the Twelve Disciples partake.

The Eucharist

The Last Supper is the basis for the ritual of communion, a.k.a. the Eucharist—the consuming of tasteless wafers and dishwater wine at the altar because they allegedly turn into the flesh and blood of Christ. Paul launches this idea in *1 Corinthians 11:24* when he breaks bread and then quotes Jesus (the only time he does): "This is my body which is for you. Do this in remembrance of me."

This miracle-in-your-mouth is called Transubstantiation, as if a big word made it more credible. But believers are not kidding about this. It's regarded as a way to achieve a kind of intimate oneness with their savior. (As a burger aficionado, I shudder to think of all the cattle with which I've achieved intimate oneness.)

If this cracker-to-Christ transformation really does happen, why don't we take a sample of it and run a DNA test? Heck, we could clone Jesus. I wonder if he'd be a copy of Mary, because he had no biological father, or would we have God's genetic code? Could we clone God? Wow...spooky thought. Somebody's got to try this, or at least make a movie about it for the SyFy Channel.

As with many Christian traditions, the Eucharist was not unique. In the Egyptian *Book of the Dead*, the deceased ate gods to acquire their powers. In the *Bacchae*, the Greek writer Euripides called bread and wine the "two powers that are supreme in human affairs." Even Justin Martyr, an early Church father, admitted that subscribers to Mithraism practiced this ritual.

Inevitably, Christians were accused of cannibalism, and it's kind of understandable. The Roman philosopher Cicero, less prone to superstition than most, couldn't believe that anyone took this stuff seriously. "Is anybody so mad as to believe that the food which he eats is actually a god?" Answer: Yes—they call him the pope.

How strange that a religion which prides itself on rising above the barbaric sacrifices of primitive faiths has, as its central icon, a dead man on whom worshippers occasionally snack. Yes, yes, Jesus calls himself "the bread of life." [John 6:35]. But come on, it's a metaphor! Maybe he was human. Maybe he was divine. Maybe he was both. We can't say. What we *can* say is that he wasn't wheat, rye, or pumpernickel.

One final note about The Last Supper before we move on. There's no mention of a Holy Grail in this scene, or anywhere in the Bible. A cup is mentioned, but that's it. It's totally unimportant. The obsession with artifacts like the Grail really took off during the Crusades, when Christian soldiers stormed into Jerusalem hot for relics from the Holy Land. The Arabs knew a sucker when they saw one and they quickly sold the Europeans any artifact they could link to Jesus with a tall tale—vials of his tears, hairs from his head, holy shrouds, and enough splinters from the cross to rebuild London. To its credit, the Catholic Church placed no importance on the Holy Grail. Most of the stories we know about it spring from more recent legends about King Arthur anyway.

Arrest

When a posse bearing swords and clubs shows up at the disciples' hiding place, Judas identifies Jesus with a kiss. Nicely ironic but a little dumb. He could just point and say, "That's the guy!" And why did the authorities have to pay anyone to identify Jesus anyway? Didn't that public dustup with the moneychangers make him recognizable to everyone?

The Gospel of Mark then offers a truly bizarre verse about a man who follows along after Jesus is apprehended:

> And a young man followed him, with nothing but a
> linen cloth about his body; and they seized him, but he
> left the linen cloth and ran away naked. [Mark 14:51]

The elusive streaker is never mentioned again, nor is he arrested for public indecency. Some claim this character symbolizes Christ's ultimate escape from his captors through death and resurrection. Maybe the guy was pledging a frat. Believe me, there are theories more fantastic than that—including one elaborate claim that says the mysterious figure was a homosexual lover. Seriously. People go nuts with this tidbit.

Once Jesus is arrested, his disciples deny knowing him and they immediately flee. What a pack of wussies. You or I might be forgiven for a lapse of faith in the face of threats because we get this whole saga fourth hand. But the disciples actually *saw* Jesus walk on water, feed 5,000 with a couple of fish, raise the dead, and glow in the dark next to Moses! What does it take to convince these people?

The story then has Jesus hauled up that night before the Sanhedrin—the Jewish rulers of Jerusalem. The authenticity of this scene is often questioned because it's unlikely such men would meet so late on the eve of Passover to deal with a rogue preacher. Yet, here they are.

> Now the chief of the priests and the whole council sought testimony against Jesus to put him to death; [Mark 14:55]
>
> And some stood up and bore false witness against him, [Mark 14:57]

Yet again, Mark is reworking Old Testament material:

> The wicked watches the righteous and seek to slay him. [Psalms 37:32]
>
> Give me not up to the will of my adversaries; for false witnesses have risen against me, [Psalms 27:12]

Determined to find him guilty of a punishable crime, the high priest asks directly if Jesus is the Christ, the son of "the Blessed," meaning God. The response:

> And Jesus said, "I am; and you will see the Son of Man sitting at the right hand of Power, and coming with the clouds of heaven." [Mark 14:62]

He's flat-out claiming to be the messianic "King of the Jews." Since only the Romans can name a king, Jesus has just committed a death penalty offense. Or so the Gospels would have us believe. I wonder if the Romans actually executed every mad prophet claiming to be royalty? I'll bet some of them just got slapped around for fun.

Consistently inconsistent, the Gospels of Matthew and Mark say the Sanhedrin tries and sentences Jesus, while Luke has him tried but not sentenced, and John doesn't mention the scene at all. It's a good thing these four never had to testify in court.

Elsewhere, Judas is so remorseful for what he's done that, according to Matthew, he hangs himself. But according to the next book in the Bible, *Acts* (written by the author of Luke), Judas retreats to a field where his guts burst out. The Gospel writers can't even agree on this.

Trial

Jesus is then brought before Pontius Pilate, the Roman governor charged with keeping order in the unruly colony of Judea. By most accounts he was a world-class bastard and even Emperor Tiberius admonished him at one point for his cruelty. Yet, after hearing the Sanhedrin carp about various offenses, Pilate refuses to condemn the maverick preacher. This even after Pilate threatens Jesus with crucifixion and his response is, "You would not have power over me unless it had been given you from above..." [John 19:11] Them's *fightin'* words to a Roman governor. Yet Pilate demands no punishment.

Wanting nothing to do with the matter, Pilate lets the crowd decide Jesus' fate. The Gospels assert that a Roman tradition allows the governor of Judea to release one condemned prisoner during the Passover—a dubious claim found in no other ancient record. The crowd cries out for Jesus' execution and instead chooses to spare a Zealot named Barabbas, a Jewish freedom fighter. To Pilate he's a terrorist. The idea that Pilate would free a violent criminal but crucify a peaceful preacher who told everyone to pay their taxes doesn't ring true.

The mob's demand that Jesus be put to death is also suspect. Over the past week, they've celebrated his arrival and marveled at his wisdom and eloquence. Now they turn on him for no apparent reason. Even Dick Cheney's popularity didn't plummet that fast.

Nevertheless, the Scripture says Pilate "washed his hands" of the matter and let the crowd make the decision.

The entire story is spin. It's crafted to make everybody look bad. "The Jews" come off as a nasty lot and the Romans seem like unthinking proto-Nazis. In reality, the Jewish leaders just wanted to punish a heretic (a hobby Christians would eventually adopt). And the Romans were not mindless fascists. They were the great civilizing force of the age. Sure, they could be merciless in war. But the Roman Empire afforded greater freedom of conscience than any of the theocratic despots or barbarian chieftains surrounding them. They permitted more religious tolerance than the Sanhedrin itself. If any of us were transported to that era, we'd much prefer life under the Caesars to life alongside the priests. Yet, in every Hollywood religious epic, Jews and Christians are the heroes while the Romans are a pack of thugs. Of course, Romans don't make the movies.

Luke is especially tough on the Jews because that Gospel was intended primarily for Gentiles. Jews who were unwilling to convert to Christianity could be vilified with this account.

While we're on the subject, we can't let this part of the story slide by without mentioning Mel Gibson's hit S&M frolic, *The Passion of the Christ*. Mel has been an outstanding director, among other things. But judging from his work on *Braveheart*, he's got a thing for over-long flogging sequences, and the Passion story gave him an opportunity to build an entire movie around a spectacle of flesh-shredding savagery. In a twisted way it was ingenious. It got Family Values voters to bring ten-year-olds to a film packed with homoerotic imagery and pornographic gore. Only Hollywood could pull that off.

For Mel and his particular religious ilk, it's all about the *suffering*; that's what will bring us eternal life. The medieval Spanish also focused on this, which is why altars throughout Latin America feature a grisly, bloody crucifix compared with the sanitized icons of the English-speaking world. Critics of Christianity note that there is a certain cult-of-death ethic that pervades the entire religion. Buddhist temples and Hindu shrines aren't accompanied by graveyards the way Christian churches are. Nor do they build countless shrines to martyrs for the faith. Hindu gods are pictured dancing, not dying. The Buddha is usually portrayed as fat and happy, and occasionally having *sex.* Imagine how much cheerier church would be if we saw Jesus turning cartwheels or making out with Mary Magdalene.

So how do the Gospel accounts of what the Romans did to Jesus compare with the horrid flogging sequences in *The Passion of the Christ?* Let's start with Mark:

> And when they had mocked him, they stripped him of the purple cloak, and put his own clothes on him. And they led him out to crucify him. [Mark 15:20]

Huh...No flogging here. Just mocking. What about Matthew?

> And they spat upon him, and took the reed and struck him on the head. And when they had mocked him, they stripped him of the robe, and put his own clothes on him, and led him away to crucify him. [Matt. 27:30-31]

A blow to the head, but no flogging here, either. So what does Luke say they did? Answer: nothing. That Gospel doesn't mention any punishment at all. As for John:

> Then Pilate took Jesus and scourged him. And the soldiers plaited a crown of thorns, and put it on his head, and arrayed him in a purple robe... [John 19:1-2]

That's it. He was "scourged," meaning severely whipped. Horrible enough. But it's not the relentless torment offered in Mel's movie. The Gospels make it clear that Jesus suffered, and countless artworks over the centuries illustrate this. But only one Gospel even mentions a beating and it does so with a single word. Everything else is dramatic license.

Another iconic image of the Passion is when Jesus drags his own cross to the hilltop site of his crucifixion as the crowds mock him. Mark, Matthew and Luke actually have a guy named Simon bearing the cross. The later two Gospels seem to base the scene on Mark's account:

> And those who passed by derided him, wagging their heads, [Mark 15:29]

But Mark, yet again, is lifting material from the Hebrew Bible:

> All who see me mock at me, they make mouths at me, they wag their heads; [Psalms 22:7]

> But at my stumbling they gathered in glees, they gathered together against me; cripples whom I knew not slandered me without ceasing; [Psalms 35:15]

The only Gospel that has him bearing the cross himself is John, which is the least biographic and the most mythological.

Crucifixion

The ancient Greeks gave us democracy, science, logic, theatre, mathematics, and free debate. Unfortunately, they also gave us crucifixion, which was later adopted by the Romans. It was a showy and degrading method of execution intended as a form of terrorism, like sticking the head of your enemy on a pike to prove you meant business. The victim died slowly and painfully from exposure to the elements, blood loss, and, some say, suffocation from his own body weight.

Crucifixion was reserved for the worst of criminals, or for offenses like treason. A slave rebellion led by the gladiator Spartacus ended in 71 B.C. with the crucifixion of 6,000 rebels along the Appian Way—the main road leading into Rome. Slave revolts dropped off quickly after that.

I've always thought it the supreme irony that a faith promising eternal life is emblemized by an image of execution. Even back then, skeptics sometimes regarded Christianity as bogus precisely because they thought no real god would die in such a humiliating way. Yet today, a Roman gallows skewers the sky of every city of

103

the Western world. Kind of a grim thought. But then, that's religion. It does things like that. Comedian Lenny Bruce once sniped that if Jesus had been born in the 20th century, Catholic kids would wear little electric chairs around their necks.

Scripture says the crucifixion takes place on a hill outside Jerusalem called Calvary, though there's no evidence to back this up despite what tour guides in the Holy Land might tell you. *John 20:25* suggests Jesus was nailed to the cross by his hands, which would not have held his body weight. A sign mocking his messianic claims is then posted above him. But once again, the Gospels don't agree on the details of a critical scene—like what the sign says:

Mark: The King of the Jews.
Matthew: This is Jesus the King of the Jews
Luke: This is the King of the Jews
John: Jesus of Nazareth, the King of the Jews

Curiously the sign is written in Hebrew, Greek and Latin, but not Aramaic, the language of the man on the street at the time.

Scripture says that, as Jesus is crucified, his executioners divide up his garments and cast lots for them, and someone offers him a sponge soaked with vinegar to drink. This crucial part of the story seems likely to be fiction, or at least an embellishment of reality, because line after line is lifted directly from *Psalms*.

> Yea, dogs are round about me; a company of evil doers encircles me; they have pierced my hands and feet— [Psalms 22:16]

> …they divided my garments among them, and for my raiment they cast lots. [Psalms 22:18]

> They gave me poison for food, and for my thirst they gave me vinegar to drink. [Psalms 69:21]

Then come more inconsistencies. All four Gospels say Jesus was crucified between two thieves. Mark and Matthew claim both men reviled him. But John never has them speak at all. In Luke, one thief jeers at Jesus while the other repents, and Jesus responds to the repentant criminal, "...today you will be with me in paradise." It's a powerful moment. Here, an innocent man in the middle of being executed is forgiving the guilty. Jesus sacrifices himself for man's salvation; he takes on the sins of the world and washes them away with his blood. Or so we are told.

Tough Questions

The scene, of course, is iconic. But even here, we can't back off questioning its credibility or what it's supposed to mean.

First, why does Jesus tell the thief they'll be in paradise "today"—Friday—when he isn't due to rise until Sunday and he won't ascend to heaven until forty days after that?

Second, if he *knows* he'll become the lord of heaven the instant he dies, doesn't this make death a lot easier for him than for you and me?

Third, why was this whole mission by Jesus even necessary? Why did we need a new Gospel from the same old god? Yahweh spent 2,000 years laying down the rules and dishing out justice to Noah, Abraham, Moses, and a dozen more pestering prophets. They even wrote most of it down. So why, suddenly, all the amendments? Why now? And why does anyone have to *die?*

This entire saga is billed as renewal of man's relationship with God. What was wrong with the old relationship? If there was a flaw in the plan, why didn't God realize it before now? And exactly what are we supposed to think when we see the ghastly image of a dead man on a cross? Even here, the major voices of the faith can't agree.

Generally speaking, the Catholic Church takes a corporate view. The crucifix is the ultimate public relations device. You don't have to know much about Jesus himself, only that he represents God's love for man and the conquest of death through belief in his son. The crucifix is a symbol around which the Church can rally the faithful, like a flag. It's a recruiting tool; a lightning rod of power and authority. All you need do is clean up your act, endure all the sacraments and church services, and you'll attain grace—God's eternal insurance policy. It's an institutional approach to salvation and Christ on the cross is the company logo.

For Protestants, however, it's personal. Jesus didn't sacrifice himself for humankind. He sacrificed himself for you. Yeah, *you!* His blood washes away *your* own miserable little sins and through him you can achieve salvation. You don't simply believe and go through the rituals. You convert. And for many evangelicals, this means a psychological high dive off the deep end. It's a profoundly new state of mind. Or state of being. Or state of something. You're born again. You're internally rearranged and you begin an ongoing, 24/7, personal relationship with Jesus. He's your walking, talking B.F.F. Your wise neighbor. You can lean over the fence whenever you want and ask his advice on anything from lawn care to group sex...though, I'd hold off on the group sex questions until you get to know him real well.

But the whole notion of one man dying to take on the sins of the world doesn't entirely add up. Theologians call it "substitutionary atonement." It's the bizarre idea of getting *me* off the hook for my screw-ups by punishing someone else. Jesus is the ultimate whipping boy, taking the rap for everyone else's wrong-doing. So how exactly does this work? How does all *my* sinful mojo get transferred to some other guy just because he threw himself into a volcano or something? What's remotely just about that? If it's such a good idea, why doesn't our justice system work this way? You could pay someone else to serve out your prison sentence. Politicians would love this.

Furthermore, why am I obligated to obey someone just because he decided to sacrifice himself for me? If some guru in Mongolia jumps off a cliff to atone for my sins, does that mean I'm obligated to live by his rules and preach to the world that he survived the fall? I never asked him to do this and, frankly, there's nothing I've ever done that warrants anyone's *death*. A few kicks in the ass maybe. But crucifixion? I don't think so.

On top of all this there's a bigger question. Jesus is saving mankind, but who is he saving mankind from? Who's demanding this sacrifice in exchange for salvation? God? Isn't *he* God? He comes to earth and lets himself be killed to save us from his own wrath? Isn't this like cutting off his own hand so he won't punch us in the mouth?

Now, if you insist he's saving us from Satan, I'm afraid you go to the back of the class. Satan is God's creation, just like the law of gravity or head lice. God can crush the devil like a bug if he wants. And he will. Satan rebelled against the Lord and the Lord will have his vengeance. So why wait so long? And why drag *us* into it?

If God wants to save us from our sins, why did he make us sinful in the first place? Because he gave us free will? Why does free will automatically lead to sin? Couldn't God make beings that freely chose to be nice all the time? Like bunny rabbits? Of course he could. He's God! So why didn't he give us all a natural impulse to be a Goody Two-Shoes? Or would that be like spending an eternity watching *Mr. Roger's Neighborhood?* Personal theory: We're God's home entertainment system and he likes action flicks.

Last Words

In the Gospel of Mark, Jesus' final words on the cross are tough to figure given that he's supposed to be the Son of God, if not God himself.

> E'lo-i, E'lo-i, lä'ma sabach-tha'ni?" which means, "My God, my God, why hast thou forsaken me?"
> [Mark 15:34]

This cry of doubt at the last minute jibes with the picture Mark paints of him as a country healer whose ministry takes a bad turn and ends in tragedy. But it doesn't sound like the all-powerful Jesus we think of today. Why would he say such words after claiming he and the Father are one? Is he complaining to himself?

What's that, you say? God is a Trinity? Maybe, but what do we usually say about someone who talks to himself as three separate people?

These last words are actually Mark making another direct lift from the Hebrew Bible, specifically the *22nd Psalm*. Because the Psalm was written centuries before the crucifixion, we're supposed to think it's an astounding prophecy of the coming of Jesus. This is silly, of course. If I'm on my death bed and decide to quote Shakespeare, does that mean he prophesized the coming of *me?*

Mark quotes the *Psalms* because they're quotable. They're supposed to be. Let's read more of the passage:

> My God, my God, why hast thou forsaken me?
> Why art thou so far from helping me, from the words of my groaning?
>
> O my God, I cry by day, but thou dost not answer; and by night, but find no rest. [Psalm 22:1-2]

This doesn't sound like a man being crucified, and it isn't. It's called *A Psalm of King David*. It was David bemoaning his own tribulations a thousand years earlier. The quote is used out of context; it doesn't refer to Jesus. So much for prophecy.

While Mark and Matthew's authors agree on Jesus' dying words, the other two Gospel writers disagree:

> "…Father, into thy hands I commit my spirit."
> [Luke 23:46]
>
> "It is finished…" [John 19:30]

This is what happens when you write about an event you haven't seen fifty years after you haven't seen it. That's what the Gospel writers did. You'll notice that the earliest of them, Mark, portrays a messiah in distress. By the time we get to John, written about thirty years later, Jesus is calm and deliberate. Nothing ruffles him, not even death. Rewrites have a tendency to smooth over things like this.

Just before Jesus breathes his last, Mark and Matthew report that a darkness comes over the land from the sixth hour of crucifixion to the ninth. Luke says the darkness covers the entire earth, though I'm not sure how the author knew this. John doesn't mention it at all. As for any evidence outside the Bible of darkness at noon on that Friday, or any Friday, there is none. Nobody in India or China or Greece or Egypt ever recorded such an event. It's more of that dramatic license.

Day of the Dead

Once Jesus expires, Matthew describes an extraordinary event:

> And behold...the earth shook, and the rocks were split; the tombs were opened, and many bodies of the saints who had fallen asleep were raised, and coming out of the tombs after his resurrection they went into the holy city and appeared to many. [Matt. 27:51-54]

Awesome! Not only is there a great earthquake that nobody's ever documented, but the deceased climb out of their graves and head for town! A kosher version of *Night of the Living Dead*. Yet, absolutely nowhere but in Matthew is this event reported. Hundreds of corpses stalking the streets is the sort of thing people remember. But no other writer, Christian, Jew, Greek, or Roman, ever does. Nor does Matthew tell us what becomes of these folks. Did they rise to heaven? Return to the grave? Go trick-or-treating? What about the graveyards they climbed out of? Who's gonna fill in all those holes?

So why does Matthew tell this story? Because the writer wants to tie his Gospel to Old Testament prophesy, and the Old Testament says:

> Thy dead shall live, their bodies shall rise,
> O dwellers in the dust, awake and sing for joy!
> [Isaiah 26:19]

Of course, when Isaiah wrote this he was referring to the resurrection of the dead at the End of Time, after the Apocalypse. Matthew's author, however, is never shy about taking quotes out of context to make a point. Sure, he may have *believed* the end was near, but it wasn't, so the zombies he describes here were not the same ones Isaiah foresaw. This means that either the author is making it up, or this sort of thing happens more often than we think.

Saturday at the Tomb

Everyone remembers Good Friday and, of course, Easter Sunday. But what about the forgotten Saturday in between? Does anything interesting happen then? Actually, a critical meeting takes place. After the body is taken down from the cross on Friday, it's wrapped in cloth and taken to a tomb. Then, on Saturday, the chief priests ask Pontius Pilate to post a guard at the entrance; they want to ensure that someone doesn't fake a resurrection by swiping the body under dark of night. So, Pilate has a stone rolled in front of the tomb and a guard is posted.

But wait a second! All this takes place the day *after* Jesus dies on the cross and is taken to the tomb. The body spends the first night in the tomb unguarded. So much for security. The Gospel leaves open the easy possibility that the body is indeed taken. Maybe there was nothing but a roll of linens in the tomb by the time it was sealed. Or maybe someone just invented the whole episode.

In any event, the priests' plan doesn't work. On Sunday morning the body is missing. The guards say they fell asleep while on post, which sounds pretty lame. But it doesn't matter.

A legend is born.

Rise and Shine

According to the Gospel of Mark, Mary Magdalene, Mary the mother of James, and Mary Salome, all come to the tomb and discover the stone has already been rolled away. A young man dressed in white is inside, but he's not Jesus. He's never identified, but he tells them that the Lord has already risen and to inform the others. The women flee in fear.

So who is this guy and how did he move the stone without the guards seeing him? Matthew's version of the tale clears this up with a simple miracle—an *angel* moves the stone when the women drop by, and the guards pass out from fear like a couple of southern belles who get the vapors. In a third version of the episode, Luke has the women finding *two* men at the tomb. And while Matthew has the women running into Jesus as they flee the scene, Luke has him approaching them later that day. At first, they don't recognize him. It's not until they all break bread later that night that they suddenly realize who he is—and then he *vanishes!* It sounds like an episode of *The Twilight Zone.*

In a completely different fourth account, John claims Mary Magdalene goes to the tomb alone on Sunday morning and finds it empty—no angel. Mary immediately tells Peter and another disciple about the empty tomb, and they both see for themselves. It's only when they leave and Mary stays behind, crying, that two angels show up and ask, "Woman, why are you weeping?" As if they didn't know. Then she turns around, and there's Jesus! But at first, she thinks he's just the gardener. (Did everyone's eyesight go bad that morning?) Later on, she tells the others that Jesus has risen.

Go figure. This is the single most important event in the entire Christian religion—the resurrection of Jesus Christ—and his biographers *still* can't get their stories straight. Yet everyone is supposed to accept these accounts as word-for-word sacred truth. Conveniently, we have four sacred truths to choose from.

Later, when Jesus is with his disciples, the one named Thomas says he finds this whole resurrection claim hard to believe. So Jesus allows him to stick his hand into the holes in his body. *Bleeech.* The doubting Thomas is finally convinced, and probably grossed out as well.

Then comes my favorite part: Luke says that Jesus asks if they have anything to *eat*—and they give him a piece of broiled fish. No kidding. He just rose from death and now he wants lunch. This incident is meant to drive home the point that he was raised up in body as well as spirit, which was a major theological issue in the early centuries. Apparently resurrection works up a roarin' appetite.

Interestingly, none of the four Gospels report Jesus actually ascending to heaven. Mark's story ends with the discovery of the empty tomb, though an extended version of that Gospel includes a few post-resurrection moments. Matthew ends with Jesus asking his disciples to preach to all nations. Luke concludes with Jesus blessing his followers, and then simply departing. Lastly, John has him saying "follow me," but that's it. No glorious exit scene. To tell you the truth, it's kind of anticlimactic.

Luke, by the way, also has Jesus misquoting the Old Testament:

> "Thus it is written, that the Christ should suffer and on
> the third day rise from the dead." [Luke 24:46]

Unfortunately, this is *not* written. Nowhere in the Hebrew Bible is there a prediction of The Messiah's resurrection on the third day. There's no prophecy of his death and resurrection at all. Yet later, in the New Testament, Paul makes this same bogus claim in his letter to the Corinthians. [1 Corinth. 15:3-4] Kind of a major point to get wrong.

So, where does all this leave us?

Astoundingly, the end of the four Gospels leaves us in pretty much the same place as the end of the Hebrew Bible: Jews in first century Judea are ruled by Rome, praying for liberation, and awaiting a messiah. So far, Christianity is a lot of running to stay in place; nothing's changed.

Well, at the very least, God's message has been clearly delivered. The jury is in. The fat lady sang. No more revelations, revisions, updates, modifications, alterations, extenuating remarks or expletives deleted. Jesus said his piece and that's the absolute, final, no-kidding, last word, that's-all-she-wrote, end of the discussion on God, right?

Excuse me, but where have you been for the past 2,000 years? The *end* of the debate? Hell, we're just getting warmed up. Strap yourself in because we're about to plunge into a hundred different ways to believe in the same Jesus.

As the small, offshoot faith begins to spread across the eastern Mediterranean in the years after the crucifixion, another figure arises who will be more critical to its success than any of the apostles. You may wonder why Jesus didn't recruit him personally. Perhaps it's because this figure will, in the view of many, fundamentally change the new religion into something that Jesus himself might not even recognize.

CHAPTER FIVE

Anno Domini

The codfish lays a thousand eggs, the homely hen lays one.
The codfish never cackles, to tell you what she's done.
And so we scorn the codfish, while the humble hen we prize,
Which only goes to show you, that it pays to advertise.

—Anonymous

From Jesus to Christianity

Mark Twain famously remarked that if Jesus were alive today the one thing he would not be is a Christian. Twain wasn't the first or the last to think this. But why is that? Apparently, people just couldn't leave well enough alone.

No sooner did Jesus depart the scene than others began to spin, modify, edit, or shamelessly twist what he had to say into what *they* wanted him to say. Believers have been doing this down to the present day. First and foremost among them was a Roman Jew who started life as Saul of Tarsus and ended up as Saint Paul. For him, messing with the word of God was clearly a good career move.

Who is this Paul and why does anyone listen to him?

It's argued that Paul changed the religion *of* Jesus into a religion *about* Jesus. He made it a genuine cult. The point of the religion was no longer the philosophy, it was the philosopher.

Paul was the first great Christian evangelist and his letters are the oldest known Christian writings. While many of us would like to, we can't ignore him because he wrote some of the most influential parts of the New Testament and he's the founding father of Christian theology.

Paul made four rather high-profile, *Up-with-Jesus* tours across the Roman Empire between A.D. 46 and A.D. 64, during which time he wrote letters to the bickering churches back home. According to scholarly consensus, his letters include those to the *Romans, 1st and 2nd Corinthians, Galatians, Philippians, 1st Thessalonians* and *Philemon.*

The man had a lot to say, and he said it over and over in a thousand heavy-handed ways. The guy was a metaphor factory. He concocted endless formulations on the theme that "I was crucified with Christ" and that Jesus now "lives within me." He was intoxicated with his love for God and denounced any concern other than being "saved through faith in Christ," as if there were only one way to do this and it was as self-evident as finding the front door to your house. Paul asked people to be like himself because he was so much like Jesus. Then he told them not to be arrogant. His idea of modesty was to call himself "the very least of all the saints." [Ephesians 3:8]. What a humble guy.

Paul was a complicated figure because he was a Jew who preached to the Gentiles. He took a backcountry faith and preached it in the big cities. He was a Roman citizen, yet he advocated a religion that put him in opposition to Roman authority. His ideas seem to fall into several categories of culture and belief of the time, so he can be puzzling to scholars and flat-out baffling to the rest of us.

Paul's Good Intentions

To be sure, Paul had a lot of nice, constructive things to say. He reiterated Jesus' gospel of love, generosity, forgiveness, and obedience to God. He wanted people to stop being hypocrites and to love and support one another. He pleaded for us to walk through life with personal integrity and to reject "immorality, impurity, licentiousness, idolatry, sorcery, enmity, strife, jealousy, anger, selfishness, dissention, envy, drunkenness, carousing," and everything else that makes Las Vegas fun. It's all solid, ethical teaching, though much of it is rather obvious. Is there *any* religion that encourages people to be selfish, carousing drunks? Do you know where they meet?

Everyone from Aristotle to Confucius to the Buddha agreed with these ideas. But Paul had a way of sounding like he invented them and that the only way to avoid being an angry, envious sorcerer was to obsess about Jesus night and day.

Paul asked that we not judge each other. He advised us to forgive, to love, and to live a life of decency, honor, and faith through Jesus Christ. But instead of emphasizing the values, he emphasized the Jesus. In fact, instead of emphasizing the Jesus, he focused on the Christ. Morality was not achieved so much through learning, discipline, or experience, as through a kind of mind-meld with a deceased holy man. We're supposed to live as if we were an organ in the body of Jesus—by which Paul meant the Church. The Catholic Church described itself as the "mystical body of Christ." Some of us are eyes, some are ears, some are kneecaps, and some are just plain…well, you name the body part.

Paul often used irony to make his point, forever twisting words back on themselves. To be free, we must be slaves to Christ. To pass judgment is to be judged yourself. Faith puts you beyond the law and thus upholds the law. Through death comes eternal life, etc., etc. "If any one among you think that he is wise in this age, let him become a fool that he may become wise." [1 Corinthians 3:18] He was a cornucopia of Orwellian logic pretzels.

Paul believed in a depraved humanity and a punitive God, though his grim vision didn't fully catch on until Augustine popularized his ideas in the fourth century. Paul is often quoted today and, for some, seems to carry the same authority as Jesus. This is curious. If some convert can revise the entire faith, what's to stop others from doing the same thing? As we'll see, not much.

Paul understood what every ad exec knows: You don't sell the steak, you sell the sizzle. It's not the product, it's the marketing. As a result, his relentless proselytizing expanded Christianity from a tiny Jewish sect to an independent religion that would eventually pester the entire Western world.

Born Saul of Tarsus in Asia Minor around A.D. 10, he was a Greek-speaking Hellenized Jew. This means he was a product of Greco-Roman life. But back in Jerusalem, traditional Jews disliked Hellenism. Yahweh had little use for Greek rationalism or Roman law. First century Jews faced a cultural dilemma similar to what Muslims confront today—a division between the old-fashioned and the new-fangled. Their way of life was at a crossroads.

The culture clash sometimes took on weird forms. The Greeks were big on health clubs, and they worked out in the nude. (The word *gymnasium,* a place to exercise, literally translates to "a place to be naked.") This practice scandalized traditional Jews, but those steeped in Hellenistic culture joined the clubs, sometimes hiding their circumcisions with fake foreskins. (And you thought your uncle's toupee was hideous.)

As far as we know, Saul never tried this particular accessory, but he was well-schooled in secular matters. He got his religious education in Judea and eventually became a member of the Pharisee sect. Despite their reputation as theocratic stick-in-the-muds, the Pharisees were actually rather open-minded about Jewish law. They opposed a rigid, literal interpretation of the Torah (the Law), and they believed in resurrection—just not the resurrection of Jesus.

Consequently, before he converted, Saul himself hounded Christians, dragging them into prison, or worse. At least, this is what the Bible purports. In reality, there is no outside verification of the Christian persecutions Saul claims he joined. This lack of evidence problem is one we run into a lot.

The Road to Damascus

According to Scripture, one day around A.D. 36, as he led his shock troops to Damascus for another round of oppression, Saul had a revelation—a great light from heaven—and the voice of Jesus telling him to stop with the persecutions already! The light blinded him for three days, ironic given that Jesus' specialty was restoring sight.

What Saul actually experienced is anyone's guess. Maybe it was a holy vision. Maybe it was an epileptic fit. The point is he was the first person to report a Jesus sighting after Christ's ascension to heaven. As we all know, he would not be the last.

After this episode, Saul did what all bipolar personalities do—he swung from one extreme to the other. He switched from a zealous persecutor of The Way, as the early Christians called their movement, to a fanatical promoter. He joined the very group he had intended to destroy and became a preacher himself—being a remarkably quick study on the subject. Jesus' disciples should have been this quick on the uptake.

Mind you, Paul (his new Christian name) never met Jesus personally. Judging from his work, he didn't know anything about Jesus' life story at all. He mentions crucifixion in his letters, but that's the only detail he seems to know about, and it comes off as more symbolic than biographical.

Hard Acts to Follow

We first meet Paul around half-way through the book that immediately follows the four Gospels: the *Acts of the Apostles*.

Acts was written by the author of Luke, who was allegedly Paul's traveling companion. Actually, there's a lot of "allegedly" in *Acts*. Most scholars are very skeptical about its historical accuracy, whether it's talking about the growth of the early churches or about Paul's evangelical journeys. It's packed with fanciful episodes that read more like propaganda than history. And yet again, no non-Christian writings verify any of it.

Acts begins with Jesus hanging around with his disciples/apostles for forty days after his resurrection. He dodges the question of whether or not the kingdom of Israel will be restored as everyone hopes and, instead, promises to send down the Holy Spirit—a kind of portable force-field to guide their actions. Then, finally, Jesus makes the spectacular exit we've been waiting for:

> And when he had said this, as they were looking on, he was lifted up, and a cloud took him out of their sight. [Acts 1:9]

Yet again, the writer is leaning on Old Testament imagery established centuries earlier:

> I saw in the night visions, and behold, with the clouds of heaven there came one like a son of man, and he came to the Ancient of Days... [Daniel 7:13]

"Ancient of Days" was the prophet Daniel's way of identifying God. And remember back when some of Jesus' followers thought he might be Elijah reincarnated?

> And Elijah went up by a whirlwind into heaven. [2 Kings 2:11]

Elijah was the only Old Testament prophet who didn't actually die. He was whisked away to heaven, which meant he might some day return. Jesus wasn't the first to create this expectation.

It is right after Jesus' breathtaking exit that two angels appear and ask a very dumb question: "Men of Galilee, why do you stand looking into heaven?" Like *duh!* Personal theory: Angels are no brighter than most messenger boys.

Fifty days after Passover, the apostles and 3,000 others are gripped by the Holy Spirit. The event is called Pentecost, and it's marked by the sort of thing that sends most of us running for cover—a rushing wind kicks up *inside* their house of worship and everyone starts speaking in tongues. This will continue to be one of the strange things new converts do as the faith spreads across Rome. It's interesting that the first sign of being born again is to start babbling nonsense.

Educated non-believers were understandably alarmed by such behavior. They had their own pagan rituals, but even so, Gentiles were often aghast at the noisy, primitive machinations of The Way. Blathering worshippers in the thralls of divine possession, touched by an all-powerful god...who became a man in order to save the world...but who died before he did...but who will come back any day now to save it for real and leave the spirit-possessed babblers in charge! Yeesh.

Well, religious rituals often mystify outsiders. Pentecostal snake-handlers frolic with deadly serpents to prove they have God's blessing. Goddess cults stage belly dances under the full moon in order to commune with Isis or Ishtar or Oprah. Tantric masters re-channel sexual energies to attain erotic transcendence, and to meet women who aren't fanatics about chastity.

Even modern Christian groups, like the Emerging Church movement, have adopted mystical, touchy-feely approaches to worship. They're turned off by stuffy, traditional church services. For them, faith is a bliss-inducing work-in-progress that involves personal connection and social activism. Priests in T-shirts and ponytails create hangouts in their living rooms where young people can kick back and rap about faith...man. Nobody has to sit up straight or polish their shoes. They sprawl out on beanbag chairs beneath glow-in-the-dark posters of the Rapture. Far out.

Jews for Jesus

Having received the Holy Spirit, it was now time for the apostles to give it a test drive. According to *Acts*, Peter ("the rock") becomes prominent in the mother church in Jerusalem, and other churches pop up across Judea. There's no archeological evidence for any of this; the oldest known ruin of a church is in Megiddo, Israel and it only goes back to the third or fourth century.

Acts claims that this new sect is in constant conflict with mainstream Judaism. Stephen, an outspoken believer, is stoned to death and becomes the first Christian martyr. With such hostility around them, virtually all services are held in private homes, believers keeping a low profile lest they make the neighbors nervous. Around A.D. 40, the term "Christian" is coined as a derisive label (like "Moonies") for the rather loopy followers of The Way. Over time, a church hierarchy emerges.

Oddly, *Acts* never says what happens to most of the twelve apostles after the crucifixion. You'd think a dozen wonder-workers with the same healing powers as Jesus would have generated serious buzz across the Near East. Yet nobody, not the Romans nor the Greeks nor the Egyptians nor even the Bible documents anything they do.

Around A.D. 46, Paul hits the road on a two-year journey that will be the first of four evangelizing missions across Asia Minor, Greece, and Italy. Most people dismiss The Way as a goofy cult. But Paul sets up house churches everywhere he goes. He preaches to anyone who will listen and even to a few who won't. It's hard to say how successful he was, but even in *Acts*, many listeners are not impressed and it seems unlikely he converted more than a few hundred people.

In any case, Paul's drive to offer the faith to all takers sparks the first great controversy of the new sect: Who gets to be a Christian?

It was a touchy subject. Jesus claimed to be the fulfillment of Jewish prophecy, so didn't this mean you had to be Jewish first? Didn't you have to observe all those nettlesome laws and statutes? Or could you be a Gentile and leapfrog over all that circumcision and no-shellfish stuff and just be born again?

After much debate and hair-pulling, the churches gradually decided to abandon the separatist tradition of Judaism and allow everyone to become a Christian, even the un-snipped. This decision was a key to their success. It expanded the potential market for Christianity from Jews to anyone with a pulse.

A Man of Letters

Paul proselytizes his way across the Roman Empire on four missionary treks over two decades. Along the way, he heals the sick, blinds the occasional sorcerer, and sends his instructive, high-minded, and sometimes spiteful letters to the home churches back east. He's appalled by the nude sculptures of Greece, sex being one of his major bugaboos. He's nearly stoned to death at one point, and he eludes other plots against his life. But he continues to establish small churches across the Empire, and they spend lots of time debating about what he writes.

His letters sometimes come off as schizoid, perhaps because Paul himself had such a mixed background. He preaches love and forgiveness. But he also rails at length against...well, pretty much everybody. We're all sinners, hypocrites, slanderers, and gossips. We're full of envy, murder, strife and deceit. Paul is big on earning God's grace and being justified by faith, and anyone who doesn't join his cause is in for a holy reaming. There's not much middle ground in Paul's world.

As he travels, Paul's evangelical zeal meets with varied results. The logic-loving Greeks think he's three columns short of a Parthenon. Jews get pissed off that he wants to rewrite the old rules or ignore them altogether. The Romans, always the Bible's disciplinarians, only take notice when he becomes a public nuisance.

Eventually, he's arrested and imprisoned, but is later released. Then, on his fourth and final journey, he survives a shipwreck and winds up in a prison cell in Rome. While there, he writes more letters that end up in the New Testament. According to *Acts*, he's eventually freed, but it doesn't say what becomes of him. One tradition claims he was beheaded around A.D. 64.

Paul on Jesus

In his work, Paul echoes Jesus' ideas about loving all, never taking revenge against the wicked, and blessing those who persecute you. But according to *Acts*, in his eagerness to say nice things he sometimes strays off the reservation:

> "...remembering the words of the Lord Jesus, how he said, 'It is more blessed to give than to receive.'" [Acts 20:35]

The Gospels don't record Jesus saying this nor does Paul himself write this in any of his letters. In several cases, Paul insists "it is written" when it isn't written at all. Further, if Paul never met Jesus, how could he "remember" the Lord's words?

Paul later explains to the Romans why all men need a healthy dose of Vitamin Jesus to live a good moral life:

> "For God has consigned all men to disobedience, that he may have mercy upon all." [Romans 11:32]

In other words, he made us heroin addicts so that we'd all seek his holy rehab clinic. Technically, God is excusing his own shoddy work. He wants moral perfection, but instead of creating it himself he churns out flawed humans and expects *us* to achieve what *he* failed to conjure up. Despite claims to the contrary, God's mercy isn't free—it has to be *earned*. A work ethic for salvation. Kind of nervy given that Yahweh is a god who takes days off.

For all Paul's insistence that Christianity be inclusive, he doesn't want to set the bar too low:

> "Do not be deceived; neither the immoral, nor idolaters, nor adulterers, nor homosexuals, nor thieves, nor the greedy, nor drunkards, nor revilers, nor robbers will inherit the Kingdom of God."
> [1 Corinthians 6:9-10]

The Vulgate—the Latin version of the Bible produced by the Church in the fifth century—adds "the effeminate" and "fornicators" to this list of offenders. This Kingdom of God sounds like a dull place. Paul continues condemning the wicked, exalting the faithful, and dreaming up a zillion metaphors for the "Christ died so we may have eternal life" idea. And again, he lapses into an Orwellian mind-frame:

> "...having been set free from sin, [we] have become slaves of righteousness." [Romans 6:18]

He makes it sound a bit creepy, especially since you don't get to vote on what constitutes "righteousness."

Paul on Slavery

While we're on the subject of slaves, how does Paul feel about actually owning other human beings?

> "Slaves, be obedient to those who are your earthly masters, with fear and trembling, in singleness of heart, as to Christ;" [Ephesians 6:5]

Remember, Jesus' statement that "the truth shall make you free" is a spiritual ideal, not an emancipation proclamation. It's about the soul. Slaves can be free from sin, but not from their owners.

> "Masters, treat your slaves justly and fairly, knowing that you also have a Master in heaven." [Colossians 4:1]

That's right. Be nice to your slaves, but don't feel obligated to free them. In Paul's brief letter to his colleague Philemon, he offers to return Philemon's runaway slave, Onesimus, whom he has converted to Christianity. He asks that Philemon accept him "no longer as a slave, as a beloved brother..." It's a hint at the Christian attitude that, in God's eyes, there is no class distinction. All souls are equal—a refreshingly progressive idea.

Yet somehow this didn't translate into action on the ground. Not only was Paul offering to return an escaped slave without demanding his freedom, but Christian Europe would eventually become the greatest slave-owning civilization in history. If we're very generous and allow that Paul was sowing the seeds of slave abolition with this story, it fell on sterile ground. Sadly, the Bible never envisions a world without slavery.

Paul on Marriage

Of course, no evangelical harangue is complete without waxing expert on so-called Family Values. Unfortunately, as iffy as Jesus was on the glories of wedded bliss, Paul is a whole lot worse:

> "To the unmarried and the widows I say that it is well for them to remain single as I do. But if they cannot exercise self-control, they should marry. For it is better to marry than to be aflame with passion." [1 Corinthians 7:8-9]

Translation: Stay single unless you're so horny the sheep start looking good. In that case, go ahead and tie the knot. He goes on:

> "The unmarried man is anxious about the affairs of the Lord, how to please the Lord; but the married man is anxious about worldly affairs, how to please his wife, and his interests are divided." [1 Corinthians 7:32-34]

And on...

> "...he who marries his betrothed does well; and he who refrains from marriage will do better." [1 Corinthians 7:38]

And on...

> "...those who marry will have worldly troubles...from now on, let those who have wives live as though they had none." [1 Corinthians 7:28-29]

Can't you just feel the Family Values? Paul also has problems with sex in general, and with women in particular:

> "As in all the churches of the saints, the women should keep silence in the churches. For they are not permitted to speak...For it is shameful for a woman to speak in church." [1 Corinthians 14:34-35]

To their credit, most churches today leave this line on the cutting room floor. But not all of them. You might want to check the by-laws before you join.

Paul on Lifestyle

For Paul, women should be seen and not heard, and maybe not even seen.

> "...if a woman will not veil herself, then she should cut off her hair..." [1 Corinthians 11:6]

Uh-huh. Any fashion tips for the guys?

> "Does not nature itself teach you that for a man to wear long hair is degrading to him, but if a woman has long hair, it is her pride?" [1 Corinthians 11:14]

Maybe Jesus had a buzz cut. Whatever he sported, this verse discredits virtually every image of Jesus ever produced.

Paul writes lines that are so poetic, half of us think they originated with Shakespeare: "Let us eat and drink, for tomorrow we die," [1 Corinthians 15:32] and "O death, where is thy victory? O death, where is thy sting?" [1 Corinthians 15:55] He also criticizes the tendency to overdo the speaking-in-tongues routine because, for one thing, it makes outsiders think they're all batty:

> "If, therefore, the whole church assembles and all speak in tongues, and outsiders or unbelievers enter, will they not say that you are mad?" [1 Corinthians 14:23]

Yeah, they will. Still, Paul supports the nutty habit of rejecting the truth of our eyes in favor of the invisible:

> "...we look not to the things that are seen but the things that are unseen; for the things that are seen are transient, but the things that are unseen are eternal."
> [2 Corinthians 4:18]

Sure, and sometimes the things that are unseen are completely imaginary, which is why they're unseen. To be fair, in this case he's referring to the spiritual rewards that are promised after we shuffle off this mortal coil. Those are certainly invisible. But he doesn't stop there. Paul gets a lot of the specifics he teaches from this unseen world as well. This is because he comes from the school of thought that says belief itself is a form of evidence. More on that in a moment.

Paul on Paul

> "For I would have you know, brethren, that the gospel which was preached by me is not man's gospel. For I did not receive it from man, nor was I taught it, but it came through a revelation of Jesus Christ." [Galatians 1:11]

I wonder why Paul has to rely on a supernatural source for his information when, according Scripture, he personally knew Peter and James, who personally knew Jesus. Paul didn't need a revelation from the dead; a simple conversation with the living would have sufficed.

Well, Paul isn't big on hard reporting. He's one of those "gut" thinkers who equates conviction with fact. He's slopping over with wisdom that just sort of comes to him. Much of it is good advice and all of it is well-intended. He wants us to be decent, honorable, and respectful. Fine. But then he gets all cultish with how we're all part of the body of Christ, washed clean by his blood. We live in him and he lives in us. We're his slaves, his servants, his body, his glory, his ambassadors, the sheep of his pasture, the fish of his aquarium, the special sauce of his Big Mac, and so on.

Paul doesn't know when to quit. Nor is he burdened by humility:

> "I have confidence in the Lord that you will take no other view than mine;" [Galatians 5:10]

There's a lot of that going around the Christian world these days. What's really frustrating is that, when Paul finally says something sensible, nobody seems to listen:

> "...there is no distinction between Jew and Greek (Gentile)." [Romans 10:12]

It's a declaration of ethnic and religious equality before God. That sentiment sure slipped through the cracks over the centuries, didn't it?

> "...never avenge yourselves, but leave it to the wrath of God..." [Romans 12:19]

This would certainly save on defense spending.

> "...if your enemy is hungry, feed him; if he is thirsty, give him drink...overcome evil with good." [Romans 12:20-21]

Really? So we start sending humanitarian aid to al Qaeda? Well, Paul is just a big-hearted guy:

> Let all that you do be done in love." [1 Corinthians 16:14]

That's sweet. But remember, it is love for God that he's talking about:

> "If any one has no love for the Lord, let him be accursed." [1 Corinthians 16:22]

See what I mean? Paul always lets you know where he's coming from, even if where he's coming from is the booby hatch:

> "We are fools for Christ's sake..." [1 Corinthians 4:10]

No argument here.

Paul's Jesus

Despite his exhaustive evangelizing, Paul leaves the world with a major question: Was his Jesus a human or something else? Paul's writings are the oldest Christian works known, yet they seem to describe a heavenly savior rather than an earthly one; a cosmic figure in a spiritual realm rather than a flesh-and-blood man.

Paul never mentions any details of Jesus' life on earth, nor does he place Jesus in any geographic place or historical time. He offers only one quote, about the Eucharist, and that's it. Otherwise, he never cites Jesus, even when the situation calls for it and even when Jesus expresses an idea more eloquently than Paul does. He never describes the particulars of Jesus' ministry. He never mentions Bethlehem or virgin births or John the Baptist or miracle healings. No mass feedings or landmark sermons. He says nothing about Pontius Pilate or Jesus on trial. He seems completely unaware of the stories that show up years later in the four Gospels.

It's argued that the people Paul was writing to already knew these stories, so he didn't have to repeat them. But he was writing before the Gospels existed, and the total lack of reference to Jesus' words and activities starts to make you wonder. It's almost as if Paul worshipped a mythical figure with no earthly biography at all—a Jewish version of an Olympian deity. The Greeks swapped legends about their gods, but they didn't always provide full back-stories. Likewise, Paul's Jesus has the supernatural persona of a Greek myth, but the details that make for a believable life story didn't hit the press until years after Paul's death.

Some of the last epistles in the New Testament, *Hebrews 5:7* and *1 John 4:2,* do mention Jesus existing "in the flesh." But these letters were produced very late in the first century and, by then, the four Gospels were already making the rounds.

Did Jesus Exist?

Somewhere along the line we have to ask the inevitable question: Did Jesus of Nazareth ever actually walk the earth?

Most Bible skeptics figure Jesus was a real guy whose life story was inflated to cosmic proportions by his fan club, or through rumor, over generations of time. But another school of thought claims that there is no historical person at the core of the New Testament at all. They hold that Jesus Christ is an entirely mythical figure created by writers who concocted a life story out of selected scraps of the Old Testament.

One compelling argument for this view is the striking absence of evidence where there ought to be some for so many details of the Gospels—the Roman census, the Star of Bethlehem, the slaughter of the innocents, miracle healings, raising the dead, the feeding of thousands, the twelve apostles, and a crucifixion drama that includes earthquakes, darkness at noon, and zombies stalking Jerusalem. You'd think there'd be *some* kind of independent record of these events. Yet, there is no contemporary evidence at all. Zip.

Even if you take into account the fact that Jerusalem and vicinity were basically burned to the ground in A.D. 70, thus eradicating both documents and eyewitnesses, most of these events would have been known about far beyond the territory flattened by the Romans. This lack of outside verification is called the argument from silence, and it's a pretty good one.

Still, absence of evidence is not evidence of absence. Many actual events have left no historical record. Problem is, even the evidence offered to *support* a historical Jesus doesn't add up. There are the Gospels themselves, with all the inconsistencies, absurdities, historical inaccuracies, mistranslations, and scientific impossibilities you have to roll with to take these stories literally. There is the lack of eyewitness accounts. The disingenuous use of Old Testament verse to make the Jesus story look like the fulfillment of prophecy. And there are the suspicious similarities between his biography and all those other resurrection myths.

Scapegoats

So, where and when do we find the first references to Jesus outside the Bible? One of the earliest was written around A.D. 115

by a Roman senator and historian named Tacitus. He tells us that, in A.D. 64, screwball emperor Nero blamed a fire he set in Rome on the little-known religious sect that followed Jesus. Because they were "infamous for their abominations," according to Tacitus, they were subjected to "the most exquisite punishments," which included being killed by dogs, nailed to crosses, or set aflame and used as night lamps.

Christians call this the first persecution and it's often trumpeted as an epic purge. In reality, the edict against them lasted only one year and only covered the city of Rome—if it happened at all. Tacitus is reporting an event he never saw a half-century after it supposedly happened. He's getting the story second hand at best. Fact is there's scant evidence that Christians were even established in Rome back in A.D. 64.

True or not, the story was useful to Christians because it suggested that they were important enough to persecute, and it never hurt their cause to be seen as victims of a cruel world.

Josephus

The earliest known reference to Jesus from a non-biblical source is a famous, or infamous, passage from a huge, multi-volume work entitled *Antiquities of the Jews* by the great Jewish historian Flavius Josephus. He was one of Rome's top literary figures and was *the* historian of first century Judea.

In one of his books, written around A.D. 93, he briefly veers off his essay on the troubles Rome is having with its occupation of Jerusalem and inserts a single, intriguing paragraph. Today it's known as the *Testimonium Flavianum:*

> "At about this time lived Jesus, a wise man, if indeed one might call him a man. For he was one who accomplished surprising feats and was a teacher of such people as are eager for novelties. He won over many of the Jews and many of the Greeks. He was The Messiah.
> When Pilate, upon an indictment brought by the principle men among us, condemned him to the cross,

those who had loved him from the very first did not cease to be attached to him.

On the third day he appeared to them restored to life, for the holy prophets had foretold this and myriads of other marvels concerning him. And the tribe of the Christians, so called after him, has to this day still not disappeared."

This passage has long been offered as the best and earliest evidence outside the Bible for a historical Jesus. There are, however, a lot of problems with it.

For one, it was written sixty years after the crucifixion and at least twenty years after the Gospel of Mark—not exactly an eyewitness report. Worse, the oldest existing copy of it was produced centuries after Josephus allegedly wrote it. Who knows what copyists might have added or changed? (They were known to do such things.)

When reading the *Antiquities*, this Jesus paragraph seems out of context. It interrupts the larger story rather than fitting into it. After it appears, the text goes back to the original subject and there's no further discussion of Jesus. Its literary style is also different from the surrounding text. If you delete it altogether, the larger work reads more smoothly. You don't miss the paragraph.

Suspiciously, the passage neatly summarizes the entire Passion story—in a couple of sentences it crams in references to miracles, The Messiah, prosecution, crucifixion, Pontius Pilate, and resurrection. It's a little too convenient. It looks for all the world like it was inserted by a later writer.

Let's apply a little common sense. Josephus was Jewish, so he'd never refer to Jesus, or *anyone*, as "The Messiah." If he did believe this about Jesus, he wouldn't describe him like a novelty act for a pack of suckers and then offhandedly claim he was the long-awaited savior of his people. This would be like a modern reporter casually writing about a local guru with a popular following...oh and, by the way, he's the Overlord who just arrived on the

Mothership to take over the earth. Journalists call that burying the lead.

Nor would a believer in Jesus call him a simple "wise man," nor would he mention "the tribe of Christians" as if he just discovered them in darkest Africa. Some argue that a Christian forger wouldn't use this term either...unless, of course, he was being crafty—a distinct possibility, as we'll see. Still others counter that *some* of this passage may have been written by Josephus and only parts of it were inserted.

Elsewhere in *Antiquities*, Josephus mentions other so-called messiahs, but he doesn't take any of them seriously. There is also one other dubious passage in which Josephus refers to "the brother of Jesus, who was called Christ, whose brother was James." But similar debates rage over the authenticity of this line.

The fact that the passage comes to us through a prominent fourth century Church propagandist named Eusebius doesn't help. He was Emperor Constantine's top religious public relations man and he had no problem putting a heavy Christian spin on most of what he wrote. Some suggest he was the guy who inserted the dubious paragraph. It's just the sort of thing he'd do.

Why Faith?

You can go back and forth on the evidence for a historic Jesus forever, but you have to admit it's all a pretty thin sandwich. It's most likely that a real person inspired the Gospel accounts of Jesus. But if he existed, his biographers really took liberties. There is no archeological evidence to back them up at all. Discoveries of a garden, or a tomb, or a tattoo parlor mentioned in the Gospels prove nothing. Fictional stories are usually set in real places; unearthing a legend's location doesn't make the story true. And every time some antique dealer comes up with a relic traceable to Jesus, the evidence is inconclusive or the guy turns out to be an established huckster.

It makes you wonder—if God was so intent on spreading his word and giving us all a shot at salvation, why do we have to work so hard to ensure we get the message right? Why do we even need biblical scholars, boring archeologists, or bullyragging preachers? Why doesn't God just appear in the sky in front of the whole world and say, "Hey! Looky here! Mystery over! Now clean up your act!" That's all it would take.

The classic response to this is that God wants us to love and obey him through faith. But why is that? What does faith accomplish when it comes to love? I love my mother. I wouldn't love her more if there were some doubt of her existence. Nor would I be more inclined to obey her rules if my belief in her was based solely on ancient stories. What good is this "have faith" requirement if it makes us less likely to get with the program? Frankly, it sounds like a load. You demand faith in an idea when you don't have anything better to support it, like proof.

> Faith is the substance of things hoped for, the evidence
> of things not seen. [Hebrews 11:1]

I like the sentiment of this verse. Faith in the future, or in yourself, or in your friends, or in your country, are all fine because it's an attitude you have based on experience. It's a sense of trust and hope, and a source of strength and optimism. But it's not proof of anything, and certainly not verification of a higher power that runs the universe. Gravity is an invisible force that governs the cosmos, too, but it took an apple clunking Newton's head and some thoughtful number-crunching before it made sense to build a space program dependent upon it.

Waxing poetic about faith has its benefits. But it's no substitute for sensory evidence or rational analysis when it comes to authenticating facts, which is what Paul is asking us to do. Faith is belief in the *absence* of evidence. When you fall back on faith, you give up the ability to distinguish fantasy from fact because you're no longer looking for proof. Faith is not a higher standard than reason, it's a lower one. It's based on feelings, and even animals have those. Your cat *believes* she can catch that fish on the TV screen. Your dog has *faith* that, when you take him to the vet, he'll come back with his balls. It ain't always the case.

Paul would have us accept faith itself as a form of evidence. Belief in the absence of evidence now becomes evidence. This is how conspiracy theorists think. If there's no evidence of an evil plot, that's proof of the plot because the conspirators are *that* diabolically good. You can never disprove the conspiracy, which is what keeps it alive whether it's true or not.

Some insist that Paul's own conversion from persecutor to evangelist is proof of his claims, as if it confirmed anything beyond his susceptibility to mood swings. They'll argue that knowledge also comes through revelation, or intuition, or authority. Empirical evidence alone won't do.

Well, wisdom or creativity clearly involve more than scientific proofs. But if you're trying to establish something as a *fact*, like a miracle or a deity, you need more than faith. Facts require evidence gained through the eyes and ears. So does knowledge of the Bible for that matter; it's not inborn. You can't act as if sensory evidence is an excessive demand made by stubborn skeptics. That's a classic dodge—if you can't prove your point, insist that you don't need to. Your *belief* is enough. Move the epistemological goalposts and equate your convictions with fact. Sorry, but this doesn't lead to truth. It just leads to Fox News.

To rely on faith means to abandon your senses, literally, and lose the ability to distinguish reality from bullshit. If faith itself is proof, then all religions would be true because they're all based on faith. If you think most of them aren't true, then you're forced to concede that faith is not reliable. It usually steers people wrong.

The Pagan Perspective

So where did the rest of the ancient world stand on all this Jesus stuff? Pagans have always gotten a bum rap from Judeo-Christian culture primarily because the word "pagan" refers to worshippers who weren't Jewish or Christian. There was never a specific religion called paganism. It is a sweeping term that refers to anyone with spiritual beliefs not found in the Bible. It originally referred to rural folks who worshipped nature gods—trees and meadows, or even houses and doors. Some use the term more loosely to refer to any non-believing Greeks and Romans—which was about 90% of them.

Today's popular image of their civilization is pretty unfair. We imagine the Greeks split their time between carving statues, gay orgies, and standing around asking, "Why is there air?" The Romans just conquered, crucified, bet on gladiators, and lounged around marble fountains being fed grapes. If the movies are right, they all spoke with British accents and had the moral sensibilities of Jabba the Hut.

In reality, what they did was invent Western civilization. From roughly 600 B.C. to A.D. 450 the Greeks, and then the Romans, dominated the scene and reinvented the way people lived and thought. It was hardly a bed of roses; life could be harsh and unfair by our standards. But the world they created would be more familiar to you and me than anything going on in ancient Judea, and their cultural innovations would eventually liberate us from the baggage of theocracy and superstition.

Greco-Roman civilization was largely secular, but there was no shortage of cults and religions scattered across the Empire, ranging from Isis worship to Mithraism to belief in the Olympian deities. Like Jews and Christians, pagans worried that misfortune would strike if their gods were not honored.

The Romans may have been liberal about religious choice but they were sticklers for ceremony, especially when it reinforced the authority of the state. Much like the United States, with its Pledge of Allegiance and National Anthem, Rome had rituals to ensure that its vast and diverse population remained loyal to the unifying symbol of the emperor.

It was here that many Jews and Christians got themselves in trouble. They wouldn't play ball and often snubbed even token recognitions of any authority but their own god. It was the equivalent of refusing to salute the flag or not standing for *The Star Spangled Banner*. They had every right to their opinion. But it made them unpopular and suspect. So, when hard times hit, they were easy to blame.

This didn't make the Romans any worse about religious persecution than anyone else, however. In the Old Testament, any disaster that befell the Israelites was routinely blamed on their tolerance of other religions. In the Middle Ages, a lack of godliness was the default explanation for every malady from the bubonic plague to impotence. Even today, many evangelical pastors keep us entertained when they characterize a hurricane or a terrorist attack as the Lord's vengeance against *Roe vs. Wade* or same-sex marriages. Interesting that they know the specific offenses that get God to blow his stack. And it's always *those* offenses. It's never war, torture, greed, or ads for Christmas gifts in October.

For most pagans the new Jesus religion was just another among the many that people fell for. Sheep herders and village dwellers were easy marks for a magic act. In *Acts 14:8*, after Paul witnessed to the Greek city of Lystra, a crippled man got up and walked and the locals shouted out, "The gods have come down to us in the likeness of men!" Later, in *Acts 28*, on the island of Malta, Paul was bitten by a snake. When he didn't die, the crowds figured him for a god. It must have been a lot easier to launch a messianic following in those days.

Josephus wrote of "tricksters" who convinced crowds of their divine authority. People reported weeping statues and wise men performing miracle cures. During the Olympics of A.D. 165, a pious nitwit named Proteus set himself aflame to prove his belief in reincarnation. Lucian, a skeptic who knew him personally, decided to test popular gullibility by spreading the story that Proteus rose up to heaven as a vulture after his death. That rumor later came back to Lucian as a "fact." In another instance, he wrote that someone stuck a puppet's head onto a snake and promoted it as the god of healing. A petition went out to rename the town where this happened in the god's honor.

There's one born every minute, and sometimes two or three.

Values Scorecard

So how did the values of Hellenism actually stack up against the ideas enshrined by the Jews and Christians of the time? To hear the believers tell it, Western history is one long glorious conquest of biblical values over the godless debauchery of paganism. Without the one true God of the Bible we'd all be groveling before chunks of marble, or fornicating in the streets, or tossing children into fireplaces like Yule logs. No Family Values, no democracy, no personal responsibility, and no god-fearing Republicans. Nothing but false deities, temple prostitutes having ritual sex, and man-boy love. (Okay, so maybe there'd be *some* Republicans.)

Fortunately, we escaped the soulless idolatry of paganism. We got a deity who established a patriarchal theocracy that kept slaves, practiced polygamy, sacrificed animals, and extinguished anyone who complained too much. Boy, did we luck out.

This was then followed by a new Gospel centered on a messiah who asked us to give up everything and follow him because he was going to change the world. But then he died, and now we have to wait for him to get back to us. That was two millennia ago. In the centuries since, his followers have provided hope for the destitute and a nice code of conduct. Of course, they've also provided persecutions, inquisitions, crusades, book burnings, witch burnings, press censorship, religious intolerance, and no talk of democracy for a thousand years. But hey, at least they didn't have sex in church.

Morality without God

News flash: You don't need religion to have morals or values. You certainly didn't need Yahweh or Jesus. Hammurabi didn't. Confucius didn't. The Buddha didn't. Babylon, Egypt, and Canaan all had codes of morality, justice, and personal behavior a thousand years before the Ten Commandments were committed to granite, and they weren't all based on a belief in the supernatural.

Nor did the ancient Greeks have an all-powerful god to lean on. Instead, around 600 B.C., they started to produce generations of thinkers who established moral standards completely independent of religion—values most of us cherish today. Some of these ideas were so appealing that Jews, Christians, and Muslims would later borrow them and then act as if they invented them. They didn't.

The foundation stones of the modern West were not set down in the deserts of the Sinai or in the hills of Galilee. They were established around the blue Aegean and half of everything we are today comes from a world of people most of whom didn't know Yahweh from a potato knish.

What's more, biblical religion has never provided the changeless, eternal values it claims. Five centuries ago, slavery and religious intolerance were acceptable. Women's equality and free speech were not. Monarchy was preferred to democracy. Where were all our Christian values then? As for the theory that, without a belief in the biblical god there's nothing to restrain our darkest ambitions, the record shows that many of history's darkest deeds were done on orders from that same biblical god. Belief in him didn't stop these deeds. It some cases it inspired them.

Of course, this is a hard notion to sell. One of the slickest tricks successful religions get away with is to take credit for every idea or development they consider to be good, and to blame everything bad on someone else. Churches are masters at this. If an earthquake hits South America and ten thousand die in the ruins, nobody blames God for the disaster—even if managing seismic events would seem to fit his job description. Yet, if an infant is found in the rubble without a scratch, everybody praises the Lord for "the miracle." We do this same sort of thing with our values— we attribute them to our faith whether or not it was actually responsible for them.

Well, why don't we look at the record and see where our most important cultural ideals originate? Let's sum up the key values of Hellenism and place them side-by-side with those found in the Bible—which are supposedly the only thing that distinguishes you from somebody raised by wolves.

	Greece and Rome	Old Testament	New Testament
Democracy	Invented it.	Huh?	Huh?
Free Speech	Necessary for democracy.	Huh?	Huh?
Religious Tolerance	Standard operating procedure.	You gotta be kidding. The worst of sins—see 1st Commandment	Fine—as long as you don't mind eternity in hell. It's up to you.
The Rule of Law	Goes back to Hammurabi; Rome professionalized it.	The law is what God's prophets say it is.	Jesus is the law, whatever that means.
Ethics	Based on rational philosophy and the Golden Rule.	Based on God's mood.	Honesty, love and forgiveness, even for people you can't stomach.
War	Peace is better, but war is okay for defense or profit.	Peace is better, but war is okay for defense, profit, or destroying idols.	Those who live by the sword die by the sword.
Property Rights	Greek law afforded property rights. Rome recognized contracts and entrepreneurs. And pay your taxes!	Don't steal or covet your neighbor's stuff, and give to a temple near you lest you be hit by a plague.	Give everything away and don't worry about money. And pay your taxes!
Slavery	No problem.	No problem.	No problem.
Individual Liberty	More than any people before them or for a thousand years after.	Fine, just obey the 613 laws, statutes, commandments, and ordinances.	Not really a priority. Be a slave to Christ.
Marriage	Greece: the transfer of a woman from father to husband. Rome: a mutual agreement between a man and a woman.	The transfer of a woman from father to husband.	Best avoided, but better than shacking up.

140

	Greece and Rome	**Old Testament**	**New Testament**
Monogamy	Generally, one wife was enough.	Take one, take four, take a dozen. Take their maids, too.	You get one spouse, and choose carefully because you're stuck for life.
Incest	Banned.	Necessary for a few thousand years, then banned.	Banned.
Prostitution	There were different categories, some legal and some not. Often stigmatized, but also accepted.	Death by stoning.	Bad, but hold off on the stoning.
Adultery	Punished by divorce or banishment.	Death by stoning.	Bad, but hold off on the stoning.
Homo-sexuality	Acceptable, with certain restrictions.	Death by stoning. (I'm sensing a pattern here.)	Not an issue for Jesus. Paul, on the other hand, was more of a "don't ask, don't tell" guy.
Concubines	On occasion.	On occasion.	Nope.
Divorce	Okay.	Okay.	Not okay. Like I said, stuck for life.
Gender Equality	Fat chance.	When pigs fly.	When you get to heaven, maybe.
Birth Control	Acceptable.	No comment.	No comment.
Abortion	Controversial but legal, as was infanticide.	No comment, except Exodus 21:22.	No comment.
Science	Invented it.	Huh?	Huh?

It's clear that Christianity did popularize some good ideas. But it's also clear that most of the values we're willing to fight for today can be had without any reference to Scripture—democracy, free expression, religious tolerance, scientific inquiry, ethics, trial by jury, privacy rights, marriage, the rule of law, the rights of man. Sorry to burst the balloon but none of these "Judeo-Christian values" originated with the Bible. They all have independent roots in Greece, Rome, and earlier cultures.

The Problem of Pagan Prosperity

So, how did the people of God deal with the success of the civilization around them? Well, back in first century Judea the Jewish priests resented Roman rule and were hell bent on reestablishing a theocracy. Christians, meanwhile, were busy spreading the word until Jesus returned. While both faiths found their supporters and new recruits, their repudiation of the larger culture confronted them with a dismal reality—everyone else seemed to be having a lot more fun.

You can slam the Roman Empire for plenty of reasons: slavery, the glorification of war, gladiatorial games, and the occasional pervert emperor. As in all societies there was poverty and social inequality. Plus they invented the legal profession, for which we can never forgive them. Even so, life was safer, richer, and freer for most Romans than it was in any of the empires that preceded them. With a vast road system patrolled by the army, a traveler could cross the Empire without getting mugged—something I can't even do in New York.

Given the incredible success of pagan civilization, what would be the attraction of two religions that were full of rules, rituals, and wrath, not to mention priests who spent half their time reminding you what a sinful prick you were?

The only way to fight the allures of the most exciting and triumphant civilization in history was to reject it altogether. To characterize its very success as a victory of Evil, and to scare the living hell out of anyone who didn't think so—especially the Hellenized Jews and Christians who managed to enjoy some of it.

What these backsliders needed was something special; a fresh dose of spiritual motivation. You can guess how much fun *this* is going to be.

CHAPTER SIX

How I Learned to Love the End of the World

Is God willing to prevent evil, but not able?
Then he is not omnipotent.
Is he able, but not willing? Then he is malevolent.
Is he both able and willing? Then whence cometh evil?
Is he neither able nor willing? Then why call him God?

—Epicurus

The End to End All Endings

Forecasting the world's utter destruction has a long and glorious history, even if the great majority of mainstream churches don't bother with this lunacy. Throughout its history the Catholic Church has routinely debunked End-of-the-World alarms. Nevertheless, books, movies and television programs about it are astoundingly popular. Certain evangelical churches traffic in it and their activism has injected these ideas into political debates on subjects ranging from the environment to the defense of Israel to nuclear war. So maybe it's worth a look.

Visions of the End Times got their start with Old Testament prophets like Isaiah, who pioneered the genre around 750 B.C. Jeremiah and Daniel were also major contributors to this grim lore, which usually cropped up in dire times, which was most of the time. When your cause seems completely lost and there's no hope the world will turn out the way you want, screw it. Let it all burn. We're talking really sour grapes here.

The Book of Revelation

Happy people don't write stuff like *The Revelation to John,* which is the full name of the Bible's last and most bizarre book. It's such an over-the-top rant it almost didn't make it into Scripture. *Revelation* is a fever dream of apocalyptic imagery written by a Jewish Christian named John. He wrote from the Greek island of Patmos around A.D. 95 and he may have been the most pissed-off man who ever lived. The book seethes with white-hot vitriol and spews hatred for just about anything you can see, touch, or enjoy. John wanted absolute spiritual purity for all humankind. Can you think of anything more terrifying?

John's problem was that Roman civilization was at its peak and he was miffed because of its worldly achievements and its refusal to be converted. What he demanded was total devotion to God, even if he had to knock off 99% of humanity to get it. That's exactly what he proceeded to do in his book.

Jesus the Terrible

John didn't credit the book to himself. According to him, it was a vision from Christ; John was just the stenographer. Consequently, *Revelation* is regarded by many as the only book in the Bible authored by Jesus himself. It's a divinely-inspired picture of what he intends to do when all shall hit the fan. What's disturbing is that the Jesus of *Revelation* is worlds away from the benevolent, forgiving philosopher of the four Gospels. Here, Jesus boils over with vengeance, walloping all non-believers with a whirlwind of unspeakable horrors, followed by unimaginable terrors, followed by eternal damnation. Woof...

Ever wonder how people can profess a love of Jesus and still end up advocating war, executions, anti-Semitism, racism, torture, or a fuming contempt for all other faiths? It's the Jesus of *Revelation* they resort to. It's a scary proposition and, if pushed to an extreme, a formula for fascism. Suddenly, believers have permission to loathe and destroy anything they choose, from political rivals to entire countries, and no one can question them because God wants it that way. It's right here in the book.

The Devil Takes Charge

A classic rule of drama says that a hero is only as compelling as his adversary. So, John launches his war saga by giving Satan a promotion. In the Old Testament, the devil was a minor league player; he was barely mentioned. Yahweh ran everything. If good things happened, it was God's doing. If bad things happened, it was also God's doing because you undoubtedly deserved it. Satan was one of God's angels. In the *Book of Job*, he was used as a surrogate to bring misery upon a man of virtue—but only with God's permission.

Now, in the New Testament, Satan no longer works for the Lord. He's a free agent, and a competitor. This way, all the misfortunes of the world can be laid at his doorstep instead of God's and it gives Jesus a supernatural foe upon which he can take holy vengeance. Few things make religious absolutists happier than a reason to dish out pitiless retribution upon those who won't subscribe to the faith.

You'll recall that Satan showed up in the Gospels to test Jesus in the desert. It wasn't much of a contest and Jesus basically told him to shove it. The book of *Revelation*, however, kicks Satan upstairs and makes him the supreme icon of Evil, then pits him in a one-on-one Smackdown with Christ for control of the universe at the End of Time. Ready to rumble?

146

John of Patmos borrows his visions of a global holocaust from the prophet Daniel and then does him one better. He forecasts the miraculous obliteration of everything he abhors—which is a *lot*—and he describes how a galaxy of terrors is heaped upon everyone who doesn't think the way he does.

Not that we have to sweat any of this. You'll recall that the Gospel of Mark got it wrong when it had Jesus predicting God's judgment before "this generation" is passed. *Revelation* gets it equally wrong. The last lines of the book, which are the final lines of the entire Holy Bible, have Jesus promising:

> He who testifies to these things says, "Surely I am coming soon." Amen. [Rev. 22:20]

As mentioned, Jesus doesn't seem to be up on the concept of "soon." The nightmares in *Revelation* are actually a wishful vision of the Roman Empire's destruction. But because John uses symbolism and offers no specific timeline, the book is forever mined for evidence that Doomsday is coming next week.

Holy Sh#%$&!!!!!!!

The Greek word for *Revelation* is "apocalypse," which means an unveiling. When the curtain rises on the book and the prophetic hallucinations kick in, John sees seven lamp stands (one for each of the early Christian churches), along with "one like a son of man" (presumably Jesus) in their midst. The "one" is in a long robe with a golden girdle, hair white as snow, and eyes like fire. In his right hand he holds seven stars, his tongue is a two-edged sword, and his face shines like the sun! Whoa...this is clearly not the Jesus who swung a hammer over leaky roofs in Nazareth. In fact, it's an image taken from the Old Testament:

> ...one that was ancient of days took his seat;
> his raiment was white as snow, and the hair of his head
> like pure wool; his throne was fiery flames, its wheels
> were burning fire. [Daniel 7:9]

147

The writer of *Revelation* is very into Old Testament justice, with all its righteousness and wrath, and he seems completely unaware of the kinder, gentler Yahweh who appeared as Jesus.

To its credit, the Catholic Church has always been leery of apocalyptic doomsayers. Passages like these are what caused the Church to waffle about including *Revelation* in the canon. Its portrait of Jesus is generally out of sync with the rest of Scripture. Bishops prefer lines about the Second Coming like "...I will come like a thief, and you will not know what hour I will come upon you." [Rev. 3:3] It's a smart position to take. It gives them an out every day they wake up and discover that the world is still here...which is every day.

John, however, excoriates the seven churches for not promoting godliness with the kind of vein-popping stridency that he does. He even quotes God on the subject:

> "So, because you are lukewarm, and neither cold nor
> hot, I will vomit you out of my mouth." [Rev. 3:16]

Yep. God blows chunks, and we're the chunks. John then likens rival religions to Jezebel, the wife of ancient Israel's King Ahab, who promoted pagan cults and persecuted Yahweh's followers. This tolerance of other religions is seen as adultery by God, who admits he's the jealous type. John then mentions the *Book of Life*, which lists the names of those who'll be allowed into heaven. It's the ultimate VIP list and, unless you're on it, no way is the doorman letting you in. It doesn't matter if you know the choir.

Throughout *Revelation* we keep reading about "the Lamb," which is a code word for Jesus. Yeah, it's a woolly idea, but farm animals are often used as metaphors in the Bible. You have to choose carefully, however, especially when representing Jesus. A pig wouldn't work; it's not kosher. Nor would a goat; it's horny. Nor a bull; that would be Baal, the Canaanite god of fertility. Nor a flamingo because...well, that's just stupid. The sacrificial lamb of the Old Testament works best because Jesus was sacrificed as well.

John sees a grand figure seated on a throne, presumably God (you have to do a lot of presuming in *Revelation*), and he's surrounded by twenty-four elders and four "living creatures, full of eyes in front and behind…" and "day and night they never ceased to sing." Crooning mutant monsters. Makes you wonder if this heaven place is all it's cracked up to be.

The Tribulation

God then reveals a scroll with seven seals. The Lamb opens them one by one and, with hooves, that's not easy. It's here that the fun begins. The first four seals unleash the star attractions—the Four Horsemen of the Apocalypse: conquest, war, famine and death. Awesome! The fifth seal reveals all the martyrs. Booooring. The sixth seal produces a great earthquake, the sun turns black, the moon becomes blood red, and stars fall from the sky. This sends every leader on earth scampering into caves. Meanwhile, 144,000 of God's chosen are marked on the forehead to protect them from the chaos. These are men "who have not defiled themselves with women." Great…the world's only survivors will be the twits who never got laid.

During the Cold War, these disasters were interpreted by evangelicals like Hal Lindsey as a forecast of a nuclear war between the United States and the Soviet Union, ignited by a conflict over Israel. In his 1970 best-seller, *The Late Great Planet Earth*, Lindsey figured the 1980s would pretty much wrap it up for humanity. The End was to unfold within forty years of the reestablishment of Israel, which happened in 1948. But Lindsey has a knack for making predictions that don't come true. Not that this slows him down. With the Cold War over, he subsequently claimed we're in the "false peace" before the Apocalypse. Sometimes prophecies require a little tweaking. At least he didn't buy into the doomsday frets about 2012 and the Mayan calendar. *Revelation* keeps him busy enough.

Once the seventh seal is broken, heaven falls silent for half an hour. Then, seven angels appear and each blows a trumpet summoning up *another* list of catastrophes: a hail of fire mixed with blood, a third of the earth burns, and mountains crash into the sea, turning the oceans blood red. A star falls from heaven and poisons a third of all rivers. Finally, a bottomless pit opens up and spews out smoke and a swarm of locusts.

> "...their faces were like human faces, their hair were like women's hair, and their teeth like lions' teeth; they had scales like iron breastplates, and the noise of their wings was like the noise of many chariots..."
> [Rev. 9:8-9]

Most interpret these locusts as satanic warriors. Our buddy Hal Lindsey likens them to military helicopters in a global war. For Charles Manson (yeah, *that* Charles Manson) this passage refers to The Beatles: hair like women (mop tops), lion's teeth (their voices), iron breast plates (electric guitars), and the noise of many chariots (that damned rock 'n roll music). Since this verse is found in *Revelation 9*, Manson equated it with the White Album song *Revolution 9*. This demented thinking inspired his "Helter Skelter" murders in 1969, which he believed would trigger a global race war and leave *him* in charge. Okay, he was nuts. But it shows how dangerous this prophecy business can be, even if it sounds less deranged coming from a king, a preacher, or the occasional president.

The nightmares continue, and 200 million warriors storm out of the East to slaughter a third of humanity. The Ark of the Covenant shows up at one point. Then, a great red dragon with seven heads and ten horns appears and tries to devour a heaven-sent infant (yes, yes, presumably Jesus). The seven-headed dragon probably stands for Rome—a city on seven hills—or perhaps seven Roman emperors. Or, if you're Hal Lindsay, it's the European Union back when it had fewer members than it does today. In any case, God rescues the infant.

A war rages in heaven. Satan and his army are booted out, so they turn their fury against man. Then, from the sea rises a *second* dragon: The Beast. The antichrist. Actually, he's a charismatic world leader (a charismatic dragon?) who rules for three-and-a-half years. And his number is 666!

Creative math worthy of a Hollywood studio accountant has been employed to link this number to almost anyone with a household name. Hebrew numerology assigns a numerical value to each letter, so if you spell out the name of your antichrist nominee just right (did you include a title or a middle name?) you can make it add up to 666. But that's only one method of coming up with the number. There are many other ways, which is part of what makes the whole business such a crock.

The earliest candidate for antichrist was Emperor Nero, the first great persecutor of Christians. His name can be made to calculate out to 666. Problem is, *Revelation* was supposed to be about the future and Nero died decades before the book was written. Not to worry, though. There are plenty more candidates where he came from, chief among them:

Emperor Caligula, Emperor Justinian, various barbarian kings, most popes, the Catholic Church, Mohammad, Saladin, Genghis Khan, King Philip of France, Martin Luther, King George III of England, Napoleon Bonaparte, Czar Peter the Great, Friedrich Nietzsche, Kaiser Wilhelm, Benito Mussolini, Adolph Hitler, Franklin Roosevelt, Josef Stalin, Nikita Khrushchev, David Rockefeller, JFK, Pete Seeger, the European Union, Henry Kissinger, Jim Jones, Jimmy Carter, Anwar Sadat, Rev. Sun Myung Moon, Ronald Wilson Reagan, Mikhail Gorbachev, David Koresh, Pat Robertson, Bill Gates, Yasser Arafat, the Ayatollah Khomeini, Saddam Hussein, Osama bin Laden, Dick Cheney, and even Barrack Hussein Obama.

Of course, it's quite possible that nobody's name fits 666, and for good reason. *It's the wrong number!* The oldest surviving copy of *Revelation*, from the third century, claims the number of the Beast is 616. This would seem to toss out all the candidates mentioned above and send *Revelation* freaks back to their calculators. But if we try real hard we might come up with something for this alternative number. How's this: The area code for Grand Rapids,

Michigan is 616. Now look at a map. Michigan is shaped like a hand—which is exactly where Scripture says we will receive the mark of the Beast! No?

> "Also it [the Beast] causes all...to be marked on the right
> hand or the forehead, so that no one can buy or sell
> unless he has the mark..." [Rev. 13:16-17]

This ominous mark gets some fundamentalists in a tizzy over things like bar codes, credit cards, and even union labels on commercial products. (They must figure Satan is a Teamster. I'm sure he belongs to the NRA.)

The reality is "the mark of the Beast" refers to Roman coins that were stamped with the image of the emperor—a false idol. As mentioned earlier, using such coins was disdained by pious Jews. Now these coins were being demonized by Christians as well in order to separate believers from the economic prosperity of pagan life. It's the biblical equivalent of cutting up your VISA card.

Armageddon

The battle between good and evil is drawn between the Beast, with its army of 200 million, and the 144,000 virgin mama's boys, plus a few warrior angels. They assemble on the field of Armageddon—a place mentioned only once in Scripture. The Hebrew term is *Har Megiddo*—an actual site in Israel where ancient battles took place. There are even road signs pointing the way, just in case you have a hard time finding 200 million warriors.

John then sees the great Whore of Babylon—a coded reference to Rome. She rides a scarlet beast, she's dressed in gold and jewels, and she drinks the blood of the martyrs. But don't worry. In the end, she'll be made "desolate and naked" and her flesh will be "devoured and burned." [Rev. 17:16] Makes you feel all Christian inside, doesn't it?

When the battle is over, Satan and the antichrist (the Beast) are cast into "a lake of fire," and for the next thousand years peace will reign on earth—the Millennium we always hear about.

But some guys don't know when they're beaten. At the end of the Millennium, Satan will be free again. (Someone forget to lock the door?) After a little more fighting, a fire consumes the armies of hell and Satan is tossed into the pit forever. *Whew!*

Ah, but don't relax yet because now it's Judgment Day. All the living and all the dead whose names are not in the *Book of Life* will join Satan in the fiery pit.

Then finally, finally, *finally*...John sees a New Jerusalem, a radiant city of crystal and gold, descend to the earth, and all the chosen will dwell there forever in eternal sunlight. God's kingdom will have come. Everyone lives happily ever after. Seriously.

As mentioned, at the tail end of the Bible there's a brief postscript. Jesus says *three times* that he's coming "soon." There's that word again. Twenty centuries later, we're still waiting.

Ends of the Earth

Though the author himself says *Revelation* should be read "spiritually" and not literally, history is lousy with self-appointed visionaries who take it literally anyway and it gets hordes of believers strangely jazzed about the end of the world.

This is not a good thing. If you think The End is near, you tend to do things that help it along and you ignore long-term problems that ought to be addressed. Obviously you don't want such people in charge. But their mixture of delusion and paranoia can be very entertaining, and sometimes dangerous. Here are just a few of the hundreds of alarmists who got it wrong over the centuries.

Raoul Glaber: This monk from Burgundy interpreted a famine, earthquakes, the eruption of Mount Vesuvius in A.D. 993, and the death of Pope Gregory V in 999, as ominous portents of The End. His forecasts had pilgrims to the Holy Land dropping to their knees in fervent prayer over every shooting star or black cat.

Joachim of Fiore: In the late 1100s, this guy launched the tradition of applying verses in *Revelation* to contemporary events instead of to ancient occurrences. During the Third Crusade he told Richard the Lionheart (Robin Hood's king) that Jesus was coming soon to battle the antichrist—who happened to be the pope.

Emperor Prester John: Around 1219, European Christians heard tales of a warrior prince who was vanquishing their Muslim enemies in the East. He was thought to be Prester John, a Christian hero whom legend said would emerge in the Last Days to reunite the Lost Tribes of Israel. He turned out to be Genghis Khan. Oops.

The Flagellants: Around 1260, this Italian doomsday cult went from town to town publicly beating themselves into spiritual ecstasy with iron-tipped leather whips. They wanted to assure their salvation by sharing the sufferings of Christ. At least, that was their excuse. Apparently, they were very naughty boys.

Christopher Columbus: Sure, he was a hard-headed navigator, but he also imagined that the gold he might acquire in the New World could finance the rebuilding of the Jerusalem Temple and thus hasten the return of Christ. The guy was always looking for a shortcut.

Girolamo Savonarola: In the late 1400s, this Dominican friar became a strident moral reformer and one of Europe's most pious pains in the ass. The Joe McCarthy of his day, he saw enemies everywhere and he believed the flourishing city of Florence would be the site of the New Jerusalem—as soon as he finished destroying everything that was good about the place. Savonarola puked up rage against the opulence of both the city and the Church. He denounced sexual pleasures (naturally), along with makeup, perfume, and most anything that made you attractive in public. He sparked the famous "Bonfire of the Vanities" that called for the incineration of fashion accessories, gambling doodads, "lewd" artworks (including a Botticelli or two), and even musical instruments. The man was a fart in a sack.

He slammed the Church so hard for its excesses that the pope offered to make him a cardinal just to shut him up. Instead, he spent three years revving up intolerance, outrage, and violence, until he ticked off so many people that he was finally accused of heresy. He was excommunicated, tortured, hanged, and then burned. Nobody seems to miss him.

Martin Luther: Only a bit less annoying was the father of the Protestant Reformation, who said, "For my part, I am sure that the Day of Judgment is just around the corner…" That was in the early 1500s.

John van Leiden (a.k.a. Jan Bockelson): This actor turned panic-peddler joined the radical Dutch Anabaptists and, in 1534, established a messianic little kingdom in Münster, Germany. He claimed everyone but his own followers were about to be wiped out and he launched his messiah gig by running naked through the streets, then falling into a trance for three days. Somehow it worked. He demanded everyone's silver and gold and advocated strict sexual behavior—until he became a polygamist. Under his regime, the people were milked for every dime and anyone who objected was beheaded. After a year of this, his rivals finally rose up, sentenced him to death, and then had him shackled to a stake, burned with hot pincers, and finally de-tongued.

The Puritans: These religious extremists established early colonies in the New World and they added a new wrinkle to apocalyptic fear-mongering by being so happily enthusiastic about Doomsday. After all, it would see the demise of all non-believers and no one would be left to interfere with their joy-killing.

In Leeds, England back in 1806, a small panic broke out when a hen started laying eggs bearing the words "Christ is coming." Turns out someone wrote on the eggs, then stuffed them back *into* the poor chicken. Note: This doesn't work with sheep.

William Miller: In the 1830s, this character built up a huge following across the U.S. by preaching Jesus' imminent return. On October 22, 1844, thousands of his followers prepared for The End; some even waited beside their own freshly-dug graves. When Jesus was a no-show, the day became known as The Great Day of Disappointment. Miller's following fizzled, but a few diehards stuck it out and morphed into the Seventh Day Adventists.

Rev. Jerry Falwell: Founder of the now-defunct Moral Majority, the right-wing reverend was among those fundamentalist frauds who had millions believing the Cold War was a preamble to Armageddon. In the introduction to his 1983 book, *Nuclear War and the Second Coming of Jesus Christ*, he wrote, "...the one brings thoughts of fear, destruction, and death, while the other brings thoughts of joy, hope, and life. They almost seem inconsistent with one another, yet they are indelibly intertwined." Falwell also suggested the attacks of September 11, 2001 on New York and Washington D.C. were God's punishment for America's tolerance of abortion, homosexuality, or anything else that personally bugged him. He could get like that.

David Koresh: Born Vernon Wayne Howell, which makes him sound like he lived on Gilligan's Island, this self-serving guru conned a softheaded crowd of believers in 1993 into burning themselves alive rather than surrender the weapons they collected on their compound in Waco, Texas. Personal theory: No good ever comes from a compound.

The Rapture

The goofy notion that all true believers will suddenly disappear just before the Apocalypse, and thus be spared all the carnage, comes out of the same fuzzyheaded Spiritualist movement of the

19th century that produced William Miller, Joseph Smith, and numberless parlor room séances. The term "Rapture" is never used in the Bible, and the concept doesn't come from *Revelation*, but from Paul in *1 Thessalonians 4:16-17:*

> And the dead in Christ will rise first; then we who are alive, who are left, shall be caught up together with them in the clouds to meet the Lord in the air;

I've met Christians over the years that were actually smug about this. They are confident that non-believers will have to face the Tribulation while—*foosh!*—they happily vanish. Hugely successful books and videos, like the depressingly popular *Left Behind* series, traffic in this nonsense. They sift through Scripture and seize upon this one verse as a landmark event of the Last Days to assure themselves that they'll be spared the horrors of *Revelation*. They'll simply beam up without warning, which means you never want one of them as your surgeon, your pilot, or your Commander in Chief.

Apocalypse How?

People love talking about the End of the World so much that there's a special realm of study about it called eschatology. It's one of those disciplines that attract both top-notch scholars and tinfoil hats. The imagination people apply to working out the details of Doomsday would make Walt Disney envious. It's a subject of staggering complexity. Not a shred of it is true, but it is a lot of fun coming up with timelines for Judgment Day and then watching people go into a pious panic about it.

One tiny taste of this eschatology business is the loopy concept of Dispensationalism. Around 1819, an Irish minister with entirely too much time on his hands named John Nelson Darby sparked a movement that sees human history as a succession of "ages" in which God dispenses, or reveals, certain rules and expectations for man to meet. Each age has a holy purpose and is a step towards Judgment Day. The movement, in its many forms, has had a major influence on American fundamentalists and, through them, on U.S. foreign policy.

Dispensationalists adhere to three basic points. First, biblical prophecies, even in the Old Testament, should be read literally. (Right away we're in trouble.) Second, God distinguishes between the "church" and "Israel." The "church" is everyone who has accepted Jesus since the first Pentecost. "Israel" refers to the seed of Abraham (I think they call them Jews) for whom the covenants of the Old Testament still count. Both groups will be saved, but in distinct ways, and they'll continue to be distinct throughout eternity. Separate but equal. Third, each dispensation is done for the greater glory of God...and God is *very* into glory.

Usually, these religious futurists break history down into seven dispensations:

1. Innocence: from the Creation to the Fall of Man
2. Conscience: from the Fall to Noah's Flood
3. Human Government: from the Flood to Abraham
4. Promise: from Abraham to Moses
5. Law: from Moses to Jesus
6. Grace: the Church Age/ from Jesus to the present
7. Kingdom: the Millennium/ the thousand-year reign of Christ

In each age, God reveals something new and tests our obedience. For instance, Noah's dispensation after the Flood was to "be fruitful and multiply" ...one of the more delightful dispensations to obey. Of course, our present age is located right on the eve of the Apocalypse. The current Church Age ends with a seven-year Tribulation, when God will pull out his cosmic can of whoop-ass. After this comes the Kingdom—the thousand-year Millennium when Jesus will rule the world and the saved will live happily in a theocratic utopia.

But at what point in this series of events will Jesus appear? At the start of the Millennium or at the end? Whole schools of thought, if you can call any of this thought, are dedicated to such questions, and none of them are easy to pronounce.

Pre-tribulational Premillennialism—Jesus will return at the *start* of the Tribulation, then comes the Millennium, and then the Last Judgment.

Post-tribulational Premillennialism—Jesus will return at the *end* of the Tribulation but *before* the Millennium. At the end of the Millennium comes the Last Judgment.

Post-millennialism—Jesus will return at the *end* of the Millennium at the same time as the Last Judgment.

Amillennialism—the whole Millennium idea is just symbolic so don't wait to see it. Jesus won't return until the Last Judgment.

And on and on and *on* you can go with this stuff until the End of Time…or your patience.

CHAPTER SEVEN

Baptizing the West

Lead me not into temptation.
I can find it myself.

—Anonymous

Preaching to the Unconverted

Okay, so we're back again in the first century. The Christians have their savior, their Gospels, and their prophecies and any day now Jesus is coming back. But as the days turn into years, and the years into centuries, living life barefoot, broke, and celibate is not turning out to be the festival of joy many imagined. It's impractical. On top of this, the years produce numerous new folktales about Jesus, many of which conflict with each other and some of which are truly bizarre. This is a problem. If every home-tooled visionary can have his own take on Jesus regardless of what his fellow Christians think, they won't have a religion for long.

They'll have the Democratic Party. Christians have got to get organized.

Why a Church?

Well, somebody had to do it. A few guys pass the time hitting balls with a stick and it isn't long before we've got leagues and commissioners and congressional investigations. Same deal with religion. You need an establishment to set the rules.

Left on its own, the Bible is like the salad bar at Sizzler—it offers such a variety of choices that you can tailor it to your liking. You can select a healthy mix of fruits and veggies, or you can lard on the Tater Tots and fried chicken wings and create a heart attack to go. Radically different results can come from the same source. Same with the Bible. Any bozo can assemble his own faith out of hand-picked passages if there is no authority to shape the big picture. Eventually, someone realized that individuals couldn't be allowed to arbitrarily troll through Scripture and focus only on the self-serving verses they liked. That was a job for a church.

As "the rock" upon which Jesus said he'd build his church, the apostle Peter leads the most prominent of the early churches, in Jerusalem. He eventually becomes the first Bishop of Rome—an office that will evolve into the papacy. It takes centuries before the Roman Church establishes formal authority over the others and, in the process, not a few bishops tell aspiring pontiffs to take a hike. But gradually, power and money accrue to an office that starts to think of itself as God's exclusive mouthpiece.

Century One

For the first 100 years of the Christian era, The Way is an unwieldy movement, with splinter groups and homespun cults. Meetings are held in private homes, sometimes in secret. Over time, a hierarchy emerges with a bishop heading up each church. Heroes of the faith become saints, complete with biographies so sanitized their subjects practically pee perfume. Unfounded legends emerge, like the story of Peter being crucified and buried in Rome. The event is not in the Bible and there's no evidence it happened, but it's a handy rationale for moving the religion's home base from the outback of Jerusalem to the Empire's capital city. One version of the tale says Peter was crucified upside-down because he didn't feel worthy to die as Christ did. Interesting that he had a choice in the matter.

The early Church adopts the no-frills aesthetics of Roman Stoics and some Greek philosophers. Christians are to exercise self-discipline, prayer, generosity, and fasting. They develop a legal system based on the Roman one, and they begin to standardize their rituals, prayers, and holidays. Towards the end of the century they also retarget their recruitment drive from Jews to Gentiles.

To spread the word, the Church promotes stories, poems, letters, and lectures in schools, libraries, temples and debating societies. In some homes the domestic slave, attracted to the underdog religion, will pass it on to the kids, and it filters up to the lady of the house who breaks the news to dad one day that the family is now Christian. Yeah whatever, honey. Is dinner ready?

Not everyone is favorably impressed by the new faith, however. Guys like Tacitus who, as we saw, was one of the first outside the Bible to mention Christians, regards them as superstitious fanatics with "shameful and degraded practices."

Century Two

As Christianity grows from a dozen wandering sages to a loosely-defined subculture, it becomes more complicated and less, well, Christian. Feuding bishops engage in professional rivalries, political intrigues, cultural schisms, and even civil wars over who knows Jesus best. It's not quite Shiites vs. Sunnis but it's the same idea. Each bishop claims exclusive authority over his church and over interpretation of the Gospels.

There are many upstart cults, but they break down into two broad categories: the Mythicists—those who see the Gospels as symbolic folktales, and the Literalists—those who read the

162

Scripture like it was the morning news. For the latter group, virgin birth is a reality and the Eucharist actually transubstantiates into the flesh of Christ. Maybe they invented dental floss. Nobody wants Jesus stuck in his teeth.

Despite their savior's nickname, the "Prince of Peace," early Christians spend a lot of time fighting over the endless interpretations of their diamond-in-the-rough religion. Just about everything we know about early Christianity comes through the filter of these characters, and some of them loaded on some major baggage.

Ignatius of Antioch (ca. 50-110) was a bishop, and supposedly a student of the apostle John. That made him one of the few Church fathers who knew someone who knew Jesus. He was among the first to quote the Gospels. Early in the second century, he was condemned to die in the Colosseum. En route to his demise he wrote seven letters that influenced early Christian theology.

He advocated loyalty to your bishop, changing the Sabbath (Saturday) to the Lord's Day (Sunday), and he was the first on record to use "Catholic" (meaning "universal") in referring to his church. A fanatic about martyrdom, he famously said, "Allow me to be eaten by the beasts, which are my way of reaching to God. I am God's wheat...so that I may become the pure bread of Christ." Unfortunately, once he reached the Colosseum, he was toast.

Polycarp (ca. 69-155) was another Church bishop who reportedly knew the apostle John. He preached against many rival sects that cropped up in the second century, he renounced financial dishonesty in the Church, and he died as a martyr for the faith in mid-century after almost being burned at the stake, and then stabbed. Tough crowd.

Justin Martyr (ca. 100-165) argued for the faith against Roman skeptics in the mid-second century. While big on philosophy, he could be confusing and inconsistent, especially when it came to understanding the Old Testament. He claimed God wanted the

Jews to be circumcised to identify them as Christ-killers. Apparently this was important to him.

Tatian (110-180) was a protégé of Justin. In A.D. 144, he tried harmonizing the four Gospels to eliminate the contradictions. Didn't really work. But his Gospels were used in some regions of the ancient world for several hundred years.

Tertullian (ca. 160-220) was an important Church father from North Africa who said of biblical miracles, *"Credo quia incredibilis est."* (I believe it because it is incredible.) Today he'd be in Vegas selling the picture of Jesus he found in his grilled cheese sandwich.

Marcion (ca. 110-160) established a brand of the faith that, according to *The Catholic Encyclopedia*, became the greatest threat to Christianity in its history. For him, the vengeful warrior god of the Old Testament was not the true God, but an inferior deity. The *real* Almighty was revealed by Jesus, you see. To make his point, Marcion wrote *The Antitheses*, a manuscript that highlighted the contradictions between the Old and New Testaments. (Don't you love books like that?)

Marcion set up an alternative hierarchy to the Roman Church, made himself a bishop, and developed a theology that seriously rivaled Catholicism. He believed Jesus' appearance on earth was an illusion for our benefit, which made events like the virgin birth or the resurrection kind of meaningless. The Catholic Church got seriously fed up with this character, dubbed him a heretic, and excommunicated him. But for a while, he really put the fear of God in the clergy.

Clement of Alexandria (ca. 150-216) was a Church father who Christianized concepts borrowed from Plato and other philosophers—ideas like the *logos* (the belief in a rational universe) and *gnosis* (knowledge). Plato taught that philosophy strove to attain perfection through union with a higher Truth—which Clement saw as the Christian god. Clement taught that faith was the foundation of knowledge and that knowledge enriched and perfected faith.

Montanus (mid-2nd century) launched a movement in Asia Minor that insisted the Second Coming of Christ was near. Yeah, well, the line forms over there. They claimed direct contact with God, and his following became famous for its ecstatic women priests (cool!) and its moral rigor (not so cool).

Celsus (mid-2nd century) was not a Christian, but he was important to the debate because he stridently took them on. He was a Greek philosopher, and a skeptic, who was famous for mocking Christians for their ignorance and superstition. He noted that a god who worked with his hands and took a day off wasn't much of a god. A real wise-ass, this guy. I like him.

The Gnostics: In 1945, writings by a prominent Christian sect dating back to the second century were discovered near the Egyptian town of Nag Hammadi. They include the Gospels of Thomas, Mary, and Philip, and they paint a very different picture of Christianity than most of us are taught. The Gnostics reveled in the mystery of the *gnosis*—that is, secret knowledge. They believed each of us contained a spark of divinity and that we needed to discover "the Christ within." For this you didn't need a church, so they were firmly in the heresy camp.

The Gnostics (a label given to them by later scholars) are a fave among New Age types because they had women priests and were of a very spiritual bent, to the point of thinking that Jesus' appearance on earth was a projection rather than a flesh-and-blood guy. Some also read into Gnostic writings the *Da Vinci Code* idea that Jesus and Mary Magdalene had an intimate relationship.

Well, this didn't go over well with the mainstream Church and, after a couple of centuries, the Gnostics were muscled off the stage. But the documents they left behind hint at the great variety of Christian religions that existed in the early days.

And the hits just keep on coming:

Origen (ca. 184-254) The most optimistic of the great Church fathers, he was one of the last to stand for rationalist thought and free debate in theology. He developed a sophisticated philosophy based on a loving and forgiving god, and thought everyone would be saved in the end—a concept called Christian universalism. He didn't think sex was demonic, as others did, but he did idealize celibacy. The first great interpreter of the Bible, he saw stories like Adam and Eve as allegories and regarded hell as a temporary punishment. The Church, wanting none of this, later turned against his ideas and deemed them heresy.

Plotinus (ca. 204-270) founded the school of Neo-Platonism, an updated version of Plato's metaphysics—the notion that a perfect, higher reality paralleled our imperfect physical existence. For every saggy butt perched on a bar stool there was an ideal J-Lo tush nestled on a throne, or something like that. Plato's metaphysics had a huge influence on later ideas about heaven and the soul.

Eusebius (263-339) was the Bishop of Caesarea, and the grand maestro of Church propaganda under Emperor Constantine—the first Christian emperor of Rome. Eusebius is hugely important because much of what we know about the other early Christian thinkers, and the Church itself, comes through him.

This is why it's unfortunate that Eusebius was a self-serving bullshit artist of the first order. He quoted letters that he claimed were written exchanges between Jesus and a certain King Abgar V of Edessa. He gave us the legend of St. Peter going to Rome, and he also believed that the John of the Gospels was the same John who wrote *Revelation*. Not so. More importantly, he helped pioneer the idea that victory in war was proof of God's blessing—a handy concept over the next thousand years.

Eusebius defended telling falsehoods in the service of God and he routinely availed himself of the privilege. In his *Ecclesiastical History*, he admitted that he would only offer details about Christian persecutions that served his purpose and that he wouldn't discuss the notorious activities of the Church. As mentioned, Eusebius may be the man who added the suspect passages about Jesus to the works of Josephus. The guy isn't even a saint and, given that there are over ten thousand of them, that doesn't say much for his reputation.

The fact that this pious liar is the conduit for much of our knowledge of Christianity's first three centuries says something about the reliability of anything we know about Jesus. It also underlines God's long disinterest in good record-keeping. Anybody know where they stashed the Ten Commandments?

Atheists for Jesus

The Romans came up with a word to describe the growing number of Jesus people: atheists. For many, the Christian unwillingness to accept the traditional gods made them immoral and a threat to society—an attitude Christians would later perfect. Pretty soon nasty rumors about them started circulating the same way urban legends did about satanic cults in the 1990s. "Did you hear? They eat babies and wash them down with body shots of blood!" Christians became the target of slanderous whisper campaigns.

Presumably, this made them easy marks for opportunists like Emperor Nero, who, if the account is true, blamed them for that fire in Rome in A.D. 64. His year-long purge against them in Rome was horrific and it convinced them that they were pitted against the civilization of Satan.

Nero, however, was the exception. Generally, the Romans allowed for religious freedom, certainly more than the Christians would allow for once they took charge. But Romans were also sticklers for ritual and, as mentioned, Christians refused to cooperate. As they grew in number, their separatist attitude alarmed the public. On a few occasions this bubbled up as persecution.

Over three centuries, ten persecutions took place, most of them likely exaggerated by Christian historians. To hear them tell it, the Romans did little more than feed Christians to lions while taking suspiciously long baths. The purges were ghastly, but most of them were short-lived (lions are an expensive way to kill people) and limited in scope, unlike the baths. Some crusades reaped as few as ten victims and some of the victims actually wanted to be martyrs—not that this was any excuse. Tertullian wrote of one group around A.D. 185 that *asked* the governor of Asia to execute them. He refused, and suggested they hang themselves or go jump off a cliff. He actually told them that. He wouldn't be the last.

To be sure, Christians were sometimes victims of diabolical cruelty. They might be covered in honey and locked up with a hive of wasps, or stuffed in a sack and made a plaything for wild bulls. Some were perched atop a metal pyramid to be split apart. Women were publicly raped. Believers were strapped into a hot iron chair and cooked to death. Eyes were gouged out with iron tools. Others starved in prison. A molten lead enema took care of the body orifices. Whips encrusted with hooks or seashells flayed flesh from bone. And so forth.

Some of these accounts are propaganda, but all too many of them are true. If they have a medieval ring to them it's because God-fearing Christians would eventually adopt many of these same methods of torture and execution once *they* got to do the persecuting.

The worst purge—The Great Persecution—was launched by Emperor Diocletian in the early fourth century. In direct opposition to the Greco-Roman tradition of tolerance, Diocletian outlawed Christianity in A.D. 303, closed the churches, and forced Christians to perform pagan sacrifices after they handed over their Bibles for burning. This went on for years and claimed some 2,000 lives. Fortunately, Diocletian fell ill in 305 and abdicated his office. But the persecutions went on until about 311, when they finally stopped.

Enter Diocletian's more reasonable grandson, Constantine—an ambitious general and builder, who became emperor. Tradition (meaning Eusebius) says that on the eve of a critical battle in 312, Constantine saw a heavenly vision of the cross, or something like it, in the sky. He placed this icon on his battle standard and when he won the conflict, he credited the victory to the Christian god. In 313, he issued the *Edict of Toleration,* which ended the attacks on Christianity and made the faith legal. Christians emerged from the shadows and the religion built up a fresh head of steam.

Constantine had a simple plan to restore order to the chaotic and divided Empire of the fourth century—use the Christian cult to his own ends. The Empire could be unified under their single, all-powerful deity: One God. One Empire. One Emperor. No arguments.

Ah, but most of the Empire was still pagan. What to do? Let's see now. Pagans worshipped a Sun God (Sol Invictus). Christians worshipped the Son-of-God. Hmm. To unify the Empire, Constantine fused these rival deities into two sides of the same coin—literally. Coinage was struck with the pagan Sun God on one side and a symbol of Christianity on the other. He melded both traditions in his official ceremonies, temple artwork, and political rhetoric as well.

By A.D. 325, Christianity was the dominant faith of the government. (It would become the official faith in 381 under Emperor Theodosius.) The success of the religion made hash of the prophecies in *Revelation,* which had Christians at war with Rome. But nobody harped on that anymore. From now on the emperors were working for Jesus.

Alas, if Constantine thought his recognition of Christianity would get everyone on the same theological page, he was mistaken. Religious guys love to argue and Christians found lots of things to argue about, even amongst themselves.

169

From the very start, Christians faced a theological dilemma that had never confronted the Jews. In the Hebrew Bible, God was God. Yahweh. One guy. Pretty simple. But in the New Testament, God is mentioned as the Father in heaven, the Son on earth, and the Holy Spirit, which was sort of everywhere. What exactly was the relationship between these three aspects of the Almighty? Was Jesus a deity, the son of a deity, or a human with godly powers? Were God and Jesus made of the same stuff, similar stuff, or different stuff? Did God create Jesus, or did they always co-exist? And where did the Holy Spirit fit in? Was God a unity, a trinity, or a barbershop quartet? Floor wax or dessert topping?

People stayed up late at night fretting over this nonsense. For three centuries these issues provoked fistfights in the streets, stone throwing, church burnings, and attempts by bishops to slander and even attack their rivals. It was the kind of insanity you get when institutions are founded upon religious speculations—a society that fights over how many angels can dance on the head of a pin. (The answer, by the way, is nine...unless the angels are really fat.)

As to the question of exactly what Jesus was made of, there were many schools of thought, and this led to a crisis which would shape the future of the faith and of the Western world. Everyone had a pet theory; here are just a few:

The Trinity: God, Jesus and the Holy Spirit were the *same* stuff—three personae in one divinity. This is the Catholic view.

The Homoean Creed: God and Jesus were *similar* stuff, but not the *same* stuff. Still, they were a lot alike.

The Dated Creed: God and Jesus were *similar* stuff, but the Son was begotten of the Father.

The Eunomian Heresy: God and Jesus were *different* stuff because the Son was begotten of the Father.

Apollinarism: Christ's body was human, but his mind and soul were divine—*two kinds* of stuff in one Jesus.

Docetism: Jesus was made of *no* stuff. He was fully divine, but not flesh and blood. What people saw on the cross was a projection, like a hologram or the Wizard of Oz.

The Logos: Jesus was *logos* stuff; the ordering principle of the universe. But the *logos* was less than God, which meant Jesus was less than God, which meant you were in deep doo-doo with the Church.

Adoptionist Theory: Jesus was *human* stuff and God adopted him as his son.

The Two Sons Formulation: Jesus had been conceived *twice*—once in divine form and once in human form. But he had only one belly button.

Sabellianism: God had three "manifestations," Jesus being one of them—like two sides of a coin. This differs from the Trinity, which is more like equating four quarters to a dollar. Get it? No?

If you wonder why people haggled over these dizzying theories, it's because they had real-world consequences. If God and Jesus were the same, and the Church was the living extension of Jesus' ministry, it put the churches and the emperors who loved them that much closer to God. People listened to you more carefully if you had divine authority. It was all about power.

The Arian Heresy

This point became clear back in the early 300s over the most controversial of all the Jesus-stuff theories: Arianism. Named for Arius (250-336), the priest who proposed the idea, it said that God created the *logos* (Jesus) out of nothingness. Therefore, Jesus was more than a man but less than God. Arius argued that God and Jesus had to be made of *different* stuff because, as mentioned earlier, Jesus called God "my Father." If they were one and the same, Jesus would be his own father, which is not even possible in Appalachia. Arius also said Jesus had to be fully human lest his suffering on the cross be just an act.

Well, this got a lot of butts in a pucker because it put Jesus in a position inferior to God. The Arian Heresy flew directly against the mainstream Church view, later represented by Bishop Athanasius, who held that God, Jesus and the Holy Spirit were the *same* stuff—equal and co-eternal. This became the single most controversial issue in the Christian world.

To settle the matter, Emperor Constantine (with the guidance of our old pal Eusebius) called a meeting in A.D. 325—the Council at Nicaea—an assembly of about 250 bishops from across the Empire. Surely they could put the issue to rest.

Unfortunately, if you laid all the bishops in Rome end-to-end they couldn't reach a conclusion. Their verdict: Jesus was both fully human *and* fully divine. Then they insisted this wasn't confusing—they actually used those words. Yet, after the Council meeting, some wanted to take back their vote. Whoops, too late. The Athanasius school won the fight and those who disagreed were about to catch hell.

Over the next five decades, the line between church and state continued to blur. Emperors sought to pin down theological issues while bishops took on governmental authority. By the end of the fourth century, the quest for imperial unity under religious conformity would narrow what you could say about the faith to the God = Jesus orthodoxy of Nicaea.

Why Christian Theology?

The entire controversy once again raises the question: Why was any of this necessary? Why four centuries of philosophical food-fights to sort out precisely what we're all supposed to understand about Jesus? Why didn't God make it all self-evident? The whole idea of Jesus' ministry was to make simple truths available to simple people so that the maximum number could avoid damnation. Why did we need experts and councils to figure out what should be obvious to a first century shepherd?

Isn't the very complexity of these ideas proof that they're not the clear truths of a perfect deity, but the work of imperfect humans? It seems crazy that we can't get religious ideas right without archeologists to unearth scraps of parchment, and linguists to figure out their meaning, and theologians to write libraries full of hair-splitting interpretations of it all.

Yeah, sure, to understand the universe scientifically we need PhD's in physics and astronomy. Puzzling out stuff like quantum mechanics, dark matter, or string theory isn't easy. But science doesn't insist the laws of nature were laid down by a loving God. The universe of science doesn't care if we understand it or not. The Christian universe does. So why is it so damned hard to figure it out and get everyone on the same page?

The problem comes from what's being sold: Faith—something that can't be proven or disproven and, therefore, an issue that can never be resolved. If you're establishing hard facts, like the sum of $2 + 2$, you reach a consensus because you can *verify* that it equals 4 and not 5. You toss out the wrong answer because you can prove it's wrong. This is why history isn't full of feuding math cults.

But religion is based on spiritual claims, which can't be proven. So, no matter how loopy a belief might be, it can be defended. Churches are free to abandon reason and evidence and insist their ideas will make sense *if* you just have faith. How else can you buy into beliefs like a Jesus who is both fully human *and* fully divine? It's like insisting $2 + 2$ equals both 4 *and* 5.

This kind of silliness calls for a theologian. Some genius who can fuzzy the issue with ramblings about how, "In Christ, $2 + 2$ lives, and transcends mere addition with a Truth beyond 'plus' that is God's grace, which is infinite, and in which dwells the sum of 4 in harmony with 5." A hundred pages of pious obfuscation later, he concludes that $2 + 2 =$ Jesus. And if you're still confused, think of it as a beautiful mystery. But don't ever ditch your nonsense belief.

Holy Payback

Anyway, once Christianity got the upper hand in the Roman government, it was time to give the pagans what they deserved. The men who had once persecuted the Christians were now persecuted themselves. Pagan priests were accused of ghastly crimes and perversions. They were tortured, chained to statues, and left to starve. Their sacred scrolls were burned and their temples were desecrated or turned into churches. They suffered horrors as bad as anything they had dished out.

Purging the pagans, however, wasn't the end of it. Christians fought other Christians over who were the genuine Christians. Sticking a Jesus fish on your bumper wouldn't cut it. During the Great Persecution (303-311), many believers had caved in to the Roman authorities—they ratted out their friends, destroyed holy texts, or participated in pagan rituals. While the mainstream Church wanted to go easy on them, independent churches full of hardliners, known as Donatists, insisted that these weak-kneed stoolpigeons be punished or excommunicated. Some of these churches took brutal actions of their own.

To put a stop to persecutions by these splinter groups, the Catholic Church decided to...well, persecute them. (Old habits die hard.) Churches went after churches. Bishops hatched murder plots against one another and, once again, the Empire was faced with the possibility of unraveling. It was a mess.

So, over the next century, the new church-state partnership flexed its muscles to straighten things out and became what history writer Jonathan Kirsch calls the world's first totalitarian state. Around 374, the sixty-six books of the Holy Bible were officially canonized. In 381, heresy was outlawed. By 386, bands of salvation-crazed monks ran riot throughout the Empire. They were described as mobs dressed in black, armed with cudgels and bars of iron. They tore down temples, demolished statues, and if the local priest objected, he was killed. By 391, Emperor Theodosius had all pagan temples shut down and all anti-Christian books burned. Unofficial concepts of God were more or less extinguished—which is why the surviving records of those days are scant and rather one-sided.

Emblematic of this great social change was the fate of a scientist from Alexandria, Egypt. In 415, a brilliant female mathematician and philosopher named Hypatia found herself on the business end of a Christian horde that didn't much care for her fame or for her preference of science over mysticism. She was stripped naked in the streets, dragged off, and flailed to death—in a church. Then she was burned.

Hypatia's death was an epic tragedy, and it's sometimes regarded as the dividing line between the end of the classical world and the beginning of the Middle Ages. Cue the creepy music.

Pagan Postscript

The popular cliché is that the Roman Empire deteriorated due to moral decay and debauchery. Many liken modern America to ancient Rome and insist that, if we simply come back to Jesus, we'll avoid the same fate. But think again. Rome grew as a pagan empire and disintegrated as a Christian one. Christianity didn't necessarily cause it to fall apart, but it didn't stop the downfall either.

In its heyday, Hellenistic civilization established roads, aqueducts, schools, currency, a justice system, religious tolerance, enduring innovations in art and architecture, and a barbarian-free zone unequalled in the ancient world. The classical era was an astounding success. It was a spectacular age of scientific discovery, political sophistication, literary achievement, and economic prosperity that would be unsurpassed for 1,500 years.

So why didn't it last if it was so terrific? Well, look around you. Essentially, it's still here. Most of our modern world is built on the foundations of Greece and Rome—science, democracy, law, free debate, medicine, sports, drama, wine-making, nude wrestling, you name it. Their political structure collapsed because of infighting among leaders, vast economic factors, and barbarian attacks. But their values are still around. All things considered, they had a pretty good run and, in a very real way, they're still going strong.

Goin' Medieval

Augustine—the Middle Age Man

Paganism was giving way to Christianity, but for some it wasn't happening fast enough. Chief among those who advocated religious militancy in the name of the Prince of Peace was a North African bishop named Augustine, who lived and worked around A.D. 400. He's advertised as the most important Church father of the ancient world because he laid the intellectual groundwork for the Age of Faith. A little more of that creepy music, please.

In 410, the "invincible" city of Rome was invaded by the Visigoths, who acted like a bunch of barbarians. Many thought this was divine punishment for Rome having abandoned the traditional pagan gods in favor of Christianity. But Augustine thought Catholicism was the "Divine Philosophy," and he re-imagined the Church as the *City of God*—a spiritual community of believers that could never be sacked by a horde of thugs. It transcended the physical world, so it would survive and flourish no matter what. And if it had to use force on occasion to drive that point home, so be it. Welcome to the Dark Ages.

Like a lot of righteous firebrands, Augustine made radical swings in his value system over the course of his life. He sired a child with a concubine he kept on tap for fifteen years, only to become a crusader for celibacy. When he turned thirty, his mother arranged a marriage into money with a girl so young he had to wait two years for her to come of age. While waiting, he found himself another cookie, during which time he famously begged God to "Grant me chastity and continence, but not yet." Apparently, God obliged.

Augustine's mother wanted him to be Catholic and he broke her heart by becoming a Manichaean Gnostic and then a skeptic. Then, in the usual trajectory for guys who become spiritual steamrollers, he had a sudden personal crisis. He called off the wedding to his child bride and pursued the priesthood. He opted for celibacy.

Though abstinence was considered virtuous by the larger culture of the time, it wasn't yet Church doctrine. Alas, Auggie helped to make it so.

Augustine was inspired to become celibate when one day he heard "a voice." (You know this isn't gonna be good.) It told him to read the first thing he picked up. Sadly, it was a copy of Paul's letter to the *Romans*, *Chapter 13*, which talked about walking soberly through life and making "no provision for the flesh, to gratify its desires." Terrific. He couldn't have found something about Solomon's 300 concubines?

From then on, Augustine was a puritanical knuckle-rapper. He gave his money to the poor, embarked on a monastic lifestyle, and proceeded to pitch for Catholicism with the zeal of a spammer for male enhancement drugs. His big contribution to theology was to revive Paul's grim views of God and man after they had been neglected for centuries. He incorporated Greek philosophy into his thought, but he rejected most classical ideals. Reason, which the Greeks exalted, was now only a handmaiden to faith; logic was the shoeshine boy to religion. Science and worldly wisdom were no longer important. What you really wanted was God's grace—and that wasn't easy to come by. Most of us didn't deserve it.

Augustine's masterpiece, *Confessions*, is regarded as the West's first real autobiography because it explored his confused inner life as much as the events around him. He decided that God lived outside of normal time. He distinguished miracles from magic. (If *his* god did it, it was a miracle. If *yours* did it, it was magic.) He condemned curiosity as a distraction from God, and called astrology the work of women taught by demons, which established a justification for medieval witch hunts.

Since he lived at a time when barbarians were literally at the gates, he came up with handy notions like "just warfare." He supported authoritarian rule to enforce theology, and he dreamt up the concept of Original Sin—a term found nowhere in the Bible and one of the issues that would ultimately split the Christian world into the Western Catholic Church and the Eastern Orthodox faith. The guy has a lot to answer for.

Augustine's pessimism fit the troubled times and others signed on to his anti-intellectualism. John Chrysostom, a theologian, asked that we all "restrain our own reason, and empty our mind of secular learning, in order to provide a mind swept clear for the reception of divine words." In other words, don't you worry your pretty little head. God will do the thinking. And who speaks for God? The same guys peddling this self-imposed lobotomy.

For the next thousand years, this faith-first, reason-second mentality shackled most critical free thought and produced the longest stretch of ignorance, poverty, oppression, and stagnation in the history of Western civilization. But hey, they had faith.

Medieval governments, many of them tiny, took a back seat to the increasingly powerful Church. Princes collected the taxes and kept the torches burning. But the Church is what gave a king his divine credibility, and it had free reign to keep his sinning little subjects on the straight and narrow with its own morality cops. Since all of humanity was headed for one common destiny and judgment, anyone who strayed from that path with an idea of their own was trouble. The West became one big faith-based initiative.

This is not to say the Middle Ages were entirely dark. The ninth through the thirteenth centuries did produce ideas like the university, small industries driven by waterwheels, and advances in architecture that produced spectacular cathedrals. There were also scholarly investigations into nature.

But medieval logic proceeded from a different premise—a biblical premise—and this only got you so far. Every object and event now had a theological meaning; every stone and blade of grass was put here to drive home some moral point. Creation was an instruction book written by God for man to read and for the clergy to interpret. Everything from the weather to the behavior of field mice had a Christian message. Life was a testing ground for admission to what was really important—the afterlife. Our time on earth was essentially a moral obstacle course, and there were plenty of experts on heaven, hell, God, and the devil to tutor you on how to maximize your chances for eternal bliss. Usually it meant doing what you were told.

Back then the cosmos was a relatively cozy place. Earth was nestled at the center, the planets orbited in perfect circles, and God looked on from beyond the sphere of the stars. Man was caught in the frontier between hell below and heaven above. The world was the battleground between the two, with God nearby to help with the odd miracle now and then, and the promise of eternal life at the end of it all. Everything had a purpose and a place.

In those days there was a comforting certainty about life, death, good, and evil that we don't have now. Some folks are nostalgic for those days, buying into the premise that certainty about something, *anything*, is better than none at all. They bemoan today's so-called "moral relativism" and rail against post-modern philosophers who claim there is no such thing as right and wrong.

Outside of a few academic circles, however, most of us don't subscribe to this. We *do* believe in right and wrong. But we also have questions and doubts, and doubt is constructive. Doubt is something grownups deal with. Doubt is what makes you think and reflect, and that's a good thing. Is this going out on a limb?

What's more, the claim that belief in God provides a moral anchor in the stormy seas of change is fiction. "God" is as subjective and evolving an idea as any. Quiz your church today on moral issues like racism, women's rights, or religious tolerance and you'll get answers very different from those you got back in the 14th century. Eternal truth isn't so eternal.

Anyway, the Middle Ages were far too long and complex to tackle here in detail. But we should touch on a few highlights to understand the, ahem, benefits of a religion-based civilization.

A Thousand Years in a Thousand Words

Rome fell.

Okay, maybe that's a little too simple. Actually, one could argue that Rome didn't entirely fall. It cleaved into other, smaller entities that carried on. Let's flesh this out a little.

Back in 330, Emperor Constantine moved the Roman capital to the newly rebuilt city of Byzantium which was renamed Constantinople (now Istanbul) after the emperor's death. The Empire became divided. Constantinople became the capital of the Eastern, Greek-speaking half of the Empire, while the capital of the Western, Latin-speaking Empire remained in Rome.

The Byzantine East continued to flourish. But by A.D. 476 the Latin West was overrun by barbarian kings and military brutes. Once these flea-bitten monarchs set up their kingdoms on the ruins of Rome, they tried to class up their act. If the Bishop of Rome would anoint them, they'd have God's blessing and the people might think of them as legitimate rulers instead of victorious gangsters. Popes like Gregory the Great, in the sixth century, were happy to leverage the papacy into a Holy-Stamp-of-Approval for these kings in exchange for money, land, slaves, or protection. God was now open for business.

To be sure, Christianity sought to push back against much of the cruelty of the ancient world. But in the process, Gregory and his team grew powerful and rich. The great palaces of classical Rome were disassembled and their parts cannibalized to build new digs for the Church. To polish up his own rep, Greg wrote a whitewashed history of Catholicism and argued for the supremacy of the papacy—that is, himself—over all other bishops.

A devotee of Augustine, he also pushed hard on the controversial Trinity theory of God, which the Eastern churches didn't like so much. This contributed to the already growing split between the eastern and western halves of the Empire.

While all this was going on, a new actor appeared on the stage in the early 600s and proceeded to hog the spotlight. Islam stormed out of Arabia and, by the year 1000, had swept across most the Mediterranean. It spread largely through conquest (not the first religion to do this), and it built the most sophisticated civilization of its day. The Arabs copied and studied the Greek classics. There was lighting in the streets of Cairo. There were scientific advances in medicine, optics, and astronomy. Words like *algebra, alchemy, zenith, zero,* and *algorithm,* not to mention our system of numbers, all came out of this period of Arabic enlightenment. They constructed magnificent mosques—architectural marvels the equal of any Gothic cathedral, which wouldn't appear for another three centuries. All this went on while most Christians were hunkered down in grimy villages fearing demons and looking for signs of the Apocalypse. What a difference a millennium makes, huh?

Christianity continued to fear its own shadow and, beginning in 726, in an effort to raise public morality, the Byzantine emperor issued a series edicts that banned worship of images and artworks, even if that meant destroying them. They were idolatry, you see, and violated the commandment against making graven images.

To its credit, the Western Church (and many Eastern ones) rejected this idea. Using images for worship was an ancient custom and few wanted to take a hammer to perfectly good works. This issue would be an early contribution to what eventually became a formal schism between the Roman Catholic Church and the Eastern Orthodox ("right believing") faith.

The Roman papacy allied itself with various Western rulers, like King Pepin, who granted the Church large territories in the mid-700s. The pope became a feudal landlord with all the lucrative benefits therein. (And in 800, he was nice enough to crown Pepin's son, Charlemagne, emperor of the Holy Roman Empire). The land grants helped establish several small Papal States in Italy. The office took on the trappings of royalty. At one point, the Church controlled as much as one-fifth of the wealth of England.

With all this going for it, the papacy became a career goal for ambitious Italian aristocrats, few of whom were interested in emulating Jesus. The office devolved into a license to steal and was hijacked by a sorry succession of criminals who were greedy, vain, and occasionally unhinged.

In 896, the vengeful Pope Stephen VII actually put the dead body of his predecessor on trial. The late Pope Formosus was from a rival family clan. His corpse had been in its tomb for eight months when Stephen had it hauled into a courtroom, dressed in priestly robes, and perched upon a throne. Stephen then railed against it and Formosus was posthumously condemned. Three of the body's fingers were cut off before it was thrown to an angry mob, then dumped into the Tiber River. Not surprisingly, the local Romans decided that Pope Stephen was crazy as a mad cow. A few months later he was strangled to death.

Over the next seven years, half a dozen short-lived popes assumed power and usually ended up dead. Finally, a controversial ally of Stephen named Sergius managed to keep the job for seven years. This set up one of the darkest periods in the history of the Church—a period later nicknamed the "Pornocracy." You're gonna like this.

Pope Joan

By A.D. 900, the city of Rome was a creaky relic of its former self. It was led by a rather spineless ruler named Theophylact, who indulged his beautiful, power-mad wife—Theodora—to the point where she essentially ran the city. The woman was a pistol.

First, she secured her clout with the reigning Pope Sergius by pimping out her young daughter, Marozia, to be his mistress. Being good Catholics, the two lovers avoided birth control and the affair produced a son named John.

Next, after Pope Sergius died in 911, Theodora used her wiles to get her own lover, Bishop John of Ravenna, elevated to the papacy. She was now screwing Pope John X.

Then, with the previous pope dead and Marozia still in her teens, mom married her off to a powerful solider of fortune named Alberic. Marozia gave birth to a second son, Alberic II. They must have been up all night with the baby name books.

In the following years, Rome was consumed with fending off invading Huns from the north and the Muslim armies from the south. During this period, Theophylact, Theodora, and Alberic all disappear from the historical record.

But not Marozia, who turned out to be a more ambitious operator than her mother. She wanted a pope in the family—namely her first son, John. But she had to get rid of the current pontiff, her mother's old lover, John X. This wasn't going to be easy because he had allied himself with a warrior named Hugh of Provence, whom John X had named king of Italy in exchange for protection.

So, Marozia seduced and married Hugh's half-brother, Guy, who happened to have his own army. It took a few years, but in 928, Marozia managed to have John X thrown into a Roman dungeon, where he died a year later. Three years after that, Marozia's twenty-something son became the next pope. From a pope's lover to a pope's mother. Pretty good. But she wasn't through.

With her son now the pontiff, Marozia dumped Guy and moved in on King Hugh himself, who was something of a horndog and an easy mark. In 932, his current wife conveniently died and he married Marozia. Now, all she needed was for her son, Pope John, to coronate her and she'd be the empress of the Western Empire.

It was all coming together with movie plot slickness. That is until her second son, Alberic II (remember him?) caught wind of Hugh's plan to *blind* him so he'd never become competition for the throne. Marozia showed no sign of stopping this. In fact, she seemed to enjoy insulting the boy, who was still only eighteen.

Then, during a feast at court, Hugh slapped young Alberic right in the face, and the boy was so humiliated that he ran out into the streets and incited a riot. The mob stormed the castle. Wanting none of this, Hugh hightailed it out of Rome and abandoned Marozia to her son, who promptly threw her into prison for the rest of her life.

Alberic II went on to rule Rome for the next twenty years and reduced the powers of his craven half-brother, John (who was still pope) to purely spiritual duties.

This sordid saga became one of the origins of the urban legend of Pope Joan—a mythical female pope. There were plenty more chapters of Church history almost as lurid as this spanning several hundred years. Life among the popes was like a soap opera with Bibles and knives.

Ironically, it was during this period that the celibate priesthood changed from a popular option to a requirement. This was partly because it symbolized purity, but mostly it was so that dying bishops would leave their property to the Church instead of to their families. This was also the era when the formal posture for prayer became that of the shackled slave—on your knees with your wrists bound together—because good Christians were slaves to Christ. Just the cheery thought you needed to get you through famines, plagues, and conquests.

Angels

One of the few sources of comfort in those days was the idea that angels were watching over you. This was a little odd since, in the Bible, angels deliver more bad news than good. But they were a convenient way for God to communicate with humans without committing to actual face time.

To this day, angels are enormously popular. You can sell anything from a coffee mug to a drum full of radioactive waste if you stick an angel on it. Some 80% of Americans believe in them. Of course, almost as many of us believe in space aliens, which are really a modern update of the same idea—higher intelligences from the sky who appear in humanoid form to help us clueless people prepare for a better world to come. They both tend to dress in simple clothes, glow in the dark, and never show up for crowds or cameras.

Now, if you're in any business long enough you inevitably build up a bureaucracy. Alas, even heaven wasn't immune to this phenomenon. By the Middle Ages, religious scholars with nothing better to do spent their time shuffling the many angels mentioned in Scripture into an organization chart of the afterlife.

Tradition describes anywhere from nine to twelve rankings in the heavenly hierarchy, with each type having their own appearance and function. None of the angels in the Bible have halos or wings. While they're often associated with music, they're never described as playing the harp. Some played the trumpet, however, and I'll bet the really cool ones blew a mean sax.

Jewish literature started these speculations of angelic organization. Centuries later, a fourth century Christian writer continued the work using passages from *Ephesians 6:12* and *Colossians 1:16* to establish nine levels of angels separated into three spheres or choirs.

The First Choir

Seraphim: These angels are the highest of the high—beings of love and light that are closest to God. They sing his praises and make the heavens turn. They're so radiant that other angels can't even look at them, which is why they're nicknamed "the burning ones." The prophet Isaiah saw them as mutant griffins with six wings and four faces, but then Isaiah saw a lot of goofy stuff. Four of them surround God's throne. Lucifer was supposedly the brightest of them until he launched his solo career.

Cherubim: In the Old Testament, these sphinx-like creatures stood beside God's throne, guarded the gates of Eden, and steered God's chariot. That was then. For some reason, they're now imagined as fat little babies with wings and no diapers, which means you don't want them perching over your car.

Thrones or Ophanim: Taking their orders from the Seraphim and the Cherubim, they serve as God's chariot, appearing as wheels with eyes around them. They carry out God's commands and keep the cosmos in order. They're described as having four wings and four faces, and they rarely interact with man—which is probably just as well because they'd give the children nightmares.

The Second Choir

Dominions: These are your classic angel types. They don white, floor-length gowns with golden belts and carry a staff of gold in one hand and God's seal in the other. Clearly they know how to accessorize. As heaven's middle-managers, their job is to coordinate the activities of the First and Third Choirs.

Virtues: Also called "the shining ones," they're sky spirits that regulate the planets and the weather. (And here you thought it was the laws of physics.) They assist people struggling with their faith, they reward worshippers with grace and valor, and they perform the occasional miracle. Handy guys to have around.

Powers: Guarding the frontier between heaven and earth, they are the border patrol of the afterlife. They guide the soul to heaven after death and stop demons from slipping in without a green card.

The Third Choir

Principalities: These hands-on entities protect human rulers, cities, and nations from *evil* angels. They dress like soldiers yet they wear girdles of gold, which makes them sound like shock troops for Victoria's Secret.

Archangels: These are the most famous angels because they deliver messages directly to man and they're the only ones with names. Theoretically there are seven of them, but we generally only hear about Gabriel and Michael. They lead the armies of heaven against the "sons of darkness," meaning those who seceded from heaven to follow Lucifer.

Angels: All other angels fall into this category. They have the thankless job of being closest to man; heaven's interns. They watch over us, offer help now and then, and work as a message service whenever something big is about to come down—like Jesus, or the end of the world, or both. Guardian Angels come from this rank, though that term appears nowhere in the Bible.

Ironically, stereotypical angels get their look from pagan mythology. The halo was originally the glowing aura of spiritual purity associated with sun gods. Their chief worshippers fashioned a crown of feathers to represent the solar disk. Later, Roman emperors and medieval kings, equating themselves with divine beings, adopted a crown of gold because gold was an incorruptible metal and because feathers started to look pretty stupid.

Christian sculptors rendered marble saints with halos on their heads shaped like flat disks, which, no kidding, had the added benefit of protecting the faces from bird droppings. In paintings, the halo was shown as a golden disk and it later morphed into the

186

circle of neon we now imagine hovering overhead like a personal UFO.

How to become a Saint

While we're on the subject of divine beings, the Catholic Church has a long tradition of turning its heroes into superheroes by elevating them to sainthood. It's a nice way to whitewash the reputation of special servants of the faith, and some of them really needed whitewashing. The bishop who ordered the death of Hypatia was made a saint.

Technically, when the pope bestows sainthood, it's simply a recognition of something God has already done. For the first thousand years of Christianity it was an informal process; more or less a popularity contest. Then, in the 10th century, Pope John XV established the official rules of canonization, which have been modified over the centuries. Until recently, there was an office of "devil's advocate" charged with making the case against the candidate for sainthood—to make sure they really deserved it. But Pope John Paul II got rid of the position, which I think is kind of disappointing.

The process of canonization can take years or even centuries. It begins at least five years after the candidate's death when a bishop investigates a candidates' life and work to see if they're virtuous enough for consideration. A report is sent to the Vatican, where a committee of cardinals and theologians review the material. If they approve, the pope declares the candidate to be "venerable." A Catholic role model.

Next, the candidate must be deemed responsible for a posthumous miracle of some kind, except if they died as a martyr, in which case no evidence is required. If they pass this hurdle they are granted "beatification."

Then, if a *second* miracle is proven to be associated with them, maybe through praying in their name, the candidate is canonized—they become a saint. But the Vatican has to verify these miracles. (I'm curious how this is even possible. Do they have a *Mythbusters* lab somewhere?)

A saint is ultimately recommended to the entire Church for veneration, and occasionally they're assigned to become the patron saint of something-or-other, like a church or a city. There are patron saints of cab drivers, accountants, comedians, earthquakes, television, thieves, and even abdominal pains. Recently, one was named for the Internet. Maybe he was prone to viruses.

A Brief History of Hell

Meanwhile, at the other end of the moral universe is the realm of the demons—hell. In the Middle Ages, hell was a big deal, and ideas about it evolved rapidly in the public imagination. What started as the gray underworld of Egypt and Greece, where everyone went after death, turned into a pit of torture exclusively for sinners, which was still almost everyone. There is no hell in Jewish belief, though some of the Israelites who bitched to Moses in the Sinai were gobbled up by the earth and landed in Sheol, also called Hades. It didn't sound like fun.

The Gospel of Matthew mentions "an unquenchable fire" that awaits sinners in the last days. This was embellished into God's penitentiary—the Evil Empire where the damned would suffer forever. Christian writers were happy to list specifically who the damned were, as if there was a membership roster, and it usually included you.

Paul included adulterers, slanderers, homosexuals, fornicators, swindlers, idolaters, thieves, drunkards, the greedy, the envious and even the quarrelsome—which takes care of all my Facebook friends. Augustine added sexual perverts to the guest list. I'm not sure if this included his concubine.

Because so much attention was paid to him, the devil took on a variety of names: Satan, Lucifer, Beelzebub, the Demon, the Dragon, Leviathan, Mephistopheles, the Serpent, Prince of Darkness, Tempter, Deceiver of Mankind, the Bogeyman, and even Dickens (as in, *"You scared the Dickens out of me!"* No relation to

Charles.). Satan assumed the appearance of Pan, the randy satyr of Greek mythology from whom we get the term "horny little devil." His pitchfork came from Neptune's trident and his voice came from *The Exorcist.*

Back around 20 B.C., the Roman poet Virgil was one of the first to describe hell vividly. It was a realm of violent earthquakes, noxious fumes, and vicious hounds, which I'll bet were those wheezing, snotty-eyed little toy poodles we'd all love to drown. Virgil was the first to locate hell geographically—under Italy. He said the entrance was in a cave outside of Naples. Consult your *Lonely Planet.*

In the sixth century, Gregory the Great collected stories of hell that included stinking rivers, cackling demons, and legions of the damned boiling in pits. One notorious work from 12th century Ireland, The Vision of Tundal, featured murderers sizzling on a grill, traitors impaled on hooks, and unchaste priests being eaten by a giant bird, which then defecated them onto a frozen lake full of serpents. Fuck.

Around 1300, Dante Alighieri added a major chapter to the lore in *The Divine Comedy.* He moved hell to the center of the earth with a sign at the entrance reading, "Abandon all hope ye who enter here." He gave us the Nine Circles of Hell, with offenders assigned to a hierarchy of specific tortures: the lustful flailed in winds of desire, gluttons sank into garbage heaps, and the slothful rotted in swamps. Plus there were the Furies, the Medusa, Harpies, boiling rivers and, at the bottom of it all, an icy lake of blood. There, Dante found those who had betrayed their lords—Judas, Brutus, and Satan himself. Et tu Beelzebub?

As the Black Death tore across Europe in the 1340s, hell visions began to include the Grim Reaper and living skeletons. Different religious orders added more details and these evolving images of damnation eventually wound up in plays and operas. John Milton elevated Satan to the glorious prince of hell in *Paradise Lost.* For Milton, hell was a kind of parallel reality rather than a geographic place, and Satan reigned from a palace called Pandemonium (meaning "all demons").

189

Fear of demons expanded to fear of everything—even old women who practiced pre-Christian folk medicine, because this sometimes involved an incantation. Pious locals would freak out about this and grab their torches and pitchforks. By the late 12th century these spontaneous panics became a big issue.

In response to popular demand, the Church established the Inquisition to handle these cases and to target heretics like the Christian Cathars in southern France. It was less about saving souls and more about spooking people into proper behavior. Speaking freely could be a death penalty offense. In 1252 the use of torture was authorized by Pope Innocent IV. While the big witch hunts of popular lore were still two centuries in the future, there was plenty of fear to go around.

Out of this same bleak era came the Crusades—Christian holy wars. In 1096 Pope Urban II launched an international assault upon the Holy Land to wrest Jerusalem back from the Muslims and to free Christians from Islamic rule. You were promised instant salvation if you died in the cause. Waves of Europeans, including children, spent the next 200 years invading Palestine in a failed campaign to "liberate" the place in the name of Jesus.

The Crusades saw the rise of one of history's great hypocrites—the Christian Soldier. Warriors for Christ, complete with the swords that Jesus said we would die by if we lived by them. These warriors passed judgment on their enemies and killed with impunity. Not a lot of "turn the other cheek" or "pray for those who persecute you" among the ranks. Yet somehow they thought they were doing God's work.

Another victim of this Age of Faith was, of course, the Jews. You know, the folks who gave us Jesus? There were many episodes of persecution. Richard the Lionheart wasn't one of their biggest fans and he banned them from his coronation in 1189. This was followed by anti-Jewish riots in London, York and elsewhere. Victims were beaten, stoned, and their houses burned until the king ordered it to stop.

Throughout this period, Jews were accused of ritually sacrificing children and, when the bubonic plague broke out, of poisoning the wells. They were expelled from England in 1290, from France in 1394, and from most of central Europe in the following decades, Christian charity and tolerance apparently in short supply.

How to End a Dark Age

Well, all this world-class stupidity couldn't last forever. But the end of the Middle Ages got its start in the *middle* of the Middle Ages. In 1085, in Southern Spain, Christian troops drove into Muslim-controlled cities like Toledo, and got busy turning mosques into churches. The Arabs had the last laugh, though, because they had been building mosques for 500 years, and what the Crusaders discovered inside those temples would eventually undo the Catholic domination of Europe.

Stored within the libraries of Islamic wisdom were Arabic translations of far older documents—the works of Aristotle, Plato, Euclid, Archimedes, Pythagoras, and a toga party full of intellectual superstars; materials essentially forgotten by the Christian world. The only reason we know about many of these guys today is because of what was preserved in those Muslim archives. By the 12th century these ancient writings were being translated from Arabic into Latin and were making their way into scholarly circles across Europe.

What the Crusaders had discovered was overwhelming—reams of Greek works on philosophy, science, history, government, mathematics, anatomy, ethics, geometry, poetry, theatre, literature, and mythology. And that was just the short list. This stuff was so advanced that European translators had to make up new words for concepts long forgotten in the West. It was a treasure trove of discovery, creativity, and wisdom unequalled in history. But for Christian scholars it was a problem.

You see, most of these documents were written centuries *before* the birth of Jesus—an astounding mass of knowledge acquired by people who worshipped pagan gods, chugged their wine, and held

191

sporting events in the buff. What were God-fearing academics to do? How could they admit that these heathens were smarter than the people of faith?

In the mid-13th century, a brilliant theologian named Thomas Aquinas figured out how to handle these pre-Christian works of genius. Instead of burning them, he baptized them. He took the braininess of Aristotle and reinterpreted his work in the light of Christian thought. Aquinas believed spiritual knowledge could only be gained through divine revelation. But rational thought could also come up with factual answers about nature. Since God created nature, man could understand God better by studying his creation. This made science and logic acceptable because they would verify the reality of God and the authority of the Church. Or so he hoped.

Thomas Aquinas thought he could logically prove the existence of God and he wrote five clever arguments to make that point. He employed Greek intellectual tools like the syllogism—the kind of three-step pocket logic you probably last used on an SAT test. Example: "Virtue deserves respect. Honesty is a virtue. Therefore, honesty deserves respect." Or perhaps less abstract: "Disco sucked. The Village People recorded disco. Therefore, The Village People sucked." Actually, this one works on several levels.

Aquinas painted Christian theology with a fresh coat of logic and lured thinkers away from Tertullian's ravings about "I believe it because it sounds nuts." Aquinas didn't think there were serious conflicts between rational thought and divine revelation—which is why he could logically prove the existence of God.

Except he couldn't. His five famous arguments are flawed and they've been refuted many times. Furthermore, his intellectual revolution would eventually hoist the Church by its own petard, and the Church had a damned big petard. If *anything* you could prove logically was true, what happens if you proved something that didn't jibe with Scripture?

This is exactly what those ancient Greek manuscripts did on more than one occasion. Yet here was Aquinas giving permission to believe in them. Add to this one final ingredient: Gutenberg's printing press, in 1439, which allowed copies of these ancient documents to spread all over Europe. These seeds of pagan knowledge were planted in the rationalist soil tilled by Aquinas, and they gradually brought forth a bumper crop of curiosity and skepticism. Logic based on nature rather than on Scripture became the new avenue to truth. People asked questions, found answers, and before you know it they had a Renaissance on their hands.

Church fathers, however, feared that all this new thinking was playing with fire. One bishop had Aquinas excommunicated shortly after his death. It took another fifty years before they got around to making him a saint. For the religious gatekeepers, the "faith-before-reason" school of Augustine was still in session. They worried that Thomas had made room for heretical thought—which he had. But it was too late. The genie was out of the bottle.

Rebirth

The word Renaissance means "rebirth," as in the rebirth of interest in the human mind and in worldly knowledge. The change that began in Italy in the early 1400s inaugurated the modern West—humanist, rationalist, and ever-changing. At first, artists and writers had to be cagey about how they revived ancient Greek ideas. Sculptors carved pagan nudes, but gussied them up as biblical characters: Michelangelo's *David*, or Mary and Jesus in his *Pieta*. Greek plays were reworked into Christian-themed dramas. Stargazers harmonized new observations with theology. It seemed to work at first.

The Church, however, saw trouble coming. Inevitably, somebody was going to cross the line and say something stupid or, more to the point, blasphemous. To head this off, the Church tried to regulate the flow of information. They esteemed intellectual ambition, but only within the bounds of religious belief. Initially, only the clergy were allowed to own Bibles. Later, heretical books were banned or burned, sometimes alongside their authors. But this could only go on for so long.

After awhile, it seemed like the Church was more concerned with its authority than with the truth. It had become enormously powerful, corrupt in some quarters, and kind of greedy. One famous method of raising cash was the selling of Indulgences— basically a get-out-of-jail-free card for a sin you hadn't yet committed. It sounds like a good deal to me, but for serious Christians it defeated the point. Repenting a sin meant vowing to never do it again. It was hard to make that case when you were buying a permission slip in advance for one more stab at debauchery.

Reformation—Like that was gonna help

The Castle Church in Wittenberg, Germany was a prime example of where the Church seemed to have lost its way. It housed a huge trove of religious art and paraphernalia that was periodically put on display—a kind of Smithsonian for religious tourists. Among the 10,000-plus holy relics were, allegedly, straw from Christ's manger and milk from the Virgin Mary herself. No joke. And get this: each donation you made bought you one hundred fewer days in Purgatory *for every relic* in the church's collection. Donate enough, help them buy enough items, and you could shave millennia off your time in the escrow of the afterlife once you died. It was a transparent sham.

Well, in 1517, ninety-five reasons for telling the Church where to stick its authority were nailed up at the Castle Church doorway. The guy who did it was a moody German monk named Martin Luther, who understandably thought that the marketing of forgiveness was a tad cynical. God's grace was supposed to be free. You were supposed to deserve it, not afford it. The Church had made it a commodity for purchase.

In challenging all this Luther launched what became the Protestant Reformation—the notion that the Church was no longer one-stop shopping for everything you wanted to know about Jesus but feared hellfire to ask. You could be Christian without being a Catholic. It was a concept with legs. Luther, never one for diplomacy, went on to demonize the papacy itself and to equate it with the Beast of *Revelation*. He also rejected the celibate priesthood (at last) and he married a former nun. Luther had issues.

Of course, by breaking with the pope, Luther opened up a massive can of theological worms. It didn't take long for this movement to proliferate a staggering number of revisions, spinoffs, and sects with a baffling assortment of claims and beliefs. Was Scripture to be taken literally or was there wiggle room? Was salvation predestined or was it up to you? Are you justified by faith alone or did good works also count? Must rituals of worship be biblically prescribed or can you make up new routines?

This denominational diversification, if you will, would only get worse until it led to the present-day potpourri that includes Lutherans, Calvinists, Presbyterians, Baptists, Southern Baptists, Congregationalists, Methodists, Quakers, Unitarians, Pentecostals, Puritans, Apostolics, Evangelicals, Charismatics, Mennonites, Mormons, Jehovah's Witnesses, Seventh Day Adventists, and hundreds of variations on each. To this you can add the Eastern and Oriental Churches, Anglicans, and thousands of modern concoctions tailored to every region, ethnicity, and political view. The result: anyone wanting to get right with Jesus might as well throw a dart at a Bible and build a faith on whichever passage he hit. It's what everyone else apparently did.

Not surprisingly, none of this went down well in Rome. Here was a hand basket and the world was officially going to hell in it.

Long story short—the Church responded to Luther with the Counter-Reformation; a wave of Catholic revivalism that ignited civil wars across Europe and produced a more centralized organization, along with some of the most gaudy, overwrought religious artwork ever created. It was a melodramatic style called Baroque—the powerful but aggressively ornate art that gluts the Vatican. Imagine if your great aunt went shopping for ceramic dolls and doilies with the budget of the Pentagon.

Wars over who loved Jesus best raged between Catholics and Protestants for the next couple of centuries, the whole idea of behaving like a Christian apparently having been lost.

195

In England, Henry VIII broke from Rome and, in 1533, founded what became the Church of England on the pretext that the stuffy old pope wouldn't grant him a divorce. This launched a century of political intrigues, persecutions, and flat out murder fests before the country finally settled on Protestantism. You know you've arrived in this world when you can start your own church over a marital dispute and everyone has to take you seriously. In fact, if you *didn't* take Henry seriously, you could be accused of treason, which would get you hanged, drawn, and quartered. If you committed heresy against his church, you were burned. Like I said, people took him seriously.

Later, in 1584, a Catholic radical named Balthazar Gerard assassinated a Protestant royal named Prince William the Silent—which he certainly was after Gerard got through with him. In revenge, Gerard's body was gouged with quill pens, and salt and vinegar were poured into the wounds. He was then stretched on the rack, his hands were cut off, and the bloody stumps were seared with hot irons. Then he was torn apart by horses.

In France, a Catholic country, Henry IV issued an edict of toleration for Protestants in 1610 to end a thirty year religious civil war. For his trouble he was assassinated by a Catholic. The assassin was subsequently tortured, his legs broken, his hand cut off, and hot oil poured into the wound. He was also torn apart by horses. These were all fights over who best understood Jesus, mind you.

Over in Spain, Philip II called for Catholics to assassinate heretical kings. Meanwhile, the religious infighting in Germany took out one third of the population—the same percentage as the bubonic plague.

Trying hard to sit on the sidelines of this madness was a growing subculture of scientific noodlers like Copernicus, Kepler, Galileo, and Newton. Some of them spent as much time on alchemy as they did on science. But they took the trouble to observe how nature operated instead of taking the Scripture's word for it, and they described what they saw with geometry and math—two disciplines every bit as boring as religion but a lot harder to argue with.

Various churches tried to shut these guys up. Gradually, however, the so-called scientific revolution swept the West in the 17th and 18th centuries. Political leaders gradually lowered the volume on spiritual issues, realizing that science and engineering could increase efficiency, create new products, expand trade, and generate more cash. That sure beat shaking down the peasants with threats of hellfire. Technology and commerce boomed. Secular life flourished. Public officials paid less attention to bishops and more attention to merchants. The town center moved from the cathedral to the city hall. The modern world had arrived.

The intellectual movement that started with the discovery of those Greek documents in Arabic mosques reached its climax in the 18th century—the Enlightenment—the era when the cult of Reason reached its zenith. The science and art of the ancients were studied, and then surpassed. Their playwrights and philosophers spurred revolutionary new ideas, and some of those spilled over into politics.

It was around this time that thirteen colonies of businessmen and farmers in North America broke away from mother England and set up shop on their own. Once they were independent, the colonists were faced with the question of what kind of government they wanted. They had lots of choices. Should it be a traditional Christian monarchy as in the countries of Europe? Or a theocracy as in ancient Israel? Or an empire such as Rome?

They scanned the millennia and reviewed the major governments throughout history. For a few years they tried the loose, decentralized structure of the Articles of Confederation. But that didn't work out. They needed something stronger.

Then, someone looked back to the same ancient Greeks who had given the West the Golden Age of Pericles and the Renaissance, and to a little experiment they had tried a long time ago in Athens. After 2,300 years, godless popular government was about to make a comeback.

CHAPTER EIGHT

America's Pagan Values

There's a phrase we live by in America:
"In God We Trust."
It's right there where Jesus would want it—on our money.

—Stephen Colbert

God's Country?

"America is founded upon Christian Family Values." How many times have we heard this mantra? It's one of those nice, flexible statements that can mean anything you want because "Christian Family Values" can mean anything you want. Choose any side of any issue, find a Bible verse that seems to back you up, and suddenly your opinion is endorsed by Jesus Christ and should rightly become the law of the land.

So what's wrong with that? How can you argue that America is anything but a Christian-based country? The Pilgrims were diehard Christians who sought religious freedom, right? The

Founding Fathers were Christians who prayed for God's help to win their revolution. The Declaration of Independence says men are "endowed by their Creator with certain unalienable Rights." We say "under God" in the Pledge of Allegiance, and "In God We Trust" is engraved on our currency. Millions of Americans think God's judgment will arrive before their next Society Security check. Hell, we invented auto gun racks and the dashboard Jesus. How much more Christian can you get?

Well, most Americans certainly call themselves Christians, and you can dig up plenty of quotes by America's founders that appeal to God or, as they put it, "divine providence." There's no doubt they believed in God, and did so sincerely. But just because they prayed for guidance back in 1787 while hammering out the Constitution doesn't mean Jesus gets the credit for it. Christians pray at the craps table, too. It doesn't mean that if you roll a lucky seven the Son of God was responsible.

Rejecting Traditional Values

The truth is, there is nothing remotely Christian about the American Constitution. It is not a product of Christian philosophy; it is in large part a rejection of it. You can't argue that America is based on biblical principles just because the founders believed God was on their side. *Everyone* believes God is on their side: the colonists and King George III; the Union and the Confederacy; Germany and the Allies, Jews and Palestinians, terrorists and troops, and both teams at the Homecoming game. They all cite chapter and verse to prove they've got the thumbs-up from heaven. No matter who wins, God gets the credit.

So ask yourself—what made the United States something *new* and *different* in 1776? What made it a revolution and not just a breakaway republic? It wasn't an embracing of Christian values. Nothing new there. The countries the colonists left back in Europe had been officially Christian for a thousand years. What made America different was its *rejection* of traditional Christian values, at least when it came to government.

From the fall of Rome right up to the American Revolution, European governments were established on Christian tradition. Monarchs reigned by divine right. Most kings ruled in the name of God. Armies marched in the name of Christ. There were official churches, religious tests for high office, persecutions against heretics, limits on scientific inquiry, plus the regulation of speech, writing, and personal behavior—all based on someone's understanding of God's holy plan. Your place was to shut up and believe.

The American Revolution threw all that out the stained glass window. The government of the United States became the first secular state of the modern world; its *lack* of religiosity is what made it unique. Its entire purpose was worldly, not otherworldly, as the preamble to the Constitution makes clear:

> We, the People of the United States, in order to form a more perfect Union, establish justice, insure domestic tranquility, provide for the common defense, promote the general welfare, and secure the blessings of liberty to ourselves and our posterity do ordain and establish this Constitution for the United States of America.

The Constitution is concerned with national defense, liberty, justice, and the rule of law. Nothing in there about God, Jesus, the Bible, faith, salvation, commandments, exorcism, crackers that turn into flesh, or sodomites boiling in the fourth circle of hell. If you want to go with all that it's your own personal goop.

Tradition said that a Christian monarch was the rightful lord of the realm. If he ruled in the name of Christ and observed the commandments, God would bless him with success in war and politics. There was no lack of faith on the king's part. Quite the contrary; tradition said God gave him his job.

America's founders didn't like God's choice of who would rule them. So, building on a couple centuries of English law and politics, the founders kept God out of the leader-choosing business and put man in his place. A leader's authority would come from the people below, not from heaven above, through a pagan ritual called voting. God could still dwell in the hearts and minds of the voters; he just couldn't work for the government.

When you read it you discover that the U.S. Constitution is essentially a set of instructions on how to organize human decision-making, in this life, on this planet. It tells us how to choose our leaders and how those leaders should do their jobs when they're not kissing babies or golfing with oil executives. It explains what they can do to us and what they can't.

The Constitution wasn't divinely inspired. Haggling humans cobbled it together while competing for power and cutting deals. It is not holy writ—that's why it can be amended. You can't do that with the Sermon on the Mount. And do you really want to credit God with the idea that slaves counted as three-fifths of a person? Didn't think so.

Values Test

The Constitution is certainly based on a set of values, but exactly which values? There are all kinds of values: religious, moral, personal, political, economic, artistic. But conservatives bring up terms like "Christian values, "moral values" and "Family Values" more often than runway models bring up lunch. Maybe we should sort these out and discover, once and for all, which values made America...America.

Christian Values

I may be going out on a limb here, but it seems to me that Christian values are those that were taught by Jesus Christ— namely, that Jesus was the son of God who sacrificed himself for our sins. Believe in his resurrection, love your fellow man, and get through life without being a complete crapweasel, and you'll have eternal life. It sounds great.

But some folks assign the "Christian values" label to *any* idea that appeals to them. If a congressman wants to legalize automatic weapons he'll try to call that Christian values. But to really earn that status an idea must either be unique to the Christian faith or essential to its teaching. Last time I checked, being armed to the teeth wasn't one of the Beatitudes.

Loving God through Jesus is perfectly nice, but it has nothing to do with the U.S. Constitution. I can be a loyal American even if the only Jesus I know is my car mechanic. Ideas essential to Christian belief are found nowhere in that document and the values that *are* found in there *do not* derive from Christianity. Read on.

Personal Values

Personal responsibility, hard work, honesty, affection for your children, loyalty to your (heterosexual) spouse, respect for your friends, and love for your country. These are what preachers and politicians usually talk about when they hawk Christian values. Christians certainly advocate them and Scripture does teach most of them.

The problem is that *none* of them originated with the Bible. They were around long before Jesus, or Moses, or even Abraham. They're moral no-brainers and they're observed today in places where the people wouldn't know a crucifix from a scarecrow.

What's more, whether you call them Christian values or not, *none* of them are in the Constitution. Yes, the framers would have recommended that you be a responsible, industrious family man. But the laws they wrote don't require it. You can be a lazy bullshitter who cheats on his wife, loathes his kids, and skips work to attend a wet T-shirt contest, and still be a flag-waving Yankee Doodle. Is this a great country or what?

Of course, there's no shortage of those who'd like to see the government *enforce* these values and demand that each of us be a loyal spouse, a doting parent, a motivated worker, and a wholesome patriot. But then we'd have to call it the People's Republic of China.

202

American Values

Representative government, free elections, free speech, free press, freedom of assembly, due process of law, the right to bear arms, the right to petition the government for a redress of grievances, the right to own property, and official neutrality toward all religions. *These* are the values we should be talking about—the ones that made the American government something new and different. The values that are actually *in* the U.S. Constitution and which were the basis for the new government.

And guess what? *None* of them originated with Christian belief, nor were they observed much by Christian governments over the previous 1,500 years. That's why they were written down. Kings tended to forget them and religious leaders traditionally opposed them.

Not buying any of this? Let's go down the list.

Democracy—In Zeus We Trust

Democracy is an idea that owes nothing to the Bible. Neither the word nor the concept appear anywhere in Scripture and it was never suggested by God, Moses, Jesus, Paul, or Jezebel as a way to organize human beings. It wasn't advocated by the ancient Hebrews or the medieval Christians. The only ones in the Bible who did practice any sort of democracy were the Greeks and the Romans, and they were usually the bad guys.

Democracy is a secular value and it got its start in ancient Athens around 507 B.C., five centuries before Jesus dropped in. Back then, voters were free adult males who participated in the people's Assembly. It met about forty times a year and had some 6,000 members. It must have been like passing laws at Woodstock. There were no speaking restrictions based on religion, tradition, or class—which also sounds like Woodstock. Hopefully they avoided the brown acid.

More to the point, democracy's creators worshipped the gods of Mount Olympus—the frat house of deities that felt at home at a

203

wine-soaked toga party. Gods Gone Wild. Christians were nowhere to be found and would probably have left the festivities early.

None of this stopped America's founders from borrowing the democracy idea directly from Athens. This is why the buildings of Washington D.C. look like the pagan temples of ancient Greece and not the Christian cathedrals of medieval Europe. It's why the key values of our government—Liberty, Justice, Democracy—are symbolized by pagan goddesses and not by Jewish prophets or Christian saints.

Of course, neither Athenians nor America's founders were sold on popular democracy, which they saw as rule by the rabble. The Greeks were more focused on serving the city-state than on individual rights. Their vision was more aristocratic than ours. And let's face it, if you've ever seen face-painters at a Knicks game, the principle of "the people" governing themselves can be pretty scary. But the Athenians tried it and it worked for two centuries in a world full of theocratic dictators and skin-wearing barbarians.

Democracy does not depend upon religious belief. That's why it travels so well. Today, it works in Catholic Italy, Protestant England, Jewish Israel, Hindu India, Shinto Japan, pagan San Francisco, godless New York, and anarchist Texas. You want to get all choked up about the roots of free debate and citizen government? Put away the Bible and pick up Aristotle's *Politics.* Yes, it does lack miracle stories, and it reads like the warranty to your iPhone. But it makes it clear that America's cornerstone values have secular roots.

Free Speech—a.k.a. Heresy

Contrary to popular belief, free speech is not a priority in the Bible. When the Israelites bitched to Moses about being dragged across the desert, they were gobbled up by the earth or hit with a plague. When Job complained about his misfortunes, God gave him a tongue-lashing you could hear from Jerusalem to Alpha Centauri. As mentioned, Jesus famously said, "the truth shall make you free," but he was talking about the soul's freedom from sin, not political free speech.

Jesus had no problem with free expression, but for the next 2,000 years, plenty of Christians did. The Catholic Church, of course, has a glorious history of silencing (or jailing or torturing or executing) people who spoke out of turn. Protestants did this as well, especially when fighting Catholics. Both faiths have undergone a big attitude adjustment over the past two centuries. But for most of their histories, genuine free speech was regarded as a *bad* thing.

This is why free speech was encoded into the Constitution—to stop all this. If I can't tell the honorable Reverend Blowdry where he can stuff his diamond-studded cross, I'm not free. Religion is not about free speech; it's about listening, learning, and ultimately agreeing with what you're told. No matter which faith we're talking about, if *it* has the last word *you* don't.

Free Press

Technically, there was no press in biblical times, though Christians are sometimes credited with the invention of the codex—what we call books. They were much easier to flip through than scrolls. But let us also remember who history's most ardent book-burners were. Churches were so anti-free press you couldn't even own a Bible in the early days. Throughout history, writing could get you in as much trouble as adultery, and it's a lot less fun. Believe me.

The Right to Bear Arms

This is certainly an American right and, for some, a psychosexual obsession. But what does Jesus say about arming yourself against evil-doers?

> "...all they that take the sword shall perish with the sword." [Matt. 26:52]

> "Love your enemies and pray for those who persecute you." [Matt. 5:43-44]

> "Do not resist one who is evil. But if anyone strikes you on the right cheek, turn to him the other also…" [Matt. 5:38-39]

> "Judge not, that you may not be judged." [Matt. 7:1]

It's hard to find a mandate for the NRA in all that. As we established earlier, Jesus didn't think you should harm anyone for any reason. Not in war. Not even in self-defense. How would his own story be different if, on the night they came to arrest him, he was packing heat? "Go ahead. Maketh my day."

Private Property

Property rights are dear to Americans, especially to the more entrepreneurial among us. But as we saw back in the *Jesus on Economics* section, Jesus was not too worried about worldly wealth. It is better to give than to receive. The poor are blessed, while the rich have a tough time getting through the pearly gates. To this we can add:

> "For the love of money is the root of all evil…" [1 Timothy 6:10]

Capitalists don't talk like that.

Religious Tolerance

It's real simple. If you pass laws to enforce a religion's ideas it means no one else's religion gets that same favor. This works well in a theocracy. In a democracy, not so much.

We sometimes hear that America needs to renew its Christian commitment to save it from decline and doom. But the Roman Empire officially recognized Christianity starting in A.D. 325; that didn't save it from disintegration. Nor did the millennium of Christian kingdoms that followed revive democracy, individual liberty, or religious tolerance. During the faith-saturated Middle

206

Ages, religious freedom was regarded as a vice rather than a virtue. Stray from the path of Christ and you were a "freethinker." Not good. Yet today, people credit God with the ideals of free thought, democratic government, and religious tolerance. Why?

The Religion of Communism

Well, it's partly due to church p.r., but you can also blame the commies. They routinely stifled freedom and then told everyone they were (gasp!) *atheists.* People naturally concluded (with the urging of their churches) that atheism led to oppression because it didn't recognize our God-given rights. Godless rationalism produced evil! Evolution led to Soviet gulags! You know the drill.

Sorry, but no. Reason doesn't lead to tryanny any more than religion does. Oppressors come in all stripes—atheist, monotheist, polytheist, Jewish, Catholic, Protestant, Muslim, Hindu, and faiths long forgotten. They've all had their shot.

In the Old Testament, God demanded total conquest. (Check out *Exodus 17:14, Numbers 33:51* or *Deuteronomy 7:2.* It's enough to make your toes curl backwards.) We saw what the Romans did to Christians and what Christians later did to pagans. Islamic armies, Catholic Crusaders, Mongol hoards, Viking raiders, Spanish Conquistadors, Sikh warriors, Latin American death squads, and the armies of Hitler, Stalin, and Mao were all murderous, whether they killed for the state, or for God, or for both.

What's more, Marxism itself was a religion. It didn't involve a personal god (many religions don't) but it functioned as a faith, which is why it was intolerant of other beliefs. It sought to define morality, guide human thought, and control behavior—a religious agenda. Sure, the Reds *claimed* to be rational and atheistic, but all they really did was gussy up mystical beliefs in scientific lingo.

Marx created a religion, which is one reason why it caught on in retrograde Russia instead of the modern, industrialized West as Marx had predicted. As with any faith, it was never practiced in its true form, which would be impossible. But there are parallels aplenty between communism and theocratic government.

In Marx's universe, events were guided by something called "the inevitable forces of history" which would eventually lead to a global communist society. It turns out history wasn't so inevitable, primarily because those "forces" existed only in his head. But for the faithful they constituted an unseen higher power which drove history forward through a process called "dialectical materialism." Two opposing forces would clash to produce the next chapter of history and ultimately lead humanity down one unalterable path to a utopian future—the perfect communist state.

Naturally, only an elite minority understood this higher power. They became the Communist Party, which had the unique authority to define the truth, interpret current events, establish doctrines, and even dictate personal behavior. They had their saints and their sacred texts, none of which could be questioned. And they demanded more than mere obedience. They wanted a personal commitment to the official mindset. If you refused and strayed off the one, true path, you became an outcast; a counterrevolutionary.

The result of all this was an authoritarian society led by one absolute ruler. He usually reigned for life. When he died, the Party elite would go behind closed doors and, through a secret process, select one of their own as the next absolute ruler.

This, of course, is precisely how they choose the pope. He and all other Christian leaders also believe in an unseen, higher power called God, who is guiding history according to his inevitable divine plan. History is a dialectical clash of Good and Evil, leading humanity down one unalterable path to a utopian future—the Kingdom of God.

Again, only an elite minority, the priesthood, understands this higher power. They constitute the Church, which has the unique authority to define the truth, interpret current events, establish doctrines, and dictate personal behavior. They have their saints and their sacred texts. And they, too, want a personal commitment to the official mindset. If you refuse, you become an outcast; a heretic.

Under both communism and Christianity everyone is supposed to be equal, yet both are controlled from the top. Both expect everyone to march lockstep into the future without challenging their leadership. Both seek to remake hearts and minds in their image; nobody asks for a show of hands before an edict is issued. They want team players, not independent thinkers. Freedom just throws a wrench into the gears.

Contrast these belief-based systems with a secular democracy, where there *is* no inevitable destiny for man. All futures are possible and each individual has a say in which one comes about. We are all the authors of our fate, which is determined by free debate, open elections, and just living our lives. No unseen powers need apply. If someone strays off the one, true path…well, there *isn't* any one, true path. Therefore, there's no outcast status such as heretic or counterrevolutionary. You get to participate even if you hate liberty and democracy. No matter what kind of useless jerk-wad you are, you still get to vote.

In a democratic country, you can live by the Bible's teachings if you want to, but you don't have to—which is the whole point. It's optional. The difference between a government that *recommends* a way of life and one that *requires* a way of life is the difference between having an advisor and having a warden.

Ten Commandments vs. Ten Amendments

So, when we run down the list of Constitutional values we don't find many of them originating with the Bible. What if we approach this from the opposite direction? When we walk through the Ten Commandments, how well do they square with the Bill of Rights? Today's morality police want to post the commandments in courtrooms and classrooms in the belief that our laws and justice system stem from this list of rules. But is this really the case?

1. Thou shall hold no other gods before me.

This commandment is the cornerstone of religious intolerance, which is why it's unconstitutional. In America, I can hold as many gods before me as I want. I can worship a lawn jockey if I wish.

Or nothing at all. Certainly the founders would have chosen God over yard ornaments. But for the first time in history, good Christians set up a government that left this decision up to me. The First Commandment and the First Amendment represent opposing philosophies.

2. Thou shall make no graven image.

The United States Government has a Bureau of Engraving.

3. Thou shall not take the Lord's name in vain.

If they could throw us in jail for this, half the public, most of the army, and all of Congress would be serving time.

4. Thou shall honor the Sabbath and keep it holy.

Cops, firemen, missile base commanders, ESPN cameramen and pizza delivery boys work on the Sabbath. No one seems to object.

5. Thou shall honor your father and mother.

Do you really want the government busting you for falling short on this one? Mother's Day visits would be a legal obligation, like jury duty. It's too much like that already.

6. Thou shall not kill.

At last, we're half way through the commandments and we finally have agreement between the Bible and the Constitution. Both regard murder as wrong. But this agreement is not because the Constitution is based on the Bible. It's because a ban against murder is a basic ingredient of *every* civilization. Nowhere in history has a culture, regardless of its faith, allowed just any loser to go kill someone without consequence. America's founders didn't need a commandment to clue them in on this point. If anyone can kill anyone, you don't have a civilization. You have barbarism.

Murder is not illegal in America because Scripture commands it. Scripture commands all kinds of things that can't become the law of the land and judges can't cite the Bible as a basis for their rulings. Murder is illegal because the founders wanted a country where you could get through the day without a knife in your back. It was about self-interest, not obedience to God. It was a political principle called the Social Contract—a mutual agreement among the citizens that everyone would be better off if murder was outlawed. It reduced stress.

Yes, the idea certainly jibed with the religious views of the framers. And that was nice. But God's disapproval isn't enough for the U.S. government to forbid something. God disapproves of people worshipping other deities and eating shellfish, but in America there's nothing he can do about it.

7. Thou shall not commit adultery.

There are many bits of good advice that shouldn't become law because they're nobody else's business. This is one of them. How many governors would be in prison if this were legally enforced?

8. Thou shall not steal.

Like the ban against murder, this idea is recognized everywhere. Even the communists, who opposed private property, didn't let anyone just walk into your house and swipe the golf clubs. For one thing, commies didn't play much golf.

9. Thou shall not bear false witness.

It's perfectly legal to lie, so long as you're not under oath or telling your customer that the Hummer he's eyeing gets eighty miles per gallon and floats. If you do lie under oath, it's punishable not because it offends God but because it offends the rights of the people you're lying to or about. Being sworn-in may intimidate you with the fear of God's wrath, but its real purpose is to hold you legally accountable for what you're about to say. If you're caught committing perjury, the government isn't going to wait for God's judgment.

10. Thou shall not covet your neighbor's property.

Forgetting for the moment that "property" included wives and slaves, coveting your neighbor's stuff is the engine that drives the American economy. Look at any TV commercial. It's all about keeping up with the Joneses, and the Joneses buy a *lot* of shit.

Three outta Ten ain't Bad

So, when we add it all up, the Sixth, Eighth and sometimes Ninth Commandments agree with the Constitution. But that's really it. Conclusion: the American Constitution can't be based on the Ten Commandments when it's clear that seven-and-a-half of them are unconstitutional. This is not advanced political science.

The Ten Commandments and the Constitution stand on separate foundations. The commandments exist to prevent people from offending God. The Constitution exists to prevent people from offending other people. God isn't involved.

A big problem with linking church and state is that it gives religion the tools of government—the power to tax, to regulate speech and private life, to throw you in jail, to start wars, or to suppress other churches. You really want to go back to those days?

Separating church and state effectively de-clawed religion in the West. If churches no longer use force it's because they have no choice; the law forbids it. Believers may still fear divine fury if their country refuses to grovel sufficiently (a constant problem with the ancient Israelites), but the only power they have today is persuasion. Preachers can scream hellfire all they want, but they can't punish you for ignoring them. You can take your business elsewhere.

The Joys of Secular Humanism

Pilgrims' Regress

Among those who understood the downside of religious oppression were the Puritans of 17th century England. These were strict, reform-minded Protestants who felt the Church of England wasn't sufficiently un-Catholic. The English Church, allied with the Crown, pushed back at them with stern rules. This got the Puritans packing for the New World.

A major reason why Americans often think their government is based on Christian values stems from events like this. It started with our earliest settlers—the Pilgrims—a pack of old-fashioned religious kooks who made the Puritans who followed them look almost post-modern. Contrary to popular legend, the Pilgrims did not need to flee to North America to find religious liberty. After leaving England in 1610, they spent a decade in Holland, free to live by their almost medieval beliefs. The Dutch, being largely merchants and traders, were too interested in making money to break a sweat about God issues.

But the "saints," as the Pilgrims modestly called themselves, were religious radicals who didn't want their kids picking up the worldly ways of the Dutch. So, in 1620, they booked a voyage on the Mayflower with a few soldiers of fortune and sailed to a remote continent. There, they established a cozy, isolated little theocracy that didn't recognize religious tolerance, democracy, or even private property at first. But at least there were no dangerous free thinkers or non-believers to influence their children. (The Indians didn't really count.)

Nor did the Puritans, who arrived a decade later, put a premium on religious freedom. They treated dissenters more harshly than they themselves had been treated back in England. You see, they wanted religious liberty, but only for themselves—a concept even the Mullahs of Iran can roll with.

When Quakers started to arrive in Massachusetts, Boston authorities passed a law in 1656 that imposed a fine of one-hundred pounds on any sea captain who brought a Quaker to their shores. If one was discovered, he was whipped. Mary Barrett Dyer, a Quaker activist who opposed this law, was hanged in 1660. She wasn't the only one to get this treatment. In other colonies, Christmas celebrations were outlawed because it was regarded as a papist holiday or too larded with pagan evergreens and whatnot.

By the time of the American Revolution, over a century later, North America was cluttered with offbeat religious groups far too weird for the mainstream churches back in Europe to stomach. With all these dizzy cults in the land it was impossible for America's founders to concoct a state religion that wouldn't piss off somebody.

Most of these churches were Christian, but that didn't mean they got along. Methodists, Calvinists, Lutherans, Anglicans, Presbyterians, Baptists, Huguenots, Quakers, Mennonites—most of them had little affection for each other. Half of them didn't think the other half were even Christian.

There was no way this smorgasbord of sects was going to be happy with a one-faith-fits-all national church. So, the framers dumped the idea of government-backed religion altogether. This didn't mean religion was removed from the public sphere. Americans could worship God in any way they wanted, including right out in the open. They just couldn't do it on the public dime or on public property. Churches would have to rise or fall on their own.

Separation of Church and State

Strange as it sounds, separation of church and state is one of America's great gifts to the modern world. Critics insist those exact words, "separation of church and state," are nowhere in the Constitution. It's true. Neither is the word "democracy," but it adds up to the same thing. The words "Original Sin" are nowhere in the Bible, but few claim the idea isn't in there.

The term "separation of church and state" comes from an 1802 letter by Thomas Jefferson to a Baptist congregation assuring them that their religious rights would be secure under the new American government:

> "Believing with you that religion is a matter which lies solely between man & his god...their legislature [the American people] should make no law respecting an establishment of religion, or prohibiting the free exercise thereof, thus building a wall of separation between church and state."

The term was coined as a *defense* of religious freedom. Of course, some folks don't want to hear this. They naturally fall back on the famous words from the second sentence of the Declaration of Independence:

> We hold these truths to be self evident, that all men are created equal, that they are endowed by their Creator with certain unalienable rights, that among these are life, liberty and the pursuit of happiness...

It sure sounds like Jefferson thinks our rights come from God. But a couple of points here. First, the Declaration was a rationale for revolution; it's not the law of the land. Second, it doesn't matter where Jefferson thought our rights came from. I'm every bit as American as he was even if I think they come from a pizza joint in Albuquerque. What matters is that our government recognizes these rights, not our personal theories about where they originated. Third, the word "Creator" is deliberately broad so it can encompass almost any belief. Some thought "Creator" referred to the laws of nature. Straining logic, am I? Let's look at the *first* sentence of the Declaration:

> When in the Course of human Events, it becomes necessary for one People to dissolve the Political Bonds which have connected them with another, and to assume among the Powers of the Earth, the separate and equal Station to which the Laws of Nature and of Nature's God entitle them...

America was entitled to separate from Britain based on "the Laws of Nature and of Nature's God." Notice that the Laws of Nature—scientific rationalism—come first. *Then* comes Nature's God. And who is Nature's God?

Well, he wasn't the faith-healing, corpse-raising, miracle-whipping guy who makes statues of Mary cry tears of blood in horror movies. He was the Deist god of the Enlightenment. The Supreme Being who created the universe, set up the laws of nature to make it run, and then let it go. America's founders believed in God, but they also subscribed to Newton's Laws of Motion. The rule of *reason* was their guiding principle of government. After all, the Declaration of Independence was not written by a theologian. It was written by a scientist.

Eleven years later, in 1787, the Constitutional Convention opened in Philadelphia without any public prayer. As the framers debated, Ben Franklin became so frustrated by their stalemated haggling that he suggested an appeal to God in the form of a morning sermon. But he also said, "I beg I may not be understood to infer, that our general Convention was divinely inspired when it formed the new federal Constitution." That's Ben Franklin saying the Constitution is not divinely inspired. His motion for a sermon never carried.

During their presidencies, both Jefferson and Madison refused to issue public prayers. Madison didn't even want chaplains in the military or in Congress.

Religion is mentioned only twice in the Constitution—both times to separate it from the government. The First Amendment says "Congress shall make no law respecting an establishment of religion, or prohibiting the free practice thereof," and Article VI, Section 3 says that members of the U.S. government shall be bound by oath to the Constitution, but that "no religious test shall ever be required as a qualification to any office or public trust under the United States." Pledging loyalty to the Constitution has nothing to do with pledging loyalty to God—even if this idea gets lost during presidential primaries.

Summing up the process of writing the Constitution, early American historian Robert Middlekauff observed, "There were no genuine evangelicals in the Convention, and there were no heated declarations of Christian piety."

In God We Trust

These words are the national motto of the United States. But they weren't always. In fact, up until 1956, the national motto was "E Pluribus Unum" (Out of Many, One). It enshrined the notion that many colonies and peoples united to form a single country. The founders didn't mention God because, after witnessing 400 years of religious warfare, they got the message. Religion divided people as much as it unified them. Maybe more.

This is why "In God We Trust" never appeared on U.S. currency during the lifetime of any of the founders. It's a religious idea stamped onto a government document—a constitutional no-no. It first appeared nearly a century after the Revolution, during the Civil War—one of those unfortunate periods of religious revivalism. After the war, cooler heads prevailed and the words were removed. But they popped up again several times until the 1930s, when they stayed on for good.

It wasn't until 1956 that Congress, in a fit of anti-communist pandering, made it the national motto. But it was never the heart and soul of the republic. It was an afterthought.

One Nation, Under God

> I pledge allegiance to my Flag and the Republic for which it stands, one nation indivisible, with liberty and justice for all.

This is the original Pledge of Allegiance as written by a Baptist minister Francis Bellamy in 1892.

A couple of details. First, the word "indivisible" was intended to emphasize national unity in the wake of the Civil War. Second, in 1923, the Daughters of the American Revolution pushed to change "my Flag" to "the flag of the United States of America," in case there was any confusion about whose flag they were pledging allegiance to. (The Daughters were a persnickety bunch, but they did have a point. The Stars and Bars of the old Confederacy still had a big fan club.)

The Pledge of Allegiance was first published in *The Youth's Companion*, a hugely popular family magazine. At the time, Bellamy was chairman of a committee of state superintendents for the National Education Association. He led a nationwide effort to celebrate the 400th anniversary of Columbus's voyage by having a U.S. flag raised on every schoolyard in America. He wrote the pledge, in part, to promote that cause.

Not coincidentally, *The Youth's Companion* was also in the business of selling…flags. By 1892 they had peddled Old Glory to 26,000 schools. Nobody said patriotism couldn't be lucrative. Wanna bet somebody's making a mint from flag lapel pins today? Wanna bet they probably live in China?

To his credit, Bellamy tried to include "equality" in the pledge (he was a Christian Socialist), but he was voted down by the board that approved it because the others were against equality for blacks and women. Makes you proud to be an American, doesn't it?

It wasn't until 1954 that Congress, in another bout of anti-communist showboating, inserted "under God" into the pledge—an addition that Bellamy's own granddaughter said he would have opposed.

I think America's founders would also have opposed those words. Pledging loyalty to the republic is not the same thing as believing in God. That's why the Constitution forbids religious tests for office. Taoists and Wiccans are Americans, too, though don't tell that to the Christian Coalition.

Oh, and for those who insist that young minds are substantially shaped by this flag-worshipping ritual, remind them that the original salute to the flag, before we started putting our hands on our hearts, involved extending the arm forward and up—like the Nazis did. It's the weirdest thing seeing old photos of kids in American classrooms saluting the Stars and Stripes like Der Führer.

Those kids grew up to become America's "greatest generation," and they all learned the pledge without the words "under God." The ones who *did* grow up saying those words were the Baby Boomers.

In Their Own Words

So, what did the founders themselves actually think about the American republic and God? Were they pious Christians bent on a Bible-based society? No. Mostly they wanted tax cuts and the vote—neither of which are in the Laws of Moses or the Lord's Prayer. Let's see what they had to say about religion.

George Washington:

There's a famous story about Washington, who attended services at his Episcopal church. He'd show up for the first half of the service, then get up and leave once the sermon started. When his bishop told him this disturbed the proceedings, Washington agreed...and he stopped showing up altogether.

For Washington, church was something you grew up with and he spoke many times of the virtue and necessity of religious belief. But he was not a fundamentalist, he did not obsess over faith, and he kept it a safe distance from his official duties. That painting of him kneeling in prayer in the snow at Valley Forge? Urban legend. This doesn't mean he didn't pray. He just didn't do it out in the snow during the coldest winter of the 18th century.

Like many of his day, Washington gave religion its due:

> "Reason and experience forbid us to expect that national morality can prevail to the exclusion of religious principle."

Fair enough. But historians see him as more or less a deist, and throughout his career he made scant mention of God or Jesus in his official capacities. When it came to religion he spoke for himself, not the country. He also told dirty jokes.

219

Ben Franklin:

Also raised in the Episcopal Church, and originally headed for the priesthood, he abandoned it for Deism. He had rather generic religious beliefs and he separated them from virtue and morality. He was hardly a model Christian. Aside from his womanizing, he confessed that he liked Christ's teachings, but did not believe in his divinity. This would get you scolded in Sunday school—which didn't become popular until the next century, by the way.

Franklin was an inventor and a man of science, and he had a few run-ins with preachers, most notably over his new lightning rod. They objected to it because lightning was regarded as punishment from God and it was out of line for man to circumvent it. Ironically, the churches that didn't use it were the ones most likely to burn down. Their pastors preferred to ward off lightning strikes with prayer, or by ringing the church bells—which sometimes got the bell-ringer electrocuted. Small wonder Franklin copped an attitude toward traditional religion:

> "Original Sin was as ridiculous as imputed righteousness."

He was not hostile towards Christianity; his views were pretty moderate. But he was not much of a churchgoer. The following may explain why:

> "I wish it [the Christian religion] were more productive of good works...I mean real good works...not holy-day keeping, sermon-hearing...or making long prayers, filled with flatteries and compliments despised by wise men, and much less capable of pleasing the Deity."

He expected a bit more from God's cheerleaders, I guess.

John Adams:

Raised as a Congregationalist, he later rejected many of its doctrines, like the Trinity, and opted for the one-god Unitarian church instead. His father wanted him to be a minister, but he thought being a lawyer was a more noble pursuit. (Frankly, "noble" is not a word that comes to mind in either case.) He felt that religion had a role in developing morals and virtues, and he was more overtly Christian in his sensibilities than many of the founders. He believed Christian morality was key to the success of his country. But in the course of his career he sent mixed messages about the relationship between church and state—understandable given that he and his pals were charting new territory and he was a product of churchy New England. Yet, he had moments when he could be very tough on the dogmas of the Old Time Religion:

> "As I understand the Christian religion, it was, and is, a revelation. But how has it happened that millions of fables, tales, legends, have been blended with both Jewish and Christian revelation that have made them the most bloody religion that ever existed?"

> "I almost shudder at the thought of alluding to the most fatal example of the abuses of grief which the history of mankind has preserved—the Cross. Consider what calamities that engine of grief has produced!"

He said it, not me.

James Madison:

The "Father of the Constitution" attended St. John's Episcopal Church while he was president, but like his compatriots, he was more likely a Deist. Actually, he's a bit difficult to figure out on the religion score. For a time he considered a career in the ministry. But he also felt that religious belief should be directed by reason and he objected to taxes being used to support churches. He had these things to say about the alleged benefits of religion:

> "In no instance have...the churches been guardians of the liberties of the people."

"...religion and government will both exist in greater purity, the less they are mixed together..."

"Religious bondage shackles and debilitates the mind and unfits it for every noble enterprise."

"During almost fifteen centuries has the legal establishment of Christianity been on trial. What have been its fruits? More or less, in all places, pride and indolence in the clergy; ignorance and servility in the laity; in both, superstition, bigotry, and persecution."

Guys like Madison didn't show up on your doorstep Sunday afternoon with pamphlets about Jesus.

Thomas Paine:

The great writer and agitator of the American Revolution also believed in a rational approach to God.

"It is only by the exercise of reason that man can discover God. Take away that reason, and he would be incapable of understanding anything;"

Sounds moderate enough. But get a few beers in him (Samuel Adams?) and he'd give you an earful of what he *really* thought:

"Of all the tyrannies that affect mankind, tyranny in religion is the worst."

Paine's landmark book, *The Age of Reason*, dissected the Bible chapter and verse, and ridiculed many religious dogmas. This didn't win him a lot of friends. (It rarely does, trust me.) He was accused of being an atheist, which he wasn't. He simply saw a huge gap between spiritual truth and what Scripture was promoting.

"It is not a God, just and good, but a devil, under the name of God, that the Bible describes."

"All national institutions of churches, whether Jewish, Christian, or Turkish, appear to me no other than human inventions set up to terrify and enslave mankind, and monopolize power and profit."

Okay, he hits religion pretty hard. But he did think it through:

"Are we to suppose that every world in the boundless creation had an Eve, an apple, a serpent and a redeemer? In this case, the person who is irreverently called the Son of God...would have nothing else to do than to travel from world to world, in an endless succession of deaths, with scarcely a momentary interval of life."

Another concept for the SyFy Channel?

Ironically, Paine's bottom line on all this sounds more like Jesus than a lot of Christians do.

"My country is the world, and my religion is to do good."

Thomas Jefferson:

While Jefferson was also raised in the Episcopal Church, we often think of him as a Deist. But he didn't belong to any such sect and some think him more a Unitarian. He believed in the morals and ethics of Jesus, but he felt that a lot of traditional Christianity was "errors and corruptions" added to the original message.

In an 1819 letter to his former secretary, William Short, Jefferson declared that the Gospels served up, "a groundwork of vulgar ignorance, of things impossible, of superstitions, fanaticisms and fabrications." While he believed they also presented "sublime ideas of the Supreme Being," which included "precepts of the purist morality and benevolence...with an eloquence and persuasiveness which have not been surpassed," he then added:

"These [ideas] could not be the intentions of the groveling authors who related them. They are far beyond the powers of their feeble minds."

It's the "groveling authors" of Matthew, Mark, Luke and John he's slamming here. To set the record straight, Jefferson edited something now called *The Jefferson Bible*, wherein he actually cut out, rearranged, and shuffled together the verses of the four Gospels into a single chronology. But in doing so, he left out all of the miracles—no virgin birth, no resurrection. He regarded all that as claptrap added by Jesus' biographers, who had distorted his original teachings:

> "...his principles were departed from by those who professed to be his special servants, and perverted into an engine for enslaving mankind, and aggrandizing their oppressors in Church and State...to filch wealth and power to themselves..."

Like the Greek philosophers he studied, Jefferson didn't see the need to support human rights with religious belief. When he wrote the 1786 Virginia Statute for Religious Freedom, he was vilified for doubting ideas like the Great Flood and the biblical age of the earth. But he did manage to include this:

> "Our civil liberties are not dependent upon our religious opinions."

Rights and freedoms do not require religion; they transcend it. Everyone deserves basic rights no matter what they believe. Nor does civil society depend upon any particular deity:

> "...it does me no injury for my neighbor to say there are twenty gods or no God."

Jefferson admired the philosophy of Jesus, but he didn't buy it wholesale, and he had some major problems with the religion it spawned:

> "There is not one redeeming feature in our superstition of Christianity. It has made one half the world fools, and the other half hypocrites."

224

Given this attitude, it's not surprising that he had no interest in mixing church and state. The history of that idea wasn't good:

> "In every country and every age, the priest has been hostile to liberty. He is always in alliance with the despot, abetting his abuses in return for protection to his own...they [the Church] have perverted the purest religion ever preached to man into mystery and jargon, unintelligible to all mankind, and therefore the safer for their purposes."

So, when someone tried to slip Jesus into the Constitution:

> "An amendment was proposed by inserting 'Jesus Christ,' so that [the preamble] should read 'A departure from the plan of Jesus Christ, the holy author of our religion'; the insertion was rejected by a great majority, in proof that they meant to comprehend, within the mantle of its protection, the Jew and the Gentile, the Christian and Mohammedan, the Hindu and Infidel of every denomination."

He believed America was big enough for all of us. Oh, and just in case you're still not clear about where our doubting Thomas landed on the issue of taking the Bible literally:

> "I do not find in orthodox Christianity one redeeming feature. The day will come when the mystical generation of Jesus, by the Supreme Being as his Father, in the womb of a virgin will be classified with the fable of the generation of Minerva in the brain of Jupiter."

There are quotes I could cite that are even harsher than these, but you get the idea.

A Step into the Future

Every revolutionary stands with one foot in the past and one in the future—the world in which he grows up and the world he hopes to create. America's revolutionaries appeared on the scene at one of those great pivotal moments in history when age-old ideas like monarchy, miracles, witchcraft, slavery, and religion-based laws were being shown the door. As with any revolution the record was mixed. But they did manage to establish a country upon ideas that most of the world didn't even have on the back burner at the time.

Sure, they went to church. They prayed to God and learned from Scripture. They believed their country was divinely blessed. Their attitudes were complex and evolving. But they were not a devout conclave of theocrats. They were products of the Enlightenment; men of reason and worldly matters. And they could be a lot of fun.

Franklin was an inventor, Jefferson a scientist, and Paine a skeptic. Washington told bawdy jokes. Hamilton was all about money. They cursed, they drank, and they had affairs. They pursued happiness! It's not that they didn't like Jesus. They did. What bugged them was what so many churches were doing with Jesus and they didn't want government shoving any of that down their throats. Anyway, they were mostly about no taxation without representation.

But here's the really important point:

It doesn't matter what the Founding Fathers thought about God! It doesn't matter what *anyone* in power or authority thinks about God. All that matters in America is what *you* think about God. When you *do* have to worry about someone else's concept of God, you don't have religious freedom.

As for the Constitution, it doesn't matter what spiritual beliefs the framers had when they wrote it. It's what they put on paper that counts. And because they couldn't agree with each other about religion, they made nothing about it official. When it came to matters of faith, everyone should decide for themselves.

So in the final analysis, where does all this leave us?

The Most Moral People in History

"Western civilization is in a spiritual crisis."

My entire life I've heard this woeful drone by everyone from academic philosophers to pestering evangelicals to inner peace creeps. My first thought is always: When were we *not* in a spiritual crisis?

According to the Old Testament, we've been wrestling with dire moral dilemmas ever since Adam and Eve committed their dietary infraction. The story of the Israelites is one spiritual calamity after another. The advent of Christianity didn't help much. Immediately there were fights over who could and couldn't be a Christian, what Jesus was made of, how many parts God came in, and whether or not the pope was his mouthpiece. Factions fought in the streets. You had challenges from Gnostics, pagans, heathens, heretics, witches, Druids, Cathars, and a growing wave of Muslims. Plenty of spiritual crises to go around.

The Christian response to all this included preaching, prayer, charity, crusades, inquisitions, persecutions, tons of baroque artwork, and a non-stop succession of end-of-the-world panics. The faith then split into Catholic and Orthodox, and later spun off into thousands of Protestant sects. Who knew *what* to believe? Then came troublemakers like Galileo, Darwin, Marx, Freud, and Hugh Hefner. And those are just the biggies. There were many smaller hiccups along the way that included false messiahs, corrupt churches, and disturbing popular trends too numerous to list. If we're in a spiritual crisis today, it didn't start with the Pill or the ban on school prayer.

The moralistic worrywarts insist that we've lost our way. They claim we're alienated from our traditions, our values, and ourselves. The family is under attack. The culture is mired in indulgence and greed. And then there are the boneheads who text while driving. We are spiritually adrift and it's all circling the drain of societal decay. What we need is a return to the traditional values that made us a better people once upon a time, whenever that was.

Well, it's my contention that the 21st century West is the most moral civilization that has ever existed and that much of this is due to our rejection of what most people think of as traditional religious values.

Now, where do I get off saying this in an anything-goes culture where you can practically GoogleMap your G-spot? We have clashes over gay marriage, contraception, stem cell research, sex education, abortion rights, and senators treating public restrooms like singles bars. Plus all the personal traumas that Oprah has spent a career talking about. How can a society carrying so much baggage call itself moral? Well, here's a final rant on that.

First of all, most of our really serious problems have been around forever; we just didn't talk about them. Take for example single motherhood. A third of the children in colonial Lexington and Concord were born out of wedlock, but nobody printed this in the newspapers. School dropout rates were higher a century ago than they are today and church attendance was far lower. The mistreatment of women, children, minorities, the poor, animals, and the environment all got much less attention. Same with most of the social ills that now get theme songs on cable news.

Second, many of the problems that dog the moral doomsayers are only problems to them. Visit the huddled masses of Bangladesh or Brazil and it's clear that birth control can be a *good* thing. Or, if two guys down the street want to tie the knot, it doesn't crimp my ability to marry a nice girl and start a nice nuclear family with nice nuclear kids. If that's a problem for some, it's *their* problem, not society's. Besides, the pious hair-pullers themselves aren't all model citizens. A Harvard study from March 2009 found that the states with the highest percentage of "traditional values" voters were also the top subscribers to internet porn. Other studies show they also lead in divorce, spousal abuse, and teen pregnancy.

Third, do we really believe our values were better in the days of grim social conformity, silence about sex, and perpetual guilt over natural human feelings? Think about the theocratic societies today that come down hardest on everything from birth control to miniskirts. You think *they* occupy the moral high ground?

Why is it that, whenever we talk about morality, sexual issues usually lead the discussion? One reason is because we've been so successful in tackling the moral concerns that pop up in most other aspects of life. Ethical dilemmas still plague us, and we hardly live up to our ideals. Nobody does. But you'd be hard-pressed to find another civilization in any other period of history that's done a better job of handling the great moral questions.

Admittedly this may be hard to believe, so why don't we give our culture a final performance review on the big issues?

Freedom: Presently, we live at the high watermark of personal freedom. In lifestyle, career, mobility, associations, self-expression, and religious preference (or non-preference), we are masters of our individual fates to a greater degree than anyone else. Many think we're a little too free; religious agendas are usually about banning things. But the record shows it's better to have a surplus of freedom than a shortage. Few would prefer that the state, the clergy, or our boss, decided how we lived, what we said, or what we could do behind closed doors without the cops showing up.

Despite the occasional hysterics about Big Government you hear from politicians or talk show hosts, freedom in the Good Old Days was far less plentiful. If you were black, female, Jewish, Native American, or just poor, ideas like living where you wanted, voting, owning property, publishing your opinions, or speaking your mind, were frequently just wishful thinking.

Sure, if you're a white guy whose highest aspirations are to pay no taxes, pollute rivers, and shoot stuff without a permit, the 19th century may have been your Golden Age. Today, that concept of freedom is pretty much limited to groups like the Alaskan Independence Party—if you can call dodging grizzly bears and black helicopters freedom.

But by most measures we enjoy greater liberty today than we ever did in the God-fearing days of church-state cooperation. In a Christian monarchy there was plenty of belief in God, but *your* freedom wasn't on the king's agenda. In fact it was often part of the problem. By contrast, we now have a secular government created specifically to defend individual liberties, and there's even a written list of them. Okay, it doesn't work as well as we'd like— what does? But it works better than anything that came before, even for free market purists. When have they ever been richer?

Government: One of the most telling measures of a country's Gross National Morality is the kind of government it has. Yeah, sure, we bitch about ours night and day because it either does too much or not enough. But in the long, harrowing history of man ruling over man, nothing has topped the justice and moral soundness of the modern West's combination platter of democracy, the rule of the law, the rights of man, separation of church and state, separation of powers, private property, freedom of the press, and free speech.

As we've established, none of these are biblical values. There is little about political rights in Scripture. We saw how the pagan culture of ancient Greece came up with democracy and free debate. The Romans pioneered the rule of the law and the rights of man. (Sorry, the Laws of Moses were meant for the Israelites, not everyone—just ask the Canaanites.) In America, it was a bunch of long-haired Eastern elites, the guys with all those choice words about religion, who liberated state from church, pinned down property rights, and guaranteed freedom of the press. They fought *against* the traditional values of Christian monarchs and official churches. That's why we call them revolutionaries.

Law and Order: While we fret today about crime like it's a new invention, a century ago newspapers decried high crime rates and politicians griped that the court system was slanted in favor of criminals. Today, conviction rates for stuff like robbery and murder are considerably higher than back then.

Of course, a moral society requires fair and just laws, and you can't name a culture that has tried harder on this count than our own. Yet the legal rights we enjoy today are not products of ancient biblical wisdom. The idea that the government needs a reason to arrest you, that you're innocent until proven guilty, or that human rights apply equally to everyone, everywhere, at all times—these are more recent innovations. They got their start with the Magna Carta in England, the Declaration of the Rights of Man and Citizen in France (yeah, that's right, the *French*), and the U.S. Bill of Rights. None of these are Bible-based documents. If they were, observing these rights would have been standard operating procedure for the past 2,000 years and neither France nor America would have needed a revolution.

Marriage and Family: As mentioned, traditional marriage was usually an economic swap arranged by others. The bride and groom were the last ones whose opinion mattered. Not a lot of moral enlightenment there. What's more, in the Olden Days, traditional marriage included polygamy. Half the patriarchs of the Hebrew Bible practiced it or were products of it. And if you're a young-earth creationist who thinks the earth is 6,000 years old, then you have to believe that Adam, Noah, and their kin populated the world through incest. Kind of puts celebrity sex videos in perspective, doesn't it?

As for the nuclear family we cherish so much, it's actually not all that traditional. It's a modern institution. In earlier eras, people lived in extended families or clans—like a tenant association except you had to remember everyone's birthday. And they sometimes practiced that polygamy thing.

It's true that half of today's households are headed by a single parent. But this was often the case in centuries past when war and illness were frequently responsible. Somehow we survived.

The good news is that nowadays our spouses don't die so often. The bad news is we sometimes wish they did. We now live long enough to get seriously fed up with one another and sometimes it's better for all involved, even the children, to let everyone go their own way. Yes, every kid wants and deserves a mom and a dad, and it would be nice if all couples stayed happily together forever. It would be nice if lollipops cured cancer. But they don't. It does no one any good to pretend a bad marriage is always better than no marriage. Besides, isn't God a single father?

Anyway, the family is not under threat. Even if marriage is the new dating for some and people bail out with little provocation, we keep making more of them. The popularity of marriage ebbs and flows, but it never goes out of style. Most of those who do try alternative arrangements come crawling back to monogamy. In fact, marriage is so popular today that Family Values shock troops are in the awkward position of *opposing* certain forms of matrimony as a bad idea. I swear there's no pleasing some people.

Children: What culture has ever been more caring, indulgent, or protective of children? Today we spend much more on their education, their health, their self-esteem, and their fashion sense than we did in the "children should be seen and not heard" days of yesteryear. Ever meet a kid who wished he grew up the way *you* did?

We worry that youth today is too exposed to adult ideas; that fashion and pop culture are sexualizing childhood. To a degree this is a valid point. But then consider what the average 16-year-old girl was doing through most of human history. Answer: serving a husband and having babies. Ah, innocent youth.

Women's Equality: You gotta be kidding. Only queens (as in female monarchs) achieved anything near equality in the centuries of traditional values and even that required a few beheadings. Throughout most of history gender equality wasn't even a goal. Today, we've come so far that even conservatives reject the "women shall keep silent in the churches" attitude espoused by Paul. Sure, we've got a ways to go, but at least we're working on it.

Racial Equality: Do I even have to make this point? For 5,000 years, being a racial minority almost anywhere meant you could be owned by somebody else. In *Exodus*, God spells out the rules for keeping foreigners as slaves and he mentions slavery in the Ten Commandments, twice. While both Judaism and Christianity contributed to the idea that all souls are equal before God, somehow this didn't translate into social policy—as a few million Africans, Indians, and victims of Jim Crow found out.

It's true that Quaker opposition to slavery goes back to colonial times and black churches, along with rare birds like John Brown, did invoke the Bible in the cause of racial equality. But they were the exceptions and they often paid a price. Most old time churches were more concerned with gambling and drunkenness than with abolishing slavery. It took a religious skeptic to write "all men are created equal" before the idea started to have a practical effect and even he owned slaves. That's how bad it's been.

As recently as the 1960s, religion and racial equality were not regarded as an automatic partnership. Martin Luther King's likening of black Civil Rights to finding the Promised Land was controversial—especially in the more churchy states. Even today, Sunday services are the most segregated hour in American life. And while the election of an African American president does show progress, it has also stirred up some ugly stuff we hoped had gone the way of witch-burnings.

Still, with all the work we have yet to do, there has never been a time when racial equality was a more widely accepted virtue than it is today. That's got to mean something.

Religious Tolerance: Across the world and throughout most of history, religious tolerance was considered a *bad* idea. Consult your First Commandment or Taliban field manual. The most enduring conflicts are over religion, and usually between two factions of the same faith. Think about what it's been like to be Jewish in the Christian world over the past 2,000 years. Or Protestant in a Catholic country. Or even Mormon in a Baptist county.

In modern times, religious freedom and tolerance have been achieved by *denying* religion its traditional power. As late as 1960, JFK's Catholicism was a major hurdle en route to the presidency, and it wasn't atheists who had their frocks in a twirl about it. It was conservative Protestants. Being Christian wasn't enough. Kennedy had to be the right *kind* of Christian, and he wasn't.

Today, many of these same evangelicals like to cast themselves as a minority victimized by secular intolerance, all because the government protects the rest of us from their social agenda. They don't count the roughly 80% of Americans who call themselves Christian because too many of them support ideas like teaching only science in science classes and saving the prayers for church. Crazy stuff, I know.

War: There's no doubt that the 20ᵗʰ century produced more war victims than any previous age. Much of this was due to the deadly combination of record size populations and more efficient killing technology. War has been taking out large chunks of humanity for a long time. But today, your chances of avoiding it are better than ever. Statistically, a male is far more likely to die at the hands of another person in a tribal culture than in the modern West. Pol Pot's benighted regime exterminated eight percent of his countrymen, while the two world wars, with all their industrial weaponry, saw death rates of less than one percent among the countries in conflict.

Of course, you might be tempted to credit that improved record to the mercifulness of the God-fearing nations involved. But that's not what history tells us about God-fearing nations.

Most of the tribes confronted by the ancient Israelites aren't around anymore because the Lord promised, chapter and verse, to wipe the earth clean of them. There's a word for that. If you believe the numbers in Scripture, the body count was a larger percentage of those populations than it is in today's conflicts. In the early 1600s, Germany's Thirty Years War sparked a clash between Catholics and Protestants that claimed 15 to 30 percent of all those good Christians. As recently as the American Civil War, a period of deep religious revivalism, righteous fervor drove soldiers into battles that routinely produced 20 percent casualty rates.

Religiosity doesn't prevent warfare; it makes it worse because it demonizes adversaries and rejects compromise. You don't compromise with Evil; you leap into the fray, ready to die in a holy cause. Today, plenty of fiery fundamentalists have no difficulty employing war as a problem-solver if they believe the cause is just. How many born-again groups have you ever seen stage a protest *against* a war?

The leading cause of war is authoritarianism, not a lack of faith. And the cure is democracy, not religion, which *is* authoritarian. Democracies are least likely to start wars because the fighters can vote. It's regimes guided by some unquestioned "higher power," be it God or the Great Leader, that cause most of the trouble.

Poverty and Wealth: Jesus was forever telling people to give their stuff to the poor, but you'd never guess this from the attitude a lot of Bible-belters have towards welfare, foreign aid, unions, universal healthcare, or universal anything. They seem virulently capitalistic. Don't sweat that "it's better to give than to receive" stuff. Yeah, it's good to be skeptical of the government's ability to administer all this public assistance. But a lot of pious resistance to it isn't so much about bureaucratic waste as it is the conviction that, if you're poor and destitute, it's probably your own damned fault and it's not up to me to bail you out. Look at your own bootstraps. Now pull.

Ironically, in quite a few religious circles the enterprising quest for riches is among the highest virtues. Money is God's reward and faith is a commodity for export. For a growing number of church-going patriots God works for a profit, so tax cuts become the Eleventh Commandment and public assistance is the devil's own work—those words in the Constitution about "promote the general welfare" apparently not a priority.

Personal Responsibility: People are people and if they can dodge responsibility for their actions or leech off the public dole, they will. 'Twas ever thus. Owning up to our failures has never been popular and blaming someone else is standard human behavior. Ask anyone who lost an election or got canned for incompetence why they got dumped. They never say, "Well, it's because I'm a royal screw-up."

Today, of course, we get the occasional "it's never my fault" dingbat who embezzles funds, gets fired, blows the money in Atlantic City, and then wants his job back because his gambling addiction is a legally-protected handicap. But that's usually lawyers at work and there's nothing new about stupid lawsuits.

Religion supposedly gets us to take personal responsibility for our failings, but is the clergy's record on this actually better than anyone else's? Think real hard. And half the time, when they *do* come clean, they end up as blubbering spectacles on TV likening themselves to fallen saints. Then they ask for donations.

As for faith teaching self-reliance over freeloading off the public, what do you call paying no taxes while benefiting from national defense, state highways, and local trash collection?

Patriotism: Love of country is as powerful today as ever, even if we're not all as loud about it as some would like. Back during the American Revolution only a third of the colonists were even interested in independence and nobody saluted the flag. I'd guess those numbers have improved since then. The fact that a flag burning makes national headlines suggests how rare it is. And if folks who proudly display the Confederate flag still call themselves patriotic Americans, love of country can't be in short supply.

Any nation that spends so much time reminding the world of how great it is doesn't suffer from a lack of self-love. If you don't think patriotism is alive and kicking, go to Paris and watch how Americans react when the locals start ragging on the homeland. Pass the Freedom Fries.

Is There Nothing Sacred?

Bottom line—if you take *everything* into account, the full range of human rights and moral concerns, we today are history's highest achievers. That's not to say we don't fall seriously short of what we could be, and there's still more than enough injustice and cruelty in this life. But considering where we've been over the past 100,000 years, or even 3,000 years, or even 300 years, we're not doing too badly. Is there any other period of history in which you'd prefer to live out the rest of your life? Think about what you'd be giving up. For me, Novocain alone makes it worth living in the 21st century. The free speech thing is nice, too.

Strange as it sounds, our modern, worldly, indulgent, individualistic, secular humanist society is the most free, fair, humane, democratic, tolerant, and happiness-pursuing civilization that has ever existed. Nobody's done it better; certainly not the societies where religion ran the show.

236

In advocating Christianity, Blaise Pascal famously wrote, "There is a God-shaped hole in the heart of every person..." Believers insist we were created with this need to seek out God. But get a grip. A healthy mind always wants something more and, if life doesn't offer sufficient happiness, or security, or a cure for that mysterious rash, we'll dream something up. If the crapshoot of evolution has produced what feels like a spiritual hole in our hearts, we'll conjure up a plug for it. This isn't proof the universe was created by a drain stopper.

So, at the end of the day, is there *nothing* sacred? Is there no religious point of view that deserves to be unchallenged by critics, skeptics, or smartass writers? No sacrosanct beliefs? No divine authority to be the unmoving polar star by which we morally navigate through the centuries?

Well, what I've tried to demonstrate with this book is that falling back on the God answer always lands us in the same stew— exactly what do we mean when we say "God"? There's no shortage of answers, and that's the whole problem. "God" is as slippery and ever-changing a concept as any. Are we talking about the god of the Jews, the Catholics, Hindus, Taoists, or that UFO cult in New Mexico with the house that smells like a reptile cage? Even if we prefer the god of Jesus, which of the estimated 36,000 Christian sects now in existence is the real deal?

Everyone is certain *they* have the right answer and it's always the other guys who are wrong. If everyone who cited God to make their point had the same concept in mind we wouldn't have so many religions. We wouldn't spend centuries debating different theories of salvation. And we wouldn't bicker over what kind of stuff Jesus was made of. (Personally, I think it was chocolate. But was it milk chocolate or dark chocolate? Guess we'll need a holy war to settle that one.)

Ultimately, the God answer isn't the be-all, end-all solution it's made out to be. It's a comforting concept, but it's not eternal truth. It's only an opinion of eternal truth.

The Greek philosopher Protagoras said it best: "Man is the measure of all things." If you think this is planting your flag in the shifting sands of human convention, then what *is* the measure of all things? God? Whose god? Define "God." And around and around we go…

We can't forget that all religious belief, no matter how popular or revered, originates with mere mortals. You may think of it as divine revelation from an infallible source, but the ideas still reach us through flesh-and-blood people; human mouths that speak or human hands that put quill to parchment. All we can do is judge what they say and write—which is what we've just done.

Spoken or written, sculpted or painted, televised or tweeted, it doesn't matter. Spiritual claims always come from a fellow traveler who is every bit as fallible as you. To hold any statement, story, or authority as beyond question is to accept someone else's opinion without challenge, without thinking—and you don't want to do that, do you? Thinking is a good thing. It's what makes us human. It's what keeps us free.

Is nothing sacred? No, nothing is. I thank heaven for that.

Also by Thomas Quinn

GOD: The Unauthorized Biography
(An Irreverent History of the Old Testament)

ACKNOWLEDGEMENTS

No effort like this book takes place in a vacuum, and certain friends were critical in helping me pull this off.

First and foremost is Tom Kelly, who knows more of this stuff than I do, and who took the trouble to read my tome before anyone else. My endless conversations with him about all things religious would have put anyone else in a coma, and he was indispensible in catching mistakes and in helping me to clarify many murky points.

Helen Stringer, who I can never forgive for getting published before me, endured my rants over computer snafus and patiently guided me through the thickets of both uncooperative technology and British history. She cooks, too.

A big thanks to Joyce Alexson, creator of the Joseph Campbell Roundtable, who provided me with a venue to field test a lot of this material, and who's been a ceaseless cheerleader of my work.

A special thank-you goes to Pat Lach, who has always believed in me, as I believe in her, and whose background gave me the confidence to tackle a lot of touchy material.

My agent, Winifred Golden, enlightened me on the sobering realities of publishing. Carol Willette's flawless eye caught and corrected my errors—something she's been doing since the day we met. Alisa Curran has been my general counsel through writing projects long before this one. And Gilda Lugo has been my supportive B.F.F. for as long as I've known anyone.

While I know them only through their work, my appreciation also goes out to the brilliant P.J. O'Rourke and the fearless Bill Maher, who taught me what little I know about writing humor.

Finally, to those who were there when this incredible trek began: Laura Alexander Evanchik, whom I met in church and who stuck by me through the most turbulent months of my life. Happy seventeenth. To Rev. Brita Gill, who pulled me back from the precipice and showed me a better way. And lastly, to my old buddy Bill Gould, whose own search for truth unwittingly launched me on this journey so many years ago.

Bibliography

The Holy Bible: Revised Standard Version, World Publishing Co., 1962.

Akerley, Ben Edward. *The X-Rated Bible: An Irreverent Survey of Sex in the Scripture.* Feral House, 1998.

Aland, Kurt. *Synopsis of the Four Gospels, English Edition.* American Bible Society, 1982.

Anderson, Ken. *Where to Find it in the Bible.* Thomas Nelson, Inc., Nashville, 1996.

Archer Jr., Gleason L. *New International Encyclopedia of Biblical Difficulties.* Zondervan, 1982.

Armstrong, Karen. *A History of God: The 4,000 Year Quest of Judaism, Christianity and Islam,* New York: Alfred A. Knopf, 1993.

Asimov, Isaac. *Asimov's Guide to the Bible, vol. 1 & 2.* Wing Books, 1967, 1969.

Bell Jr., James S. and Campbell, Stan. *The Complete Idiot's Guide to the Bible.* Alpha, 2003.

Binswanger, Harry. *The Ayn Rand Lexicon.* Meridian Books, 1986.

Brown, Lewis. *This Believing World.* Macmillan Publishing Company, November 1944.

Callahan, Tim. *Bible Prophecy: Failure or Fulfillment?* Millennium Press, 1997.

Cavendish, Richard. *The Black Arts.* G.P. Putnam's Sons, 1967.

Catholic Encyclopedia, The., Online Edition.

Chamberlin, E.R. *The Bad Popes.* Barnes and Noble Books, 1969.

Dawkins, Richard. *The God Delusion.* Black Swan/Transworld Publishers/Bantam Press, 2006.

Doherty, Earl. *The Jesus Puzzle: Did Christianity Begin with a Mythical Christ?* Canadian Humanist Publications, 1999.

Ehrman, Bart D. *Misquoting Jesus: The Story Behind Who Changed the Bible and Why.* HarperCollins, 2005.

Freeman, Charles. *A.D. 381: Heretics, Pagans, and the Dawn of the Monotheistic State.* The Overlook Press/Peter Mayer Publishers, Inc., 2009.

Freeman, Charles. *The Closing of the Western Mind: The Rise of Faith and the Fall of Reason.* Borzoi Book/Knopf, 2002.

Freke, Timothy and Gandy, Peter. *The Jesus Mysteries: Was the Original Jesus a Pagan God?* HarperCollins, 1999.

Fremantle, Anne. *The Age of Belief: The Medieval Philosophers.* Meridian Books, 1954, 1982.

Friedman, Richard Elliott. *Who Wrote the Bible?* HarperSanFrancisco, 1987.

Forty, Jo. *Mythology: A Visual Encyclopedia.* Barnes & Noble Books, 1999.

Fox, Robin Lane. *Pagans and Christians.* Knopf, 1989.

Geoghegan, Jeffrey and Homan, Michael. *The Bible for Dummies.* Wiley Publishing, 2003.

Greenberg, Gary. *101 Myths of the Bible.* Barnes & Noble, Inc., 2000.

Hansen, Chadwick. *Witchcraft at Salem.* Mentor Books, 1969.

Helms, Randel McCraw. *The Bible Against Itself: Why the Bible Seems to Contradict Itself.* Millennium Press, 2006.

Hill, Jim and Cheadle, Rand. *The Bible Tells Me So.* Anchor Book, 1996.

Hitchcock, Mark. *The Complete Book of Bible Prophecy.* Tyndale House Publishers, 1999.

Hitchens, Christopher. *Thomas Jefferson: Author of America.* Atlas Books/HarperCollins, 2005.

Holzer, Hans. *The Directory of the Occult.* Henry Regnery Company, 1974.

Hornblower, Simon and Spawforth, Antony. *The Oxford Companion to Classical Civilization.* Oxford University Press, Oxford, 1998.

Hull, R.F.C. *The Portable Jung (Answer to Job).* Viking Press, 1971.

Jefferson, Thomas. *The Life and Morals of Jesus of Nazareth (The Jefferson Bible).* Beacon Press, Boston, 1989.

Jones, Judy and Wilson, William. *An Incomplete Education.* Ballantine Books, a division of Random House, New York, 1987.

Kirsch, Jonathan. *The Harlot by the Side of the Road: Forbidden Tales of the Bible.* Ballantine Books, a division of Random House, New York,1997.

Kirsch, Jonathan. *Moses: A Life.* Ballantine Books, a division of Random House, New York, 1998.

Kirsch, Jonathan. *God Against the Gods, The History of the War Between Monotheism and Polytheism.* Penguin Group, New York, 2004.

Kaminer, Wendy. *Sleeping with Extra-Terrestrials: The Rise of Irrationalism and Perils of Piety.* Vintage, a division of Random House, New York, 2000.

Küng, Hans. *Great Christian Thinkers.* The Continuum Publishing Co., 1995.

Kugel, James L. *The Bible As It Was.* Belknap/Harvard University Press, 1997.

Lang, J. Stephen. *The Complete Book of Bible Trivia.* Tyndale House Publishers, Inc., 1988.

Marquand, Ed. *The Devil's Mischief.* Abbeville Press, 1996.

Martin, Thomas R. *Ancient Greece: From Prehistoric to Hellenistic Times.* Yale University Press, 1996.

McGinn, Bernard. *Anti-Christ: Two Thousand Years of the Human Fascination with Evil.* HarperSanFrancisco, 1994.

McWilliams, Peter. *Ain't Nobody's Business If You Do.* Prelude Press, Los Angeles, 1993.

Metzger, Bruce M. and Coogan, Michael D. *The Oxford Companion to the Bible.* Oxford University Press, 1993.

Miles, Jack. *God: A Biography.* Vintage Books, 1995.

Morgan, Genevieve and Tom. *The Devil: A Visual Guide to the Demonic, Evil, Scurrilous and Bad.* Chronicle Books, 1996.

O'Grady, Joan. *The Prince of Darkness: The Devil in History, Religion and the Human Psyche.* Barnes & Noble, 1989.

Pagels, Elaine. *The Origin of Satan.* Vintage Books, 1995.

Paine, Thomas. *The Age of Reason.* Citadel Press, Kensington Publishing Group, 1948, 1974.

Plato, translated by W. C. Helmbold. *Gorgias.* The Bobbs-Merrill Company, Inc., 1952.

Ridenour, Fritz. *So What's the Difference?* Regal Books, 1967.

Roberts, Henry C. *The Complete Prophecies of Nostradamus.* Crown Publishers, 1947, 1994.

Rodgers, Nigel. *Ancient Rome.* Lorenz Books/Anness Publishing, 2005.

Rubinsky, Yuri and Wiseman, Ian. *A History of the End of the World.* Quill, 1982.

Schonfield, Dr. Hugh J. *The Passover Plot.* Bantam Books, 1966.

Shaprio, Max S. and Hendricks, Rhoda A. *Mythologies of the World: A Concise Encyclopedia.* Cadillac Publishing Co., 1973.

Shenkman, Richard. *Legends, Lies and Cherished Myths of American History.* HarperCollins Publishers, Inc., New York, 1993.

Shermer, Michael. *The Science of Good and Evil.* Henry Holt and Company, New York, 2004.

Smith, Ken. *Ken's Guide to the Bible.* Blast Books, 1995.

Stanton, Graham. *The Gospels and Jesus (2nd Edition).* Oxford Bible Series. Oxford University Press, Oxford, 2002.

Strozier, Charles B. *Apocalypse: On the Psychology of Fundamentalism in America.* Beacon Press, 1994.

Teel Jr., Rev. Roy A., *The Way, the Truth and the Lies: How the Gospels Mislead Christians About Jesus' True Message.* NarroWay Press, 2005.

Turner, Alice K. *The History of Hell.* Harcourt Brace & Company, 1993.

Vidal-Naquet, Pierre (ed.). *The Harper Atlas of World History.* Harper & Row Publishers, 1986.

Werner, Werner. *The Bible as History (2nd Revised Edition).* William Morrow and Co., 1981.

Willmington, H.L. *The Complete Book of Bible Lists.* Tyndale House Publishers, Inc., 1987.

Who's Who in the Bible. Publications International, Ltd., 1995.

ABOUT THE AUTHOR

Thomas Quinn is a writer for print and television, as well as a documentary producer and director. He received an M.F.A. in writing from The American Film Institute, worked as a story analyst for Universal, DreamWorks and HBO, and was an entertainment reporter for a weekly Los Angeles magazine.

Quinn has traveled the world writing and producing for the Discovery Channel, the History Channel, National Geographic, the Science Channel, BBC, and others. His programs investigate strange cultures, bizarre beliefs, and deconstruct everything from famous urban legends to supernatural events to conspiracy theories. He also presents humorous lectures on these same subjects.

In 2005, Quinn received two Emmy Award nominations as a writer and producer for the History Channel documentary, *Beyond the Da Vinci Code*.

Originally from New Jersey, he now lives in Los Angeles.

For more author information and blogs, please visit:
TRQuinn.com

CPSIA information can be obtained
at www.ICGtesting.com
Printed in the USA
LVHW032156231220
675035LV00029B/169